Starting Science from God

Rational Scientific Theories from Theism

IAN J. THOMPSON

EAGLE PEARL PRESS

Pleasanton

EAGLE PEARL PRESS
Pleasanton, California
Theistic Science Series

Eagle Pearl Press
PO Box 250, Pleasanton, California 94566, USA

www.eaglepearlpress.com
Information on this title: www.eaglepearlpress.com/ssfg
Website associated with this title: www.beginningtheisticscience.com

Cover photo courtesy PhotoXpress.com

Set in 11 point Palatino; Layout with LATEX2e
Typeset November 29, 2011

Publisher's Cataloging-in-Publication

Thompson, Ian J.
    Starting science from God / Ian J. Thompson.
    p. cm.
    Includes bibliographical references and index.
    LCCN 2011942981
    ISBN-13: 9780984822805 (pbk.)
    ISBN-10: 0984822801 (pbk.)

    1. Philosophy and science. 2. Religion and science.
    3. Theism--Philosophy.   I. Title.

B67.T46 2011   501
                      QBI11-600220

Ebook available for kindle, nook and iBooks.
ISBN-13: 9780984822812 (epub.)

Disclaimer:

Dr Thompson is currently employed as a theoretical nuclear physicist at the Lawrence Livermore National Laboratory, California, and is Visiting Professor at the Department of Physics, University of Surrey, England, where he was Professor until 2006.

This book is not supported or authorized by any of the organizations or institutions at which he is employed and/or with which he is affiliated, and does not represent any position or policy of those institutions.

Contents

Preface

I BELIEVE in God. I am a nuclear physicist. Those two things do not conflict in my mind, but instead they enhance each other.

Most of us have some idea about God and about how there might be such a being rather different from those we see every day. The concept of God has varied widely among religions over centuries, and it still varies among religions today. I subscribe to 'theism', in which God is seen as having created and as now sustaining the world. In the Judeo-Christian-Islamic tradition—the 'religions of the book'—this God is an eternal, omnipotent and benevolent being who transcends the temporality and limits of the world, but who still seeks a relation with the persons within it.

Theism has been continually supported by the religious traditions, and it was often used as a reference point in discussions between religions and the sciences. The early scientists such as Newton and Leibniz started from theistic frameworks, but science now presents purely naturalistic explanations that make no reference to God. Science now does not even assume any dualist distinctions between mind and nature.

The intellectual support for theism has thus been crumbling over the last two centuries. It is under a concerted attack today from many quarters. Newton and Leibniz thought that further scientific developments would support theism, but in fact many later scientists have turned actively against it. Sam Harris[1], for example, claims that religious ideas are "mere motivated credulity" that should be subjected to "sustained criticism" for their lack of connection with evidence. Richard Dawkins[2] argues that the God of religion cannot be simple but must be of enormous complexity. Since God's existence can never be supported by finite scientific evidence, Dawkins claims that believing in his existence would be "a

[1] Harris, *The end of faith.*
[2] Dawkins, *The God delusion.*

total abdication of the responsibility to find an explanation". Robert Pennock[3] concludes that any explanation of nature that appeals to supernatural causes is invoking causes that are inherently mysterious, immune from disconfirmation, and that give no grounds for judgment in specific cases. Without the binding assumption of uninterruptible natural law, he claims, there would be absolute chaos in the scientific worldview. These are the challenges to be addressed in this book.

Outside of theology, theistic beliefs are typically professed, if at all, only in private or only on Sundays. Dualist or non-materialist understandings of the nature of mind are not valued. In most academic and intellectual activities, there is no public discussion of theism. Cosmology and evolution theories are formed without theistic considerations. Little public mention of dualism is allowed in biology or neuropsychology.

There is a place, therefore, for a robust statement of the foundations of theism in which logical and clear connections can be made with the sciences. That is my goal. I use the framework of a realist ontology where only things with causal effects are taken as really existing. Such an ontological approach follows the path started by Aristotle and further explored by Aquinas. Existing things constitute substances, and thus mere Platonic forms, idealistic consciousness, mathematics or information are not claimed to be that out of which things are made.

Scientists have various religious beliefs. Many scientists are happy with the great simplification of the world that can be achieved once non-physical things are excluded, whereas many others have feelings or intuitions that there is more to the world than the purely physical. One result of this tension has been the progressive simplification of religious beliefs, especially concerning their ontological claims, in order to shoehorn them into the restricted framework apparently allowed by science. I hope that this book will allow many of these simplifications to be reversed.

Starting science from God is a reasonable way to proceed.

---

[3] Pennock, "Supernaturalist explanations and the prospects for a theistic science."

Acknowledgements

MANY discussions with Jim Lawrence and Leon James over the years have kept me focused on these issues and encouraged me to get it all together in one book.

I would like to thank very much the people who have helped me in the writing of this book and who have read and commented on earlier versions: Irene Alexander, Jim Beattie, Jeremiah Bodnar, Leon James, Jim Lawrence, Mark Oldaker, Tom O'Neill, Robert Selvendran, Susan Sup, Ed Sylvia, and Marilyn Woolford. We may perhaps not all agree with this final version, but being on the way with them has been endlessly instructive and enlightening.

I acknowledge again that this book is not supported or authorized by any of the organizations or institutions at which I am employed or with which I am affiliated, and does not represent any position or policy of those institutions.

Part I

Preliminaries

1
Introduction

1.1 Theistic postulates

IN THIS BOOK, I will formulate a *theistic manifesto* that makes explicit the foundational postulates of a scientific theism. On this basis, I will then show how deductions from these postulates give rise to the regularities of the physical world and how they generate psychological and physical structures and processes that can be confirmed from what science already has discovered. The essential theistic postulates are:

1. God is love which is unselfish and cannot love only itself.
2. God is wisdom as well as love and thereby also power and action.
3. God is life itself: the source of all dispositions to will, think and act.
4. Everything in the world is a kind of image of God: minds and also natural objects.
5. The dispositions of an object are those derivatives of divine power that accord with what is actual about that object.

On the basis of such postulates, I claim that we can understand how the world appears to function with considerable regularity in its underlying principles. It is from these principles that everything has its nature. There are laws which describe how these natures operate.

In a 2011 article at Salon.com, MIT physicist Alan Lightman[1] recognizes what he calls "the Central Doctrine of science", that "All properties and events in the physical universe are governed by laws, and those laws are true at every time and place in the universe." Theists do agree with that.

---

[1] Lightman (*Does God exist?*)

However, in theism, the laws themselves are not physical. Lightman later refers to "physical laws", but he had not mentioned that qualification to start with. He only inserted it without argument. This question, of the physical nature of laws, illuminates the difference between the existing sciences and what I show is possible for science within theism.

Our discussion will focus on the features of God that are dynamic and therefore have an effect on the world. The relevant dynamic features may have higher priority in practical religious life than in traditional philosophy since they will often be outside the 'essential divine attributes' traditionally considered. That traditional list of divine attributes includes infinity, eternity, omnipotence, omniscience, immutability, impassivity, simplicity, necessity, etc., but not many of these have consequences for the way the world functions. In this book, therefore, I do not want to talk about merely the God of philosophy, but the 'God of the living'. We will discuss for example how God is Love, how God is one into whose image we are growing, and how God is one who is delighted when we are happy for the longest period. These facts may appear to be less a part of philosophical than of vernacular religion, but they are no less important or true for that and they should be an essential part of any successful theism. I will lead up to a 'living theism', the view that God is that Person who is a necessary being, who is unselfish Love itself, Wisdom itself, and (in fact) Life itself.[2]

1.2 Theism and science

According to theism, God is responsible for both creating and sustaining the world. The theistic God is omnipotent, having at least powers far beyond those of humans. It is commonly believed by scientists that if God were allowed as an explanation in science, then an 'anything goes' attitude would prevail. They believe that the explanation of 'God did it' could be used for any event whatsoever, however regular or irregular and however comprehensible or incomprehensible. They reject the idea of God as some arbitrary and capricious old man who can do what he likes. A theist claims, in reply, that this reason for opposing theism in science arises from misunderstandings about the nature of God. We already know that there are considerable regularities in the manner of sustaining the world, so we

---

[2] Most often divine attributes will not be capitalized, except (as here) sometimes for emphasis, or for marking some important distinctions.

should instead explain the source and nature of those regularities. That source, for example, might be the constancy and eternality of the love and wisdom of God.

Allowing science to consider that God is the life of the mental and natural worlds would be a big mental jump from any naturalistic starting point. It would change the kinds of scientific theories that would be permitted. We will thus introduce a new kind of science called *theistic science*, as suggested by Plantinga[3]. You may argue that there is in fact only one kind of science, and that there is no sense in talking about e.g. 'Australian science,' or 'theistic science'. However, there are ways in which plurality can and should be part of science. In particular, there can and should be multiple sources of ideas that lead to scientific theories. This means that we can consider theistic science a branch of each theoretical science that derives general theoretical principles from theism and which begins to give the results described later in this book. I argue that we should encourage 'ontological pluralism'.[4] Some may respond that this pluralism only makes sense in the initial stages of a science but not in its mature stage. I reply that neither fundamental physics nor psychology—the subjects of this book—are mature sciences in the required sense. Some may argue that we should stick with the framework we have to see how far it will take us. There is always the possibility, they say, that materialist science will in the future give a complete and adequate account of mental processes, of the creation of the universe, and of the creation of life, so in the meantime we should not be impatient. I reply by asking that we consider the possibility that theism is true, and that God does make a difference to the world. Must we then wait 100 or 200 years until the naturalists have finally given up seeking natural explanations of those differences? Can we not start thinking now about these matters? To do so is to encourage ontological pluralism in science, especially concerning foundational questions. As Feyerabend[5] says in *Against Method*, in science there are in fact no fixed rules, and successful explanation is what counts. If some of us want to seek alternate explanations on the chance that we may be more successful in producing scientific predictions, then we should be able to do so. This is pluralism.

---

[3] Plantinga, "Evolution, neutrality, and antecedent probability."

[4] This is already explicit in the foundation of physics and in psychological modeling. Basic physics, for example, considers strings or spin foams or deformed space as alternative possible ontologies. Psychology can consider symbols or functions or network connections in alternative possible ontologies. There is no principle of science that forever forbids such ontological pluralisms.

[5] Feyerabend, *Against method*.

We give the name theistic science to the kind of scientific activity within ontological pluralism that develops theoretical ideas for the relation between God and the created world and for how they function together. This enterprise starts by rigorously formulating and examining a 'scientific theism'. It then leads towards theistic science that gives rise to 'theistic psychology', 'theistic biology', etc., within an environment of ontological pluralism. If successful, we might one day begin to call these just 'science', but that, of course, remains to be seen.

Theistic science simply starts with the postulate that there is a God, according to the living theism defined above. Just as naturalistic physics starts from the a-theistic assumption of God *not* existing, I start from the assumption of God *existing*. We have to assume that something exists to start with, so both these ontological approaches should be allowed within science as long as they produce good explanations. Science by itself should not prejudge the kinds of ontologies to be assumed in the best theories, since that should depend only on the *results* of the investigations. The earth will not disappear from under our feet if we consider the possibility of God existing and see what conclusions might follow from that assumption.

You may be puzzled that I begin with theism rather than something simpler. Do we have to start by assuming an infinite God in order to do basic physics? I will discuss questions of simplicity and infinity in Chapter 13. For now, I only ask that I be awarded at the beginning the same deferred judgment as is awarded to superstring theory (for example). In the first step of an *ab initio* or fundamental theory, scientists write down the basic postulates from which they want to start and then proceed to derive from these as many conclusions as possible about the visible world. If they make predictions about something new or explain known facts in a new way without contradiction, this is regarded as a success. I ask that theistic science be allowed to follow the same pattern so we can judge at the end whether observations confirm or refute the theory. If they confirm theistic theory, then they may be regarded as evidence in favor of theism, otherwise not. This is different than the way that religious people regard theism[6], but that does not stop us doing theistic science using the standard

---

[6] Some religious believers are reluctant to expose the foundations of theism to possible scientific investigations for fear that theism may be refuted. In reply, I would quote Socrates on the 'unexamined life' and furthermore note that many refutations are even now being attempted, for example by Stenger (*God, the failed hypothesis*) or Coyne (*Seeing and believing*). Ignorance hardly makes a good defense. Also, if I am wrong (whether in science or in religion), I want to know about it since I do not believe religious belief is only for other people.

scientific pattern. It is also possible that one day other non-theistic theories may be supported by the same evidence. I therefore challenge anyone to produce such other theories, similarly comprehensive, that are equally or more effective or better confirmed with respect to the predictions that this book will make on the basis of theism. Since in science the primary assumptions are not provable but are just that, assumptions, we should be allowed to consider alternatives.

When comparing theory with observation, we need to realize that every interpretation of observations depends on what prior theory we have in our minds, especially concerning how observations work and how it is determined that they are accurate. Observations are always 'theory laden' since their interpretation is not given by the observation itself but by previous theories. Without a method of interpretation, an experiment means nothing at all. It is therefore essential to consider alternative starting points so we are not saddled forever with what may be called a 'departure bias'.

Theistic science, as defined above, is different from traditional religion, theology or philosophy in that it attempts to describe the mechanisms by which God sustains or manages the universe and sustains or manages all the cause-effect relations within the universe. This is what makes the project scientific and thereby allows theism to enter science.

Throughout this book, there will be a number of recurring themes and ongoing conversations. These primarily relate to topics of continual debate among scientists, philosophers and theologians. The themes include:

- Is the world constructed as a monism, dualism, or theism?
- Can there be multiple levels or planes of existence?
- How can there be mind-body connections without denying the fully-fledged existence of minds or of brains?
- How can there be a Personal God, a Living God?
- How can we distinguish between divine and human actions in the world?
- How do physical, biological and mental structures come into existence? Are they created, gradually developed, or evolved?

These themes are listed here since I believe that the theism and science now being developed will, by the end of the book, suggest new answers to these queries.

Many scientists and philosophers resist this kind of theistic science. One reason is because those with a naturalist view have a negative bias concerning all things related to God, spirituality, and even mind.[7] Another reason is because there is a logical impossibility of proving that something non-natural exists when the proof allowed is limited to natural measurements or abstractions based on them. This is related to another reason: that science does not have the *methods* to investigate spiritual or divine things. Many might ask, for example, how can we perform experiments or tests on God? How can we investigate things that cannot be seen empirically? Surely science and religion are the 'non-overlapping magisteria' (NOMA), as advocated by Gould[8], where science is concerned with 'what is', and religion is concerned with 'what should be' (morality, ethics, and metaphysics beyond observations)? Many of these logical objections have been answered already by the skeptics, such as Stenger[9], Coyne[10], and summarized by Boudry, Blancke, and Braeckman[11]. They argue, and I agree with them on this point, that while science may adopt a *pragmatic methodological* naturalism, its naturalistic claims should not be stronger than this. We should not insist, for example, that science is forever barred from considering non-physical realities such as minds, spirits or God.[12] I agree with them because if these things are to make any practical difference, it must be possible for them to have effects in the natural word, and those effects must be able to be examined by scientists. If an angel appeared to heal the sick, then science should be able to investigate it rigorously. The above skeptics go on to argue that since such angels never appear, the theistic predictions fail and therefore theism should be rejected. I respond by arguing that theism was most often not correctly understood, and so the predictions were not correctly made. I will present new predictions for confirmation or falsification.

---

[7] This is to be contrasted with a 'positive bias', whereby anything proposed is provisionally accepted to see whether it is true. Those with a negative bias provisionally reject something new, even before considering whether it is true.

[8] Gould, "Nonoverlapping magisteria."

[9] Stenger, *God, the failed hypothesis.*

[10] Coyne, *Seeing and believing.*

[11] Boudry, Blancke, and Braeckman, "How not to attack intelligent design creationism."

[12] One consequence of adopting a pragmatic methodological naturalism, however, is what we already see: there are animated debates about what kind of evidence should be allowed in science, and what methods should be used to investigate the fringes of science such as parapsychology, near-death experiences, etc. Many scientists may, if pressed, admit that, if the same standard of evidence were to concern natural processes, then the already-existing evidence would be sufficient to prove the case. But still there is opposition.

1.3 Laying the foundations

This book sets out the structure of a theory that includes theism, then draws systematic conclusions from this theory, and only towards the end gives more details about our experience and observations. Part III contains a series of postulates that lay the foundation for the theory. The preliminary discussion surrounding each declared postulate is not meant to justify that assertion but only to make sure that it is understood correctly and that its declaration is plausible within a fundamental theory.

This will seem strange to many philosophers and theologians, especially those who have devoted their life's work to finding arguments, justifications and/or proofs for the existence and nature of God. I, by contrast, start in Part III by simply *assuming* that God exists and then follow that with claims about the nature of God—and all with no visible justification! How can I hope to get away with such audacity? The reason is that I am laying out the foundational postulates for a scientific theism as if it were just another scientific theory. Only after the postulates are complete and understood do we try to see what follows in detail, and only much later do I compare those predictions with observations. This is standard procedure in science, though perhaps not in philosophy and theology where more attention is paid to each claim in isolation. In today's scientific practice, whether we are theorists or experimentalists, we do not develop standalone arguments for the existence of (for example) quarks or superstrings. Rather, we only argue within the context of an overall theory that makes predictions on the basis of such existence claims. If the predictions prove correct, then this, we argue, allows us to legitimately claim support for the existence of what was postulated to exist at the fundamental level. This approach is particularly necessary if we are dealing with entities like superstrings, quarks (and now, even God) that will almost certainly never be observed with the naked eye.

There will therefore be few attempts to justify theism except by the results of the whole book. There already exist various attempts in ontology, from Aristotle, Anselm, Aquinas and others, to prove various properties of God from the existence or change or contingency of bodies in the world. Many of these proofs depend on a particular analysis of causation in nature, and since the analysis presented in this book is slightly different from Aristotle's, the details of the proofs do not proceed in the same manner. Investigating the various proofs, therefore, is beyond the scope of this book.

Part I continues in Chapter 2 with a short historical review of how monotheism has developed in Western thought and how it is presently suffering in competition with a modern science that remains based on naturalism. Chapter 3 outlines some minimal changes necessary in our views of both science and religion in order to bring them closer together. We will see the important role of 'love' in the constitution of beings, and multiple 'levels of existence' will be considered.

Part II develops the relevant concepts of dispositions and multiple generative levels, using examples entirely from existing science. There is no mention of theism whatsoever. The notion of disposition is found to be an essential 'unit of understanding' in all kinds of science, from physics to biology to psychology. It has the benefit of being largely content-neutral in the division between physical and mental properties. Chapter 4 considers all these kinds of dispositions and how science relies on them to provide the causal explanations that it seeks in order to gain understanding of the nature of things. This chapter claims, moreover, that the concepts of dispositions and of forms are sufficient together to construct a concept of *substance*. Substance is a serious philosophical problem that should be solved in any comprehensive account of ontology. Part III begins by laying out the foundational postulates for a scientific theism. By 'scientific' here, I simply mean the systematic attempt to think clearly, logically, without contradiction and in such a way as to make predictions whose validity can be confirmed (or not) by observation. There are many steps in making such predictions which therefore only follow in Part IV.

We will see that there is a logical gap between Parts III and IV. Part III produces an abstract and formal structure for what the world would be like under theism. It leaves open the *identification* of parts of that structure with what we experience and observe and does not declare what is mental or physical. Part IV, therefore, has to make some contingent identifications, and this is where *empirical scientific activities* enter in. I present my own judgements for what parts of abstract theistic structure should be lined up with the many physical and mental processes we see around us, but I always allow that I may be mistaken. Assuming that I am not wrong, in successive chapters I propose derived scientific theories for the nature of spiritual, mental and physical processes. I look forward to seeing whether they are (or are not) confirmed by experiments.

Part V follows the consequences of these theistic theories for topics of current public interest and scientific investigations. These topics include the question of how life has developed on earth: have living creatures been created specifically or have they evolved according to mutations and natural selection? A second topic, much debated in recent years, concerns the nature of our conscious awareness and how it is related to the neurochemical processes in our brains. The connected topic of spirituality and spiritual growth is also discussed, in particular as to whether that growth depends on only mental influences or whether it also depends on actions in the world. Finally, Part V touches on the problem of evil in the world and how it could exist when God is both omnipotent and wholly good. No final resolution of this problem is given, only considerations about the nature of the world and of God's interaction with the world, things which need to be known before the problem can addressed properly.

Part VI examines how these ideas fit into existing accounts of metaphysics, in particular with the relations of this theory with those of past philosophers as they dealt with similar problems about spirituality, minds and nature. Since many scientists prefer their theories to be formally expressed by mathematics, Chapter 31 discusses what the prospects are for such formalizations. While no completely formal version of theism can be given—it describes both God and persons who have their own free wills— there are various aspects of theism which could be expressed mathematically, and I make suggestions for further research. Part VI ends with a collection of possible objections to theism. Each point is stated and answered rather briefly. Again, most of these questions deserve a more full and comprehensive response.

The reader may in the end wonder what claims or predictions I can make to justify the 'extraordinary claims' to be made about God. Will I have produced 'extraordinary evidence' to prove these demanding claims? One answer is that the determination of what is 'extraordinary' relative to 'normal' is itself theory-laden: it depends on our previous theoretical suppositions. Many of the claims of modern science, for instance that material objects may possess consciousness and intentionality, are themselves equally extraordinary and so should require extraordinary evidence and not merely promissory notes that 'one day in the future' science will explain how this is possible.

I am not ever going to logically prove the basic features of theism that are needed for theistic science. There are in fact many attempts in other places to prove the existence and attributes of God from what we know and maybe from what we already know outside of religion, but that is not my approach. I do not argue in a natural theology from nature and science to God. Instead, I start from God. Indeed, I propose to start science *from* God and theism. You will see what theistic science looks like. Perhaps you will consider that this theistic science has provided retroactive evidence for God: just as a successful string theory will provide evidence for the existence of strings. Like all inductive arguments from observations to ontologies this is not an absolute proof. You are free to declare (or delay) your own decision.

2

A Short History of Theistic Ideas

PHILOSOPHICAL theism was built on the the first articulated monotheism that dates from the late Second Temple Jewish period of the prophetic tradition. We will see how the ideas of Greek philosophy came to be used to understand this Semitic theism and also the theism of Christianity. We will trace its development within Western philosophy and explain how it produced, and was then influenced by, scientific ideas and investigations. The exposition here is brief and takes the place of a more complete account which would include more of the Islamic and Indian contributions to theistic thought. Each era had its own underground currents, many of which were influential and even popular. Those currents were often hardly recognized by philosophy and were regarded as heterodox by the churches.

Every ontology, whether explicitly theistic or not, addresses similar issues. We want to see how the various recurring themes of Chapter 1 have been dealt with in the past. We also want to clarify the opposing tendencies in seeking explanations or resolutions of those problems. We will examine the tension between those philosophies that start from God and those that start from nature.

2.1 Greek philosophical foundations

The Greek philosophers wanted to know how the changeable world they saw around them was related to the world of knowledge which contained immutable and eternal truths. Plato (c. 427-347 BC) thought that what we knew truly were the *forms* of things, since these eternally existed whether or not physical objects existed to embody the forms. The contemplation of forms as such, Plato thought, was the proper intellectual activity. In particular, the contemplation of the 'form of the good', which he took as the 'good itself', was an experience akin to uplifting mystical insights. This kind of quasi-religious experience lead Plato to place greater emphasis on forms rather than on the physical world.

The result of Plato's emphasis on the pure forms as being what were absolutely real was an implication that the physical world was a 'poor shadow' of what was real. This shadow is what we would see on a cave wall when we are not facing the light. The physical universe is perhaps created by a subsidiary god or demiurge, not by the Absolute itself. Our task in life, according to Plato, is to love wisdom in order to raise ourselves out of immersion with everyday concerns. Philosophy enables us to live properly in our souls, which are 'self-moving' and hence have life in themselves and are capable of perceiving rational and transcendent forms. Our souls are certainly not the 'harmony of our body', Plato insists, since sometimes they act contrary to bodily inclinations.

Aristotle (384-322 BC) was a student of Plato but took the opposite down-to-earth approach to philosophy and knowledge. He directly examined physical objects, biological creatures, and human beings, which are all beings with potentialities for change and function. He said that each of these has a 'soul' which enables it to function in its proper manner. Plants, for example, have vegetative souls, animals have animal souls, and humans have rational souls. All these souls, according to Aristotle, should be conceived as the form or essential function of their respective organisms. That form is the form of the matter of those creatures, and the matter is that material out of which they are made. He was insisting on the reality of the natural world as that which has its sources of change within itself. Forms themselves do not exist externally to the beings that embody them. They may be intellectually distinguished—in the mind of the knower— but this does not mean that we can ever (as Plato thought) see forms as existing in a world of their own. Aristotle did develop the idea of a Divine Intellect which we share when we perceive rational truths, but in general his emphasis was on particular existing beings, not on absolute forms in some kind of intellectual or 'Platonic' heaven.

Although neither Plato nor Aristotle was a theist as we now understand the term, their agreements and disagreements set the stage for many long-running debates. One tension has continued for millennia: the tension between emphasizing some eternal source (or 'firsts') as what is most real and active (as Plato did), in contrast to emphasizing everyday objects in our physical universe (or 'lasts') as what are most real and active (as Aristotle did). A full account of theism has to integrate these two approaches, I believe, so that both God and the world have significant roles.

2.2 Christian theism

The first centuries of Christianity were profoundly influenced by the Second Temple Jewish monotheism. Much philosophical effort effort was put forth to comprehend, not theism itself, but rather the natures and relations of Jesus and God. The influential thinkers here were Justin Martyr, Tertullian, Origen, Athanasius (culminating in the Nicene Creed), and Augustine. Their formulations included many individual terms of Greek philosophy, but these terms were not included within a systematic framework.

The first comprehensive attempt to understand something like theism in terms of Greek philosophy was that of Plotinus (204-270), who used ideas from Plato to view the creation of the world as an emanation from God the Absolute One. In this 'Neoplatonism', the Absolute One contains no division, distinction or multiplicity, not even the distinction between being and non-being. Yet by emanation or 'overflowing', it produces a created universe that descends by degrees eventually to the material level. The world is not created from love, and it does not even act freely, but follows necessarily from the One. This Neoplatonism proved attractive to many Christian and Islamic thinkers such as the Alexandrians, Augustine, and pseudo-Dionysius, even though it was initially opposed to Christianity and not generally accepted as orthodox because of its non-dualist and gnostic tendencies. It was not thought to allow sufficiently for the distinction between God and humans. Also the route it described for religious salvation was through esoteric knowledge and mystical union rather than by means of a religious or social life accessible to everyone.

Thomas Aquinas (1225-1274) was the first to take seriously within Christianity the works of Aristotle. Islamic philosophers and the Jewish monotheism of Maimonides had already been influenced Aristotle's books. Aquinas showed how Aristotelean concepts may be used to formulate a metaphysics in which Christianity may be understood. At the

time, the general opinion was that a Platonic formulation would be easier, but Aquinas showed that, with only a few extensions, Aristotle's approach was very useful. Aquinas used Aristotle's analysis of organisms in
terms of function and form. He again described these functions as caused
by vegetative, animal and rational souls. However, he decided that since
forms must always be forms *of* some substratum, that substratum cannot
be matter in general (as Aristotle thought) but instead must be whatever
exists that has *no* form or property. The underlying substratum or substance must therefore be *pure potency*: just and only that capacity to receive
and embody forms. Aquinas viewed the causal powers of objects and organisms as arising from the forms (that is, souls) of those beings, since
pure potency is too indeterminate to generate specific powers. This view
requires attributing causal powers to forms which must therefore be somehow more than 'shape' and 'structure'.

In order to adapt Aristotle's philosophy to Christian theology and the
survival of bodily death, Aquinas took the *rational* soul of humans to be
not a form of the physical body but rather a form which is immaterial in
some way. He was not clear concerning the nature of this immateriality,
only saying for example, that an angel can be formed as an immaterial
substance by conjoining an intellectual soul with an 'act of existence'. A
whole person needs also a physical and biological body to function, but
the intellectual soul can persist somehow as some immaterial aspect and
be influential as a 'formal cause' in some way.

God was conceived by Aquinas in the full theistic manner as Perfect
and Immutable Being Itself, Truth Itself, along with the attributes of Im-
passibility, Transcendence, Immanence, Omnipotence, Omniscience and
(Omni)benevolence.[1] What is new with Aquinas is that God is conceived
as Pure Act and is completely devoid of potentiality.[2] 'Love' gets added
in as one more perfection. We may reasonably ask, however, whether
Aquinas had the correct way of conceiving God to be a creative power,
considering that the formulation of 'Pure Act' excludes all concepts of potentiality and hence of power and therefore partly contradicts the view of
God as powerful.

Aquinas' philosophy (Thomism) subsequently became orthodox within

---

[1] All capitalized here to emphasize their leading roles in Thomist metaphysics and theology.
[2] If God had potentiality, Aquinas argued, then he could change and therefore would not be immutable.
Or he could improve, in which case he would not previously have been perfect. And God certainly
cannot change for the worse.

the Catholic church. Because it was based on Aristotle's approach rather than that of Plato, we can argue that this scholasticism laid the first foundations for a scientific revolution that starts not with God but by examining nature itself.

2.3 The scientific revolution

The first work of René Descartes (1596-1650) was in mathematics and science. He is well known for the 'Cartesian coordinates' used in drawing graphs in all kinds of mathematical physics. He formulated theories for how the internal organs of animal bodies operate from natural causes. He took these causes as operating according to a mechanical philosophy, where the sizes and shapes of components of systems are what determine their operation.

Later in his life Descartes wanted to make a new foundation for philosophy, in particular one that kept natural science separate from the human souls responsible for rational thought and hence also separate from religion. His philosophy took the (by now well-known) skeptical approach in order to see what can be known when conventional knowledge is not taken for granted. By means of his 'Cogito, ergo sum', he concluded that we have a separate 'rational soul' by means of which we can have intellectual logic, thought, and comprehension. He contrasted this soul with the extended objects he had used in his mechanical philosophy. He concluded that there exist two types of substances: rational souls which are constituted by thought and physical objects which are constituted by extension. Rational souls are not extended, and physical objects cannot think rationally. All *non*-rational processes in humans and animals (reflexes, sensations and feelings) are to be entirely explained by the mechanical operation of extended bodies and their parts. As many have pointed out, however, Descartes did not explain the connection between souls and the natural world.[3]

Descartes was merely formalizing what had already been believed since even before Aquinas: that there was a natural world of causes and effects and, in addition, a set of human souls of some immaterial nature and ca-

---

[3] It is probable, in retrospect, that in a metaphysics where 'thought' and 'extension' are the only two essential principles no bridge between them can be found apart from a simple declaration (unexplained) that such a connection exists.

pable of rational thought. The fact that Descartes brought this distinction clearly into the open has effectively made him a scapegoat for everyone who has complaints about our understanding of mind and its relation to the body. The name 'Cartesian dualism' has become a term of derision.[4] However, Bolton[5] points out that when we "attribute the influence of Dualism to Descartes, we are implicitly attributing to him the power of imposing his own peculiar way of thinking on a whole civilization for three centuries together. In reality, this kind of power is so rare that it is usually considered an attribute of the founders of religions, not of philosophers."

In an attempt to unify what Descartes left separate, Baruch Spinoza (1632-1677) concluded that whatever exists must have the properties of *both* extension and rationality. Furthermore, it is the single God which exists with this combination of attributes, a God which exists impersonally. All of us apparently separate beings are in reality modes of existence of that One God. This again is explicitly a non-dualist and pantheist view of reality and is hence distinct from theism. However, it is a demonstration of what kind of theory might have to be conceived of in order to be logically and philosophically consistent. Spinoza's work demonstrates again the importance of considering the nature of God if we are to have any satisfactory account also of the physical world.

Isaac Newton (1643-1727) is famous for having developed mathematical treatments for many natural phenomena, especially concerning mechanics, gravity and optics, and he is seen by many today as the prototypical modern scientist. However, he adhered to a very strict monotheism wherein God had absolute Omnipotence. Since this was not orthodox from the Christian point of view—he did not allow that Jesus could be divine—it was hidden from the public even in his own lifetime. Like Nicodemus, he came to God in secret.[6] Though many today think of Newton as a deist, he in fact followed theism rather diligently. He took God as sometimes

---

[4] As, for example, Paley ("Cartesian melodrama") discusses: "There is, of course, a small paradox in all of this. If the hostility to Descartes has been so widespread for so long, in what sense has he been influential? How can it be said that Cartesianism permeates the modern world if virtually no one has had a good word to say about it? To take one obvious example, mind/body dualism never caught on, and for three centuries it has been dismissed by the vast majority of philosophers who have considered it. So why is it routinely assumed to be the 'traditional' view? Is it possible that Descartes could somehow have influenced 'the common man' (a familiar figure, once upon a time, in analytic philosophy), even though 'intellectuals' were queuing up to refute him? Did the idea that there were two forms of substance, one material and the other immaterial, somehow seep into western culture, like a disease poisoning the water supply, while philosophers, physicists and biologists were all looking the other way? How exactly is that supposed to have happened?"

[5] Bolton, "Dualism and the philosophy of the soul."

[6] See Snobelen ("Isaac Newton, heretic").

directly active in the world in order, for example, to reward moral behavior. Because Newton hid this theism, this aspect of his thinking had little public influence. This split within Newton between theism and naturalism was sustained by the public perception of him as a natural philosopher (physicist). His reluctance to publicly bridge this gap was a precursor to many later divergences within philosophy and science between theories of theism and of nature.

Gottfried Leibniz (1646-1716), a contemporary of and a competitor to Newton, developed metaphysical ideas that had great influence on early scientific Enlightenment but which were less than a full theism. Leibniz viewed God and nature as operating in parallel, with a perfect God creating the best possible universe that functioned perfectly on its own. He had all of nature consisting of atoms or 'monads', each of which had some kind of basic mentality and each of which lasted forever. This is a kind of pan-psychism, but the scientific public preserved only the idea that atoms last forever and do so independently of God. There is no room in Leibniz's system for God to influence the world, and this was one reason for his arguments against the theism of Clarke and Newton, as will be further discussed in Chapter 30. Leibniz may have wanted to preserve some kind of non-denominational theism in the interests of civil liberty and tolerance, but, because he wrote both God and minds out of causal influence on the world, the long-term effect of this writings was to maintain a 'two kingdoms' approach to scientific and religious knowledge. In the end this favored naturalism.

2.4 Insights and critiques

Instead of following or inventing a rational system of metaphysics, David Hume (1711-1776) was more skeptical and wanted to ground his beliefs only on what could be empirically observed. He attempted to form an entirely naturalistic 'science of man' that described the psychology of human nature. He saw this nature as based on desires rather than on reasons, in contrast to the rationalists of the previous generation. He was skeptical of religion, especially its more metaphysical assertions and its acceptance of miracles. He wanted, with John Locke, to keep religion separate from civic activities.

Emanuel Swedenborg (1688-1772) started out similarly following the new scientific philosophies and wanted to understand how all of nature, organisms and even the soul functioned in the world. To this end he began to develop theories based on the observations of his contemporaries. However, in midlife he experienced a kind of spiritual awakening that led, he said, to his constant presence in a spiritual world as well as in the physical world. He then published many works detailing a religious and theistic philosophy, from which I have learned a great deal. In fact, I find in Swedenborg[7] the clearest presentation of the arguments within theism that I use in Part III, in particular the arguments from love and from life, and also the universal three-fold subdivision of parts. It continues to surprise me that his theories are not more widely known. One reason for this may be that his philosophy was bound up with specifically religious content which made historical and particular claims. His views were also expressed in the terms of the science of his day that we know is no longer adequate. Furthermore, his supporting evidence consisted of his spiritual explorations which are difficult or impossible to replicate, though some reports of near-death experiences show a commonality. Perhaps there will need to be further independent support for Swedenborg's claims before they can be generally accepted today.

Immanuel Kant (1724-1804) was a philosopher who was of two minds about Swedenborg. Kant had also started out thinking about physics and nature, being an enthusiastic supporter of the new sciences from Newton. Kant (1929) tried to develop science along these lines, with several attempts to form realistic ideas of space, forces and motion in nature. He wanted to include religion (or at least the good effects that it has on practical reason for society), but, in the new scientific age, he was unable to find a realistic basis for this in ontology or metaphysics. He saw that Swedenborg claimed to have precisely what he needed here—an empirical basis for a spiritual reality—but was unable to go along with him for fear of disapproval by his academic peers. The product of this conflict in 1766 was the anonymous[8] book of Kant (2002), where he more-or-less accurately describes Swedenborg's theory but in the end ridicules Swedenborg and his claims. In private he was more accepting. Palmquist[9] and Thorpe[10] both explain how Kant's later philosophy of an 'intelligible world' can

---

[7] Swedenborg, *The divine love and wisdom.*
[8] Kant cannot have expected complete anonymity, since, for example, he lists the names of his friends whose queries prompted him to write the book.
[9] Palmquist, *Parapsychology, philosophy and the mind.*
[10] Thorpe, "The realm of ends as a community of spirits."

be usefully regarded as an attempt to construct a view that has the same *practical* effect as would follow from Swedenborg's religious philosophy but with neither the ontological commitment nor the allowance of any evidence not based on sensory inputs. In, for example, his metaphysics lectures of 1782-3, given between the publication of the first and second editions of the *Critique of Pure Reason*, Kant argues for ideas rather similar to those of Swedenborg. Kant argues in favor of the concept of a moral community not governed by physical separations but by qualitative moral relations. Thorpe points out a significant difference, however, in that Kant later arrives at a position where that community in the intelligible world is determined by the free choices of autonomous agents and hence not influenced by God. Such autonomous existences, we note, are not really possible within theism.

2.5 Creation and evolution

With the progress of the scientific revolution, the need for any influence of God on daily events became less and less obvious, culminating in Laplace's claim that "I had no need for that hypothesis" to describe the evolution of the physical universe. Others, however, still saw evidence for God in the detailed nature of that universe, especially in the existence of living creatures that appear to be wonderfully made, as if designed. William Paley (1743-1805) published *Natural Theology; or, Evidences of the Existence and Attributes of the Deity* in 1802. He argued from the perfection of living creatures to the existence of a good Deity who made them. Arguments in this manner of 'natural theology' were then very popular. Hume had in fact already presented counter-arguments to many of Paley's claims, demonstrating the weakness of arguing from nature to God. Paley's argument presupposes a general belief in the 'goodness of nature', or else, as Hume says, God becomes responsible for the unpleasant natural phenomena as well.

Charles Darwin (1809-1882) was predisposed at an early age towards naturalistic explanations but still took seriously Paley's arguments from design. Then Darwin conceived that gradualist processes of natural selection were responsible for producing the great variety of biological species and also the appearance of design within them. In this way, he was able to counter Paley's argument. Even the possibility of natural processes was

presumably sufficient to rebut his inference about God. Darwin was effectively advocating a deism, because, he said, he did not want any God to
exist that would be responsible for the suffering, predation and parasitism,
etc., which he saw everywhere in nature. Others point out that if God was
not involved, there could be no reason given for retaining a divinity at all.
Darwin was claiming that God does not influence the world after creating
it, and such claims reduced public support for theism.

2.6 Consciousness and process

Even if biological evolution could be explained, there were still many
questions remaining about the nature of mind and consciousness, questions which theism once might have been called upon to answer. There
began to be much public interest in spiritualism and psychic phenomena, and the Society for Psychical Research was founded in 1882. These
activities were not now based on theism but rather on phenomena that
were not explained by either the religious or scientific establishments.
William James (1842-1910) was not religious, for example, though from his
father he had been exposed to Swedenborg's ideas. He wanted to know
about minds, took the question of human immortality very seriously, and
published the first comprehensive description of religious experiences.
James[11] proposed a 'transmission theory' of human consciousness, con-
trasting it with the theory that it is generated by the brain. He lacked,
however, a theory of what might *exist* to account for human consciousness
or immortality, and in the end, James[12] even asked "Does 'consciousness'
exist?", seeming to reply in the negative. Unless there is *some* ontology, I
will counter, the possibility of a proper science fades away.

Alfred North Whitehead (1861-1947) was a mathematician who became
interested in the foundations of physics. He first followed interpretations
of special relativity, in which only events existed. Then in 1929 Whitehead
published a fully-fledged 'process philosophy'. According to this mature
viewpoint, the world consists of a succession of 'actual occasions' that develop and become actual by 'perceiving' their predecessors in a way reminiscent of conscious perception. Within his philosophy there is also the
beginning of a 'process theology' whereby God is involved in creation,

---

[11] James, *Human immortality*.
[12] James, "Does 'consciousness' exist?"

having both a primordial and a consequent nature, and whereby God develops along with the world. God's influence on the world is first by the 'ingress' of forms for actuality (as with Plato) and second as a 'lure' to humans for what is good. In both cases, there are no directly causal influences. In fact, there are no active causes anywhere in his ontology, not even in the physical world. Rather, everything, even physical processes, is modeled on perception by organisms, resulting overall in a panpsychist view of the entire universe.

Whitehead's philosophy can be called theistic, but only in a weak sense because the positive influences of God on the world are limited to those creatures with desire and with a conscience. His ideas were developed by Charles Hartshorne[13] and by John Cobb[14] into a 'process theology' that has became popular. It seems to offer consistency with modern physics. It has an emphasis on 'becoming' rather than 'being', along with explanations of how consciousness might arise in organisms. It also has an explanation of why Darwinian natural selection may have been necessary.

2.7 Quantum influences

Questions of how mind or God may influence physical reality have remained alive since Whitehead's era and seem to be a focus of thoughts for those who might be inclined to theism but who do not find any suitable general framework. In modern times, physical reality tends to be described by quantum mechanics. One topical question is whether quantum mechanics allows the physical world to be influenced by consciousness or by God. Since quantum theory is indeterministic by itself—it only predicts probabilities—and since the existence of a conscious observer is often invoked to solve the measurement problem in quantum mechanics, it does seem that these influences on physics are possible.

Amit Goswami[15] recently appears to be explaining theism, for example, when he says that "God is the agent of downward causation". One reading of this is true in theism, but Goswami turns it around. According to him, every instance of downward causation is God, so any experiment which demonstrates non-local correlations is therefore a proof of God. That is

---

[13] Hartshorne, *A natural theology for our time.*
[14] Cobb, *A Christian natural theology.*
[15] Goswami, *God is not dead.*

not the God of theism, and I find it farfetched to claim to have thereby 'rediscovered God within science'.

Quantum physics may be indeterministic about the detailed choices between different outcomes for some classes of microscopic events, namely decoherent measurements, but it is not completely arbitrary. It makes very precise predictions for the probabilities of those outcomes, and, furthermore, the evolution of these probability distributions is completely deterministic.

Either mind influences the choice when decohering measurements occur (as Stapp[16] suggests), or it changes the probabilities of different outcomes (as Saunders[17] and Bielfeldt[18] also consider). In the first case, the range of influence is extremely limited and hardly plausible in a dualist theory. In the second case, the non-physical input changes the probability rules of quantum physics in just the same way as dualist input would change Newton's laws of motion if it were to influence classical systems. I conclude therefore, with Saunders and Bielfeldt, that it is very doubtful that any dualist or divine input into the operation of the natural world proceeds by exploiting the small residual indeterminism of quantum physics. Dualist control in quantum physics is no easier than in classical physics. That is, any influence of a dual degree must affect those properties of objects that are also measured by physics.

The challenge is to find a coherent theory which explains what, when, how and why those physical properties are changed. In order to meet this challenge, we first need a coherent and realistic account of existence and causation, preferably one that can be used for both physical existence and for minds. That is the task of Part II.

Before such an account of causation can be used within a scientific theism, there are several fundamental issues that need to addressed, especially where science and theism presently disagree. Several of these issues are addressed in the next chapter in order to find a new way forward to a theism that will give an account of God and nature and of their connection.

---

[16] Stapp, *Mindful universe.*
[17] Saunders, "Does God cheat at dice?"
[18] Bielfeldt, "Can western monotheism avoid substance dualism?"

3

A Way Forward

3.1 Conflict or integration?

The previous chapter described a decline in theism within intellectual and scientific circles. It became more and more discredited to use theism in a realistic manner to describe how God exists in relation to the world, especially to the details of the world as found by the sciences. This decline is a consequence of the many objections put forward by scientists and philosophers since the time of Kant and of the related dissatisfactions with the kind of explanations put forward within theism. In light of this diminished acceptance and these dissatisfactions, it may seem doubtful that a way could be taken to an integrated understanding of the world together with God. Is it possible to find a view which includes both science and theology in a fully-fledged manner without doing violence to either? The theology to be advocated should describe a living God, rather than a merely metaphysical Absolute.

In this chapter I will describe a way forward to such an integration. It will be better explained in later chapters, as then the various suggested changes and methods to be advocated will be justified in terms of the theoretical structure. The purpose now is confined to outlining a series of small changes, both to science and to theology, which need to be made to understand the arguments to be presented. The small changes are modifications which, I claim, will not in the end affect the essences of science and theology but will, in fact, improve them.

3.2 Changes to science

Scientists should consider the possibility of as-yet-undiscovered dependencies of physical processes on such things as our individual minds or even on the transcendent mind of God. Such dependencies should be intellectually evaluated and evidence considered which might confirm such theories. We should *not* refuse to consider evidence because of a denial in advance of the very possibility of openness. In the end, any actual changes in science will be made only in the light of new theories and new evidence which properly describe and confirm how such influences operate, but at least evidence will not be denied a hearing according to normal standards. Scientists, in this new context, will still retain the ability to examine the regular and law-like behavior of material processes. It is only that, sometimes, the *causes* of those processes will not be previous material powers but something new to be investigated. A change needed is for science to *give up assuming the causal closure of the universe*. The likelihood of some causal openness for the universe should be admitted.

Some (perhaps many) scientists will respond with "Over my dead body! Did not we get rid of occult influences five centuries ago, and look how much better we are for that!" The theistic reply to this is "Fear not!" We are *not* asking for a return to the Middle Ages, to witchcraft or magic or anything similar, and moreover not to a 'new age' in which 'anything goes' and in which 'we make whatever reality we want'. Rather, the civil contract between secular citizens of good will should remain untouched. Any new science should be entirely robust and transparent and subject to public confirmations or disconfirmations. Admittedly we will be advocating immanent theism, rather than the deism in which God does not interact with the world, so the world will not be so simple, but it will not be the end of civilization as we know it.

In fact, it is likely that whole new sciences will be formed after we begin to understand the interactions between mental and physical processes. Many present-day scientists suspect that such interactions exist but are reluctant to admit this in public, at least on weekdays, for fear of ridicule. This reluctance is not actually based on evidence against such interactions. Every physical scientist feels pressure to assume causal closure in order to belong to the profession.

It seems to me that scientists are afraid of something: of the possible incursion into the world (into the world of thought, if not the real world) of new powers which they have traditionally ignored and over which they have no control. They fear that even *thinking* that minds or God have influence would be to encourage an acceptance of what they think of as 'black forces'. I once thought like that, but I could not make sense of the world if neither minds nor God could influence it. Some scientists may be relaxed about the prospect, but they are not a majority in research circles. The theistic response, to assuage these fears, is to emphasize that these new influences of the mind and of God are *not* arbitrary, violent, or disruptive. Rather, the opposite. These influences, in theism, will be regular, will be conditioned in many ways, and will be supportive rather than upsetting. There is nothing to be afraid of within science: these are white rather than black forces, and in fact are largely responsible for generating the enormously complicated biological, psychological, sociological and civil structures we see in the world and certainly not for breaking them down.

One related change needed in science is to consider multiple levels of reality, where such levels are related by specific causes and specific laws that scientists will investigate. Such levels are not to be taken as merely distinct levels of explanation or of different microscopic vs. macroscopic levels of description but as multiple derivative levels that exist concurrently with and interact with each other. This change in science will be relatively easy. Chapter 5 shows that many of these levels are already known to science in some detail, though not recognized as such.

3.3 Changes to theology

Religious people might also benefit from making some changes in their theology. This is a delicate process, but, I believe, the changes to be suggested here can be justified with no loss of glory to God. Rather, it will turn out, there will be much gain. It is not a coincidence that the changes to be recommended here are a mirror of those required above for scientists.

The theological conflict arises because the God described in this book is a being composed entirely of Love, and, moreover, a completely unselfish love. To such a God, we assert that anger, jealousy, exclusiveness and selfishness are completely foreign, and that God is, rather, patient, merciful, compassionate, and accommodating. Many people will question whether this is the same as the God of the Bible (Old and New Testaments) and of the Qu'ran. Those books claim to describe the same good God, but the God they portray does *appear* to be angry, jealous, possessive, selfish and vindictive. Which view is true, which view is appearance, and why? Let me give one possible resolution.

The theology in Part III will claim God is life itself: the very source of love and wisdom for all beings in the world. It will go on to explain how God is the source for all derived willing, thinking and acting in the universe. All power and glory should be attributed to God, as there is only one God and thus no other source of life. The divine Love of God in Himself can be viewed as similar to a brilliant source of light and glory before which nothing selfish or impure can stand if not shielded or otherwise aided. If unregenerate or selfish persons are in the presence of God, they will be extremely uncomfortable and pained. To such persons it truly *appears* that God is angry with them.[1] But, in reality, it is their *own* anger and selfishness which generates these discomforts and pains: real and powerful feelings. To them it does feel that God is angry and, in fact, angry with them personally. However that anger is certainly not from God but is a consequence of their own partial state of religious maturity and the manner in which God's glory is hence received imperfectly by them.

This reasoning explains why it only appears that God is possessive of his religious flock and jealous of other gods and that he selfishly believes that only his way is the truth and the life. Since there *are no other gods*, it is for *our* benefit that he deflects us from seeking them. It is a simple theistic fact that God is the one life and that this is not an arbitrary megalomania on God's part. It is actually a direct consequence of God's unselfish, compassionate, and perpetual care for everyone's individual wellbeing.

Therefore it is *our* variations which lead to God having varying appearances to us, while he is actually always constant and unselfish. Just as our sun is fixed, but we experience (real) days and seasons as our earth varies, so is it with God.[2] Since God is of Love and hence relates to us by means of our loves, it is our *deepest religious loves* which are varying, and thus drive the differing appearances. These deepest loves are what we will call spiritual loves.

If we can allow this explanation of the cause of the difference between

---

[1] By 'true appearance', I mean not a 'mere appearance' which has no effect, but something which has real effects, at least in our minds and bodies.

[2] "He causes his sun to rise on the evil and the good", Matt. 5:45

reality and appearances, we should feel free to affirm the purity and unselfishness of the God of Love as fundamental in theology. This affirma-
tion will be made in Part III, and it will be the basis for many subsequent
deductions within theism and science. It implies that God is continually
trying to provide us with as much life as we are able to receive, retain
and use. It is primarily we who vary.[3] Equivalently, we can take God as
always doing everything that he can to help us but as still respecting our
free choices. Once we can rely on God to act constantly and unselfishly for
what is best in the long term, we have a good possibility of finding laws
that relate theism and science and also a good prospect of discovering a
science based on regular structures, dispositions and predictions.

Accepting the fact that God's love is good has important consequences
for the concerns of scientists in the previous section. Many scientists worry
about possible incursions of arbitrary powers by an omnipotent God. If
God's omnipotence is ruled (as it should be) by his constant and unselfish
Love acting by means of divine Wisdom, then the influences of God on
the world will be good and constructive rather than destructive. The fact
that some less-mature persons see those influences as fearful merely reflects their own spiritual states, in accordance with the principles outlined
above.

3.4 Religious scriptures

Let us briefly discuss the consequences of the above account for how religious scriptures may be produced and read. The influence of God must
have been received and filtered according to the spiritual and religious capabilities of the persons involved in the reception. When prophets produce
religious scriptures inspired by God, they present a moral vision which
reflects their own internal spiritual loves at the time. Historically religions
did not *begin* by understanding the above facts about love and how our
spiritual loves govern the way God appears to us. Rather, the written historical scriptures have an external moral character whenever the religious
temper is external, with correspondingly more emphasis on ritual purity
than on spiritual honesty.

The purpose of such divinely-inspired scriptures is to lead us toward
life and love that are closer to God. This leading is typically from external

---

[3] As argued in Thompson ("The consistency of physical law with divine immanence").

toward more internal understandings and loves. The earliest scriptures present an external moral character that is less developed than that produced by later spiritual repentance and regeneration. Such early scriptures should still be understood as embodying the Word of God, but in a more hidden or obscure manner that is necessarily limited by the loves of the original recipients and writers. This implies that successive scriptures will be different in character. Later productions will embody God's love and wisdom more accurately than the previous writings.

3.5 New frameworks

My purpose is to follow through with the above theistic account of God and to use it to describe in simple (and perhaps somewhat bare) terms a new framework of theistic science that enables an integration of theology and the sciences. By the sciences, I primarily refer to physics and psychology.

The first step toward this integrated framework is to formulate a clear idea of causation, especially an idea that may be generalized to include physics, psychology, and perhaps theology. The preferred concept of causation, to be developed in Part II, treats 'dispositions' as the primary feature of objects (both physical objects and minds). Although Part II contains no theology, this focus on dispositions arises because of the underlying theism in the whole project. The theism suggests love as the underlying reality for persons, and hence, in a derivative manner, suggests that dispositions and powers are the reality underlying both minds and nature. A concept of *substance* can usefully be developed and defined in terms of dispositions. Ideas of *multi-level* and *derivative* causation may also be defined and recognized in physics and psychology. Part II is required because changes in the philosophy of science need to be integrated within the new framework. Some likely predictions in science will be presented in Part IV.

This book describes, by deduction from postulates, a *framework* for theology and science and *not* theologies and sciences themselves. I do not predict quantum mechanics, quantum gravity, or detailed theories of thinking and memory in particular. I only provide a general framework in which such theories are to be expected and show how much I believe a theistic framework might ideally constrain the details of scientific theories. Those future theories are thereby expected to happily link up with theism in general, as well as, I hope, with all verified empirical observations from scientific research.

3.6 Authority and evidence

If theistic science is to be in fact a science, it will be *only a theory*, and it will need to be justified by evidence and by rational logic and consistency. It cannot assume anything just on the basis of authority, neither the authority of a person nor of a book. It cannot, in advance, take anything as a proven fact. This applies to all scriptures, all revelations, and indeed to all experience. They cannot be authorities for theistic science. They are only evidence that may or may not support theories. Individual investigators will have their own beliefs, even their own firm convictions, but these can only be motivations and not proofs. This book will make and clarify some of the basic postulates of theism, but these postulations will not be automatically taken as proven. They are only the initial skeleton of an overall theory. Evidence and confirmation refer only to a theory as a whole or to the comparative evaluation of two competing theories.

Even if God speaks to someone in (say) a revelation, we still (as in any science) have to evaluate the likelihood that it *was* actually from God, that the person remembers it correctly, and that he did not distort the content of the message. Evidence and rationality enter into each such evaluation of the true nature of the revelation. Evaluation requirements still apply even if that person should be ourself. It applies even when the message is internally consistent and even when it has good effects. Such considerations will improve its evidential quality but can never automatically override the other considerations that should be part of the discernment. Personally we may be certain of something–and even build our lives on it–but such certainty is not part of any public science.

Part II

Ontology

4

Power and Substance

4.1 Substance

IN ORDER to understand the existence of physical and mental things, even of divine things, we need to treat them as actually existing. They cannot be merely concepts, hypotheses, forms, or information. We may describe some of them by mathematics but actual things are not constituted by mathematics. This amounts to taking an Aristotelian view of reality, wherein every real thing is some kind of substance and has powers for change. This can immediately be contrasted with an extreme Platonic view, wherein only ideal forms are real, and things in our world are merely some kind of image or shadow of those ideal forms.

Following Aristotle, we can analyze the nature of individual things. We see how they all have some *form* and are all composed of some *matter* (Greek *hyle*). I am going to say that objects all have some form, and that form is a form *of* some underlying substance or stuff.[1] By the term 'form', I refer not just to the external shape of an object, but to all the internal structure and descriptive details necessary to make a full account of what actually exists at a given moment. Spatial structures are forms, and so also are any other structures needed, whether they are spatial or not.[2] This use of the term 'form' refers only to static or categorical properties that can be attributed at any one time. It therefore excludes causal principles since

---

[1] Note that the word *substance* has two useful meanings here. The first, as Aristotle's *ousia*, refers to specific objects, as in 'this substance' and 'that substance'. The second, as in *hyle*, refers to the underlying stuff, as in the underlying substance of which objects are formed. In this chapter, the word 'substance' will usually have this second meaning. I also avoid using the term 'matter' since it has too many unwanted connotations and is difficult to generalize beyond the physical.

[2] As an example of non-spatial structures, we could take the 'internal spins' of elementary particles or their internal group identity. These in general have no uniform projection onto physical space, if only for not having the correct number of coordinates to map onto three dimensions.

these describe what *might* happen at later times.[3] The form and substance of each thing can be intellectually distinguished, but they never exist apart in reality. It is never the case that the form of a thing is here and the substance of it is over there.

This is to adopt a realism that takes seriously the need for substance and also for changes and processes involving substantial objects. Each object cannot merely exist self-sufficiently but must be closely linked to others by causes and/or effects. We therefore need a serious account of how causes exist and operate and how the causal powers of objects are related to their substantial nature. Because science is continually discovering new kinds of causes and new ways of causation, the realism here is not a naive realism wherein we take as real just what appears to our senses. There are enormously many things and causes that science postulates that are not apparent to our senses but are inferred from empirical or theoretical considerations.

The present realism, because it stresses the leading role of causes and powers in generating new processes, is going to be called 'generative realism.' If we want a slogan, we could say "No process without structure, no structure without substance, no substance without power, no power without process."

4.2 Dispositions

In order to understand causation and develop our generative realism, we must recognize that dispositions have a leading role in all kinds of causation processes. Dispositions such as fragility, mass, and electric charge are those features of a thing which describe what it *can do*, not just what it *is* categorically. Understanding the nature of dispositions will help in comprehending the theses of this book.

Dispositional properties of objects—also called propensities or causal powers—appear to be crucial parts of any kind of causal explanation, whether we talk about the fragility of complex objects or about the mass and charge of an individual electron. We include as propensities those dispositions which have probabilistic manifestations.

---

[3] This exclusion of 'causality' from within 'form' implies a different approach to that of Aquinas, as will be discussed in Section 4.5.

There has been considerable debate among philosophers concerning the true basis of the dispositional properties of objects. Are dispositions grounded in a base reality as described by physicists, or do they exist on their own in some way? And if physical laws are sufficient to explain the behavior of objects, are dispositions really needed in themselves, or can they be eliminated with the help of Occam's razor? Or, is it perhaps the other way around, with physical laws depending on dispositions? In order to get some answers, let us see how dispositions are analyzed and explained by science.

4.3 Scientific analyses of powers or dispositions

Consider how science might analyze the fragility of a glass vase, namely the disposition to break after small external pressures. The very *first* analysis would be to treat the vase as a whole with mass, shape, rigidity and fragility. The fragility is then a property of the vase. The vase is therefore an object with specific dispositional properties and, as well, with a shape and orientation. The *second* analysis would be to consider that the vase is made of glass, where the glass is a continuous solid with various mass, elastic and fracture properties. A computer finite-element model of the vase might then explain its fragility in terms of the stress and fracture properties of the constituent material. In this case, the *glass* is the dispositional material, to be arranged in the shape of the vase and thereby to explain the properties of the vase. A *third* level of analysis might be a molecular simulation, where elasticity and fractures are properties derived from the strengths of interaction potentials between molecules. Now, the *molecules* are the objects constituted by those interaction potentials, which are dispositions, and they are arranged to make macroscopic glass-material. And so on: a *fourth* level may consider the potentials between individual *electrons and nuclei*, where now those electrons and nuclei are constituted by mass, charge, spin, magnetic moments, etc.: all dispositional properties. Surely quantum mechanics is also needed, which introduces its own set of probabilistic dispositions (propensities).

We see that at each stage of microscopic analysis, the presented objects are diagnosed as structural forms of some more fundamental disposition. Whether the stages reach the most fundamental level is not the issue here. Rather, at each level, the result of the analysis is to attribute existence to some 'stuff' with some causal powers held essentially. First, the vase as a whole was the existing stuff; in the second analysis, the glass with stress-strain powers is taken as the stuff of the vase; later it is electrons, etc., with electric charges; and the final stage listed here has electrons with propensities to emit or absorb virtual photons.

The attribution of dispositions in all of the above cases is according to the following logical template:

"Object S has the disposition P to do action A" is equivalent to "*if* S is in some circumstance C, C depending on P and the character of A, *then* there will be a non-zero likelihood of S doing A".

For example, "A vase object has the disposition to break" is equivalent to "If the vase is in some circumstance of being struck forcefully, this circumstance depending on the precise fragility and the character of the breaking, then there is a non-zero likelihood of the vase breaking".

Here, the 'action A' can either be a change in S itself or an interaction with other objects. The suitable 'circumstance C' is usually defined by multiple spatial relations to other objects and will be different for different dispositions and for different actions. The circumstance C is said to depend only on the 'character' of the action, and not on the action itself, because possibly, if the disposition is never manifested, there may exist *no* such action at any time in the past, present or future. Finally, the phrase 'non-zero likelihood' is designed to be sufficiently general to allow both sure-fire dispositions and probabilistic propensities. It has the consequence that if the probability of an event (while varying with time) touches zero, then there is no propensity at that particular time, but this is surely a reasonable feature.

In all cases above, we never avoided dispositional properties again in the explanation of the first disposition to be explained. Dispositionality (of some kind) never seems to go away because of physical explanations! We seem to have some kind of 'dispositional essentialism', a claim which asserts that that each object has some properties that are inherently dispositional, and that these include the causal base properties that enter into scientific laws. Since Ellis and Lierse[4], many have supported this argument.

---

[4] Ellis and Lierse, "Dispositional essentialism."

Similar views are advocated in Bird[5], Bird[6], Cartwright[7], Chakravartty[8], Elder[9], Ellis[10], Ellis[11] Fetzer[12], Harré and Madden[13], Molnar[14], Mumford[15], Mumford[16], Shoemaker[17], Swoyer[18], and Thompson[19].

An opposing view is given by Ryle[20], who sees dispositions as merely 'inference tickets' or 'promises', even when science gives perfectly good explanations! There is another tension between accounts of nature based on dispositions and accounts based on laws. Armstrong[21] and Katzav[22], for example, see dispositions as derived from universal laws combined with non-dispositional properties, but, as Bird[23] points out, this does not solve all the philosophical problems. Either Armstrong must concede that some properties are not categorical but instead have essential powers, or he is faced with a regress. I adopt the above type of dispositional essentialism as the basis for further developments in this book, claiming that every object has some dispositional properties that enter into its causal relations.[24]

4.4 Dispositions in nature

This dispositional essentialism leaves two important questions still unanswered. The first question is whether *all*, or *only some* of an object's properties are dispositional. We would naively think that structural properties such as shapes, sizes and arrangements of parts are not dispositional prop-

[5] Bird, "The dispositionalist conception of laws."
[6] Bird, *Nature's metaphysics.*
[7] Cartwright, *How the laws of physics lie.*
[8] Chakravartty, "The dispositional essentialist view of properties and laws."
[9] Elder, "Laws, natures, and contingent necessities."
[10] Ellis, "Causal laws and singular causation."
[11] Ellis, *Scientific essentialism.*
[12] Fetzer, "World of dispositions."
[13] Harré and Madden, *Causal powers.*
[14] Molnar, *Powers.*
[15] Mumford, "Ellis and Lierse on dispositional essentialism."
[16] Mumford, *Dispositions.*
[17] Shoemaker, *Identity, cause, and mind.*
[18] Swoyer, "The nature of natural laws."
[19] Thompson, "Real dispositions in the physical world."
[20] Ryle, *The concept of mind.*
[21] Armstrong, "Dispositions are causes."
[22] Katzav, "Dispositions and the principle of least action."
[23] Bird, "The ultimate argument against Armstrong's contingent necessitation view of laws."
[24] Dispositional essentialism does *not* assert that all dispositions of an object are held *essentially*, since that, for example, would not allow water to lose its liquidity when it froze or evaporated. Rather, every object has *some* dispositions which are essential to that object.

erties, but Bird[25] argues that we cannot be sure of this. It would be useful to have a clear understanding of how (or whether) dispositional and non-dispositional properties can be simultaneously instantiated in an object. The second question concerns ontology: what is the relation between dispositional properties and the being (or substance) of the object with such properties? Menzies[26] doubts, for example, that *properties* can be correctly construed as causal powers. Surely, he says, it is *objects* rather than properties which are the correct bearers of enduring causal powers.

In the previous section, we saw how science analyzes and constitutes dispositional properties and how those properties are explained as forms of some essential more-fundamental dispositions or propensities. We can now philosophically generalize that analysis in order to formulate a new view of the constitution of objects, such that dispositional essentialism logically follows. This new constitution is to *take powers or propensities themselves as the persisting 'stuff' of which objects are made*. That is, I argue that we should identify 'propensity' and 'substance' so that natural objects, as 'forms of propensity', are then 'forms of a substance' in nearly the manner of Aristotle.

It is admittedly a large metaphysical leap to identify propensity as substance, but I will argue that the identification is grammatically correct, philosophically sound, historically defensible, and physically correct, and that it even helps clarify interpretations of quantum physics. It furthermore agrees with the Eleatic Principle: that existence should only be given to that which has causal power. In a more modern age, this would be called a 'pragmatic' view of substance, as attributing significance not to what something merely *is* but to what it can *do*. The identity of substance and propensity is claimed in the same sense that, while the morning star and the evening star are initially known independently, they turn out to refer to the same (ontological) being. This identification should be the next development for those who adhere today to dispositional essentialism. Instead of worrying about 'ungrounded dispositions', we will see that dispositions are able themselves to be grounds or bearers of properties.

---

[25] Bird, "The ultimate argument against Armstrong's contingent necessitation view of laws."
[26] Menzies, "Nature's metaphysics."

4.5 The proposed ontology

On the basis of the previous scientific analyses and the above generalization, I claim first that *every* existing object is composed of some underlying stuff or substance with some given set of causal powers or propensities, and that it is moreover composed according to some form or structure. We may think of those forms as being spatial[27] arrangements or fields. This can be done at any stage of scientific analysis, wherever we believe we have a complete set of the causal powers exhibited by an object. We may or may not think we have knowledge of some fundamental level.

Let us make a second philosophical step and consider that substance itself. What *is* it? Its essence is some set of causal powers. Therefore, from the Eleatic and pragmatic points of view, all we can (and need to) say is that the substance *is* that set of causal powers. This is to identify complete sets of causal powers as substantial objects and such objects as complete sets of causal powers.

We are thus making an ontological move, as powers are no longer all *properties* or properties of properties. More fundamental powers are taken instead as the substance of which objects can be made. This will also suggest a grammatical move of the powers, from being adjectives within predicates to being subjects and objects. We have now to envisage powers and propensities as nouns, as discussed below.

While this approach and that of Aquinas are both inspired by Aristotle, we end up with different formulations. We distinguish form from underlying substance, but we differ in where we attribute an object's causal principle, the active powers that lead it to act and interact. For Aquinas, the object's form is a description of everything that makes the object what it is and so includes its causal principle. His underlying substance is what is left, namely the 'pure potency' that is in-formed to make a specific object. In this book, by contrast, 'form' is taken to refer to purely static or categorical properties, and an object's causal principle – its active powers – is taken to be a certain feature of its underlying *substance*, not of its form. Aquinas groups causal principles and anatomical shapes together within 'form' and distinguishes both from substance as pure potency, whereas I group causal principles and substance together and distinguish both from anatomical shapes. In my opinion, Aquinas has too many concepts packed

---

[27] Spatial relations are assumed here, since (after Kant) they appear to be the prerequisites for any possibility of interaction.

within the meaning of 'form'. This not only often leads to confusion for readers but also hinders the scientific investigation of details of microscopic structures and of powers of those structures.

4.6 Discussion

But are propensities (powers, etc.) *the right kind of thing* to be substance? One might object that propensities do not appear to have enough *being*, as they appear instead always to point to an incipient state of becoming. Are they, as Armstrong[28] claims, always packing but never arriving? Would objects made of such substance as proposed here actually exist, or only potentially exist, or (perhaps) exist potentially? Bird[29] responds to this by pointing out that this objection assumes that powers or dispositions are not fully actual. Rather, he says, we should insist that powers are actual full-blooded features of objects and that what *is* merely potential are their manifestations. I would respond slightly differently: powers are the actual full-blooded substance of objects and are not merely the 'features' or 'properties' of objects.

Perhaps we wonder whether objects made of such substance are really 'full-blooded'. Do such substantial objects persist as objects should? *How* do they have being? Can they be individuated properly? Are they simple units, or can they be divided? Could elementary particles be of such substances? Could *we* be such objects and still feel our own reality? Let us discuss some of these issues.

Do these new kinds of substance persist? There is certainly no need for them to persist forever, but can they persist through accidental changes while maintaining their essential nature? To answer the question about persistence, we note that dispositions are possessed even when they are not being manifested. A vase is still fragile when it is not breaking. The fragility persists for a finite duration: at least from one contact event until the next. What I am asserting is that the corresponding substance of the glass persists for at least exactly that same duration. In that duration, it may change its position, orientation or illumination. These are the variable accidental properties that vary while the underlying substance (fragility and the other dispositions) remain the same. Whether the underlying sub-

---

[28] Armstrong, *A world of states of affairs*.
[29] Bird, *Nature's metaphysics*.

stance persists forever is the same question as whether the fragility (etc.) persists forever. That can be answered by looking at the future adventures of the vase in the world.[30] If the fragile glass ceases to exist, then the substance ends, perhaps by being changed into another kind of substance. That substantial objects might persist only for a finite time does not render them any less enduring or persistent objects during that time.

How do these substances have 'being'? The recent dispositional essentialists have taken all properties as 'powers, and *nothing but* powers', so we wonder if we can take all objects similarly. The claim was thought by Bird[31] to include *all* properties, including all those previously thought categorical such as position, shape and structure. I do not hold such a strong view. Particular objects have *both* dispositional and categorical properties, once we understand how this is to be conceived. The dispositional properties are instantiated by the underlying dispositional substance, whereas the categorical properties are instantiated by the *form or structure* of that substance which makes up this specific object. In this way we have what Martin[32] calls a 'Janus-faced' or 'dual-aspect' view, but of objects rather than of properties. We are thereby constructing a notion of substance wherein substantial objects legitimately have both dispositional and categorical aspects. We do not follow Jacobs[33] in having 'powerful qualities' that have both dispositional and qualitative sides. Rather it is the *substantial objects* that have both. Now, some but not all properties are dispositional. We do not deny the semantic distinction between dispositional and categorical properties but rather reinforce it. Neither do we have a 'neutral monism' whereby the dispositional and categorical are 'modes of presentation', following Mumford[34], of the same instantiated properties.

Many philosophers since Prior, Pargetter, and Jackson[35], and recently, Rives[36] have argued that dispositions are 'causally impotent' following the argument that "if dispositions are distinct from their categorical bases, and their bases are efficacious, then the dispositions themselves are impotent." Rives explicitly assumes that "the causal efficacy of categorical properties is not in question". I disagree. I think categorical properties such as

---

[30] I would doubt that vases are eternal. I not believe that electrons or nuclei are necessarily eternal either.
[31] Bird, "Structural properties revisited."
[32] Martin, "The need for ontology."
[33] Jacobs, "Powerful qualities, not pure powers."
[34] Mumford, *Dispositions*.
[35] Prior, Pargetter, and Jackson, "3 theses about dispositions."
[36] Rives, "Why dispositions are (still) distinct from their bases and causally impotent."

size, shape, structure are by themselves never causally efficacious. We saw that above. Such properties are only efficacious when they are shapes or structures *of* some substantial object, and this requires the participation of dispositional properties. A 'base' can never be a structure *per se* and hence never purely categorical.[37]

A summary of the new position is to say that specific objects are *unions* of form and power, of qualitative and dispositional aspects.[38] Objects are structures of propensity, namely forms of substance, in a good Aristotelian manner. Forms may be examined in great detail by *form*-al sciences such as mathematics and logic, but no natural changes can be generated by formal constructions. For example, contemporary attempts in physics to construct 'it from bit' (to derive existence from form) can only produce a static (timeless) universe without changes or causes of change. I would instead say that forms are *the means by which* dispositional powers operate, since the power-substances can only operate if they are arranged in some form or structure that allows for interaction and movement. Conversely, forms can only have an impact on the world if they are the forms *of* some propensity, as thereby a physical object in the world is in existence and has powers to influence others. This is why I said that objects in the world are required to be unions of form and power: they require powers to be in some form and require forms to be of some power. The resulting union has an existence that goes beyond either ingredient by itself.[39] In a natural object, the power and form are actually inseparable and only abstractly distinguishable. We can (and should) intellectually distinguish them—as recent philosophers have emphasized—but that does that mean that they can ever exist apart.

Can these substantial objects be individuated? Can we identify individual objects made of such substance? It certainly does *not* seem that we can divide powers or propensities themselves into parcels, with some for each individual object in the world. I can only see individuation proceeding via the *specific* forms or *trope* that the substance-stuff has in specific

---

[37] Psillos ("What do powers do when they are not manifested?") also makes this mistake, when he argues that "fundamental properties [..] flow from some fundamental symmetries," for symmetries, as purely mathematical structures, can never physically 'flow', and can never produce physical objects. Rather, in our Aristotelian framework, they describe the properties of objects and, here, relations between those properties. It cannot be that "elementary particles are the irreducible representations (irreps) of a group," again because groups (or even their representations) have no causal powers.

[38] Neither can exist by itself. No dispositions can exist except in a form, and no forms exist except as forms of dispositions.

[39] Ellis ("The metaphysics of powers") has recently written in support of this view of forms as being both categorical and necessary for the operation of powers.

objects. That is, identifying individual objects, as forms of the underlying substance-stuff, can only proceed by identifying those particular forms used in each individual object. We may say that even the individual and specific *existence* of an object depends on the specific forms that inform the essential underlying powers/propensities of the substance.

Some scientists may be suspicious of the idea that there is a fundamental level where objects are composed of dispositions directly and do not have parts in substructures. Would that not be the end of science? No, because science's task is to first determine *which* is the fundamental level. Secondly, scientists try to exactly characterize and understand all those dispositions, both common and uncommon, in order to predict their exact operation. Any such claims are subject to empirical verification or revision.

Finally, we must consider the *logical* plausibility of this proposed identity. Grammatically, nouns in sentences are the agents of actions and refer to the bearer of causal influences. The object of an action must cooperate in the operation of those influences.[40] This is entirely consistent with the present claim that subjects and objects are themselves forms of propensity. It is the nature of powers and propensities to be causal influences, so any thing constructed from them will be the bearer of causal influences. We must agree, therefore, to a grammatical move of powers from being adjectives within predicates to being the substance of subjects and objects. Then we must envisage as nouns the forms of such powers and propensities. This seems to me to be quite feasible.

4.7 Quantum physics

In the above sections, power and propensity have been described generically, where propensities are those powers that manifest themselves in terms of probabilities for different outcomes. To allow for *quantum physics* and its probabilities, we need just such propensities. The question of whether propensities are in fact needed for describing nature is linked to the accuracy of quantum physics. I will not decide that question now. I only wish to argue that quantum processes can be described by means of propensities, and that quantum substantial objects can be identified as

---

[40] A hammer and a vase must have powers to interact with each other if fragility is to be manifested this way.

those more fundamental propensities which appear in some form or structure.

Quantum mechanics describes the probabilities of actual outcomes in terms of a wave function or at least of a quantum state of amplitudes that varies with time. The public always asks what the wave function *is*, or what the amplitudes are amplitudes *of*. Usually, we reply that the amplitudes are 'probability amplitudes', or that the wave function is a 'probability wave function', but neither answer is ontologically satisfying since probabilities are *numbers*, not *stuff*. We have already rehearsed the objections to the natural world being made out of numbers, as these are pure forms. In fact, 'waves', 'amplitudes' and 'probabilities' are *all* forms, and none of them can be substance. So, what *are* quantum objects made of? What *stuff*?

According to Heisenberg,[41] the quantum probability waves are "a quantitative formulation of the concept of 'dynamis', possibility, or in the later Latin version, 'potentia', in Aristotle's philosophy. The concept of events not determined in a peremptory manner, but that the possibility or 'tendency' for an event to take place has a kind of reality—a certain intermediate layer of reality, halfway between the massive reality of matter and the intellectual reality of the idea or the image—this concept plays a decisive role in Aristotle's philosophy. In modern quantum theory this concept takes on a new form; it is formulated quantitatively as probability and subjected to mathematically expressible laws of nature." Unfortunately Heisenberg does not develop this interpretation much beyond the sort of generality of the above statements, and the concept of 'potentiality' remains awkwardly isolated from much of his other thought on this subject.[43] It is unclear even what he means by 'potentia'.

Herbert[44], in describing Heisenberg's ideas, imagines them to describe a world more ephemeral than substantial, imaging that "the entire visible universe, what Bishop Berkeley called 'the mighty frame of the world,' rests ultimately on a strange quantum kind of being no more substantial than a promise." (p. 195)[45] We instead argue that, far from being 'as

[41] W. Heisenberg, 'Planck's discovery and the philosophical problems of atomic physics', pp. 3-20 in Heisenberg[42].

[43] Heisenberg, for example, brings into his thought on quantum physics the Kantian phenomena/noumena distinction as well as some of Bohr's ideas on 'complementarity' in experimental arrangements.

[44] Herbert, *Quantum reality*.

[45] Note that he here uses Ryle (*The concept of mind*)'s account of dispositions as 'inference tickets.'

ephemeral as a promise', the propensities of the physical world are perfectly real and substantial and may in fact be the very substance of all
things.

We now propose, according to our pragmatic realism, that *propensities*
can be the stuff of quantum objects. We describe those objects as having the
forms of wave functions spread out in space and time. Such forms, with a
spatiotemporal range, are best viewed as *fields*.[46] Quantum objects themselves can be conceived of as 'fields of propensity' according to the general
manner of this chapter. This concept of substance is similar to Nicholas
Maxwell's notion (1988; 2010) of *smearon* or *propensiton*. Substantial objects
with such natures are particularly relevant for quantum mechanics, since
it is now found that the concept of a corpuscle with definite extension,
hardness, etc., is markedly inadequate. As yet, however, no philosophically adequate replacement has been generally accepted. With the help of
the new proposal of 'propensity fields', we can try to understand some of
the more puzzling quantum features such as the reason for 'non-localities,'
and the nature of 'measurements.'

One feature of the present account of substance is that such objects need
not be located in small fixed volumes of space as, for example, the corpuscles or particles of classical physics would be. The propensity fields that
have been defined do not need to have any special 'center' distinguishable from all the other places in the field. They may have no center at all
that could be regarded as the 'true substance' whereby the surrounding
field could be regarded as just the 'sphere of influence' of the central substance.[47]

It is commonly believed, e.g. by Molnar[48] and by many physicists, that
high energy scattering experiments allow us to conclude that fundamental particles like electrons, quarks, etc. are *point particles*, like real objects
of zero size. However, this inference is incorrect. What the experiments
show is that there is *no lower limit* to the size that the wave packet of an
electron (for example) may be compressed. They never show that there
is actually a point particle, as this would contradict the Heisenberg Un-

---

[46] We are talking still of ordinary quantum mechanics, not yet of quantum field theory (for which, see
Chapter 24). By 'field' here, I simply mean a realistic interpretation of the wave function that is the
solution of Schrödinger's equation: it is extended in space as a field and carries energy and
momentum.

[47] This was Boscovich's conception, and it slowly percolated into physics, resulting in the 'dynamic
matter' of the mid-nineteenth century. This view was popularly summarized by the aphorism "No
matter without force, no force without matter".

[48] Molnar, *Powers*.

certainty Principle by requiring infinite energy to be used in producing it. Some other objects (e.g. atoms or nuclei) *do* have a lower limit of compression, and this is interpreted as arising from a composite internal structure. No matter how small we then compress the wave packet for an atom's centre of mass motion, the atom as a whole cannot be made arbitrarily small. At all times, both fundamental particles and composite objects have some varying finite size that depends on time and circumstances and may be legitimately said to occupy the volume of this size in space. Whether they also *fill* that volume depends on the probabilities of interaction with instruments, which may be small or large and so are a matter of degree in a similar manner to the way that air 'fills' a room according to its pressure.

A substance-field of propensities may have a variable spatial size. Sometimes it behaves more like a spread-out wave, and when at other times it interacts, it behaves like a localized particle. A propensity field can have practically any extensive shape over the places that are possible for it. We can allow that propensity fields are described by some kind of field equation such as the Schrödinger or Dirac equation including interaction potentials. The fields would be subject to boundary conditions set by the results of past actions. This gives continuous and wave-like propagation into the future, and it allows them to propagate as wave packets around obstacles or potentials which would stop classical atoms. They can even tunnel through barriers, as the probability for a definite interaction may be reduced but will still be non-zero. It becomes reasonable to expect the diffraction, interference and tunneling effects we know in quantum physics from the solutions of Schrödinger's equation, even though we have no general grounds yet for choosing any particular equation.

We do not now need to believe that somewhere, as it were hidden away behind the propensities, there really exist particles waiting to appear. This is not the case. Questions like 'Where is the electron and what is its speed?' have no answer, because there never exists such a thing as a small corpuscular electron. The only things that exist are propensity fields and the inter(actions) they produce. Propensity fields are not vague, indeterminate or smeared-out particles. They are perfectly definite entities in their own right. It may not be determinate in advance which actions a propensity field will produce, but that does not mean that the propensity field is any the less real or definite when considered as a thing in itself. Its field structure can be described using perfectly definite mathematics. Its existence is as real and substantial as any existing object. In fact propensity fields are the very substantial ingredients out of which all things are made. Nothing can be more substantial than them.

Kaempffer[49], for example, after pointing out the "erosion of naive pictures of particles" goes on to suggest that the word *particle* stand for a *quantum mechanical state* [a wave field], characterized by a set of quantum numbers, which is associated, in principle, with an identifiable event such as the momentum transfer in a "collision". We can follow him as he redefines the meaning of the word 'particle' to refer to something like propensity fields.

The concept of substances as dispositional contains the essential idea that they *do something*: that the dispositions are *for* some kind of event. Such events are characterized generically as 'actual events', because they have definite properties once they exist and are selections between distinct possibilities that are arrayed like a field. In quantum mechanics, these actual events are just the process of 'reduction of the wave packet' that physicists and philosophers have long discussed and sought for both theoretically and experimentally. The treatment of quantum objects as substance-dispositions implies that such reduction or selection events *do* occur.

4.8 Dispositions in psychology

Psychology also deals with dispositions and not just with what events actually occur. Even the behaviorists recognized that they should study *tendencies* to behavior and not merely the behavioral events themselves. The question, therefore, concerns the ontological status of these tendencies or dispositions.

Ryle[50] takes the view that dispositional ascriptions "assert extra matters of fact" and claims that they are *only* "inference-tickets which license us to predict, retrodict, etc." He quite explicitly denies that one should look for either causal or mechanistic explanations of the dispositions. This holds even in cases in physics and chemistry where there are explanations in terms of constituents and their propensities to attract and repel each other. His restriction against looking for explanations in terms of internal dynamics is, fortunately, largely disregarded in scientific practice.

[49] Kaempffer, *Concepts in quantum mechanics.*
[50] Ryle, *The concept of mind.*

We could interpret psychological dispositions in the same way that physics interprets potential energy. Bawden[51], for example, claims that "the role of the psychical in relation to the physical (in the living organism) is essentially the relation of the potential or incipient to kinetic or overt action." I respond that potential energy is (again) a kind of disposition that must in some way exist, as a substance. This will be considered further in the next chapter.

In cognitive psychology it is a common starting point that mental activities consist of functions of information-processing modules, engaged, for example, in signal or symbol processing. This description refers only to the structural or formal aspects. Admittedly, structural *changes* are described, but no specific powers or dispositions for those processes are admitted. This is inadequate from the point of view of any causal realism. Any account based on computation can only be realistic if it at least allows that the hardware implementations use objects with powers, as then physical symbol processing is consistently possible.

So, what is the actual nature of the dispositions that are operative in mental activities? Are these just aggregations of physical dispositions, or are there 'true mental dispositions' that are distinct from the physical? If the later were true, we would ask what impact the true human substances have on cognitive processing, since they will have their own characteristic powers and propensities not necessarily present in computers. The issue in psychology is thus whether the dispositions and powers that constitute the substance for mental objects and processing are related to the dispositions and powers manifest in the mind itself. I am thinking specifically of the emotional and motivational dispositions that make up the apparent life of mental feelings and intentions. These are powers that appear on first phenomenological analysis, so psychology should consider whether they could be the first 'more fundamental' underlying stuff of which cognitive and symbol processing is the activity.

According to Descartes, the soul (mind) is a substance and thought is the mode of its operation. This might explain what constitutes minds. However, Descartes does not offer a dynamical account to explain the operations of the soul. (On the contrary, he was pleased that the rational soul, as he conceived it, was completely outside the scope of the new empirical sciences and could be made subject to the edicts of ethics and religion.) In

---

[51] Bawden, "The psychical as a biological directive."

the end, Descartes never discusses reasons for the details of mental powers or capacities.

4.9 Intentionality of the mental

The traditional way of distinguishing the mental from the physical has been to point to the *intentionality* of the mental. This is the name given to the ability of the mental to 'point beyond itself' and so to be *about* something different from itself. Sensations, for instance, appear as sensations *of* something, and thus they are different from after-images. Ideas and thoughts are also intentional since they are ideas about something else. It does not appear that anything physical can do this. Desires are another intentional component of mind (perhaps that for which the name 'intentionality' is the most appropriate). They intend to produce what does not yet exist.

The existence of a stone, by contrast, does not by that fact alone refer to something apart from that stone. All mental states and speech acts seem to be intentional. They are like signs, gestures and sentences that indicate or represent the things they are about. In a famous declaration of Brentano[52], "intentionality is the mark of the mental".

When philosophers examined dispositions, many were fascinated by the fact that even physical dispositions seem to be dispositions *for something else*, namely for their effects, and thus by their nature were capable of indicating something apart from themselves.[53] Place[54] hypothesized that there was something fundamentally intentional about all dispositions: that "intentionality is the mark of the dispositional". If this were so, we might be seeing some primitive kind of intentionality in physics. This 'physical intentionality' could emerge perhaps in larger systems as the fully-fledged intentionality that we attribute to the mental, by a kind of panpsychist hypothesis.

There has been debate, starting with Mumford[55], on whether this idea of physical intentionality is useful or even correct. Most recently, Bird (2007, §5.7) offered a series of arguments for a permanent distinction between

---

[52] Brentano, *Psychology from an empirical standpoint*.
[53] Feser (*Aquinas*) takes this dispositional indication of a future effects to be an Aristotelean 'final cause'.
[54] Place, "Intentionality as the mark of the dispositional."
[55] Mumford, "Intentionality and the physical."

physical dispositions and mental intentionality. He argues that direction of causality is different in the two cases. Taking sensation as an example, he points out that sensations are caused by what they refer to whereas physical dispositions are the opposite: they *cause* the effect that they may be said to 'refer' to. Bird also notes that, with mental intentionality of sensations and ideas, the object of reference may be inexistent, may be indeterminate, and may be referred to only extrinsically. The linguistic context of mental reference in a person's mind is logically intensional, by which is meant the referenced object cannot be replaced by something to which it is in fact identical, since the person may not be aware of that. With the exception of possible inexistence, none of these characteristics applies in the case of physical dispositions. Bird concludes that mental intentionality is not a relation between between a thought and an object. It is more akin to a mode of representation which is quite unlike causation.

I agree with Bird that mental and physical intentionalities are not the same, and I will go back to Brentano's emphasis on the distinct nature of mental and physical being. I do not want to reduce physical causation to mental intentionality or even explain (somehow nonreductively) the mental intentionality in terms of the physical, as then (I find) whatever is reduced no longer has its original character but is replaced by some poor shadow of its previous nature. Bird[56]'s reasons are essentially structural, whereas I hold that the arguments from *content* are sufficiently strong to maintain the difference between mental and physical dispositions. They may both be dispositions, but they are not intentional in the same way.

Not all of Bird's structural arguments will be followed in this book. The reason is that, as even he realizes, the argument about different directions of causality does not hold for the intentionality of desires, emotional and motivational dispositions, etc. Desires do cause what they refer to intentionally, rather than the opposite as for thoughts and sensations. In Chapter 25 I will present a theory of how thoughts and sensations can be generated on the basis of desires and dispositions. In that case, not even sensations and thoughts have reversed causality compared with physical dispositions. The result is that mental and physical dispositions are more similar causally, although their contents are completely different.

As a reminder of this difference, I will list those capabilities of mental processes that are unavailable to physical processes. Apart from the inten-

---

[56] Bird, *Nature's metaphysics*.

tionality already described, there are the remaining items on Bird's list, namely that minds can think of an object that may be inexistent, may be indeterminate, or may be referred to only extrinsically. Lund[57] lists the further facts that mentality can think of truth or falsity and may think with vagueness or ambiguity or with logic and argument. Logical principles, meanings, abstractions, and moral principles are all capable of being only in minds and not in physical systems. Our challenge is to relate such minds to our natural world of physical dispositions.

[57] Lund, *Persons, souls, and death.*

5

Multiple Generative Levels

5.1 Beyond simple dispositions

MOST EXAMPLES of dispositions in the previous chapter were those, like fragility, solubility, radioactive instability, whose effects (if manifested) are changes or events of some kind. If a glass exercises its fragility, it breaks. If salt shows its solubility, it dissolves. The manifestation of radioactive instability would be a decay event detected with a Geiger counter. Physicists want to know not merely that these events occur, but also how the dispositions themselves may change after the manifestation event. In the cases here, the fragility of the parts or the stability of the nuclei may change as a result of those manifestation events, and it is an important part of physics to describe the new (changed) dispositions as accurately as possible. Such descriptions are part of more comprehensive dynamical theories, as distinct from descriptive accounts of events.

Sometimes, new dispositions may be ascribable after an event that could not have been ascribed before the event. The fragments of a broken glass may be able to refract light in a way that the intact glass could not. The dissolved salt may be able to pass through a membrane, in contrast to the disposition of the initial salt crystals. The fragments arising from a nuclear decay may decay by emitting electrons in a way the parent nucleus could not.

It often appears that new dispositions may be ascribed as the result of a prior disposition's operation. It then appears that new dispositions come into existence as the manifestation of previous dispositions. Since now one disposition leads to another, some philosophical analysis is called for.

The existence of some of these new dispositions may be successfully explained as the rearrangement of the internal structures of the objects under discussion, when these are composite objects. The refraction by pieces of broken glass, in contrast to the original smooth glass, has an obvious explanation in terms of the shapes of the new fragments. Salt's diffusion through a membrane, once dissolved, is presumably because of the greater mobility of salt ions in solution compared with the crystal form.

Science is largely successful in explaining such dynamical evolutions of empirical dispositions of natural objects. It bases the explanations in terms of changes to their structural shapes and arrangements of their parts along with the fixed underlying dispositions or propensities of these parts. It is from the dispositions of these parts that, according to the structure, all their observed dispositions and causal properties may be explained.

The existence of new dispositions by rearrangement of the parts of an object is non-controversial within existing philosophical frameworks. It appears that typical philosophical analyses of an *aggregate* can readily accommodate the way its derivative dispositions are explained in terms of recombinations of the dispositions of its parts.

However, not all dynamical changes of dispositions occur by rearrangements of parts. Those that are *not* rearrangements are what I call *derivative dispositions*. There are some cases, to be listed below, where new dispositions come into existence without there being any known parts whose rearrangement could explain the changes. The next section gives some examples from physics and psychology of what appear to be such derivative dispositions. This is followed by an analysis of how these might work.

5.2 Derivative dispositions

Energy and force

If we look at physics and at what physics regards as part of its central understanding, we see that one extremely important idea is *energy*. Physics talks about kinetic energy as energy having to do with motion and potential energy as energy having to do with what *would happen* if the circumstances were right. If we look at definitions of force and energy which are commonly used to introduce these concepts, we find definitions like

- **force:** the tendency F to accelerate a mass m with acceleration F/m.
- **energy:** the capacity E to do work, which is the action of a force F over a distance d, according to $E = Fd$.
- **potential energy field:** the field potential $V(x)$ to exert a force given by $F = -dV(x)/dx$ if a test particle is present.

Furthermore, we may see a pattern here:

- **potential energy field:** the *disposition* to generate a *force*, and
- **force:** the *disposition* to accelerate a mass, and
- **acceleration:** the final result.

We cannot simply identify 'force' and 'acceleration', because, as Cartwright[1] points out, force is not *identical* to the product *ma*: it is only the *net force* at a point which has that effect. An individual force is only a tendency which may or may not be manifested. It is a disposition, as is energy generically, as well as is potential energy. It is generally acknowledged that 'force' is a disposition: my new point is that it cannot be reduced either to 'acceleration' or 'energy'.

I take these as examples of two successive *derivative dispositions*, where the effect of one disposition operating is the generation of another. An electrostatic field potential is a disposition, the manifestation of which— when a charge is present—is not itself motion, but is the presence now of a derivative disposition, namely a force. The manifestation of a force— when acting on a mass—may or may not occur as motion, as that depends on what other forces are also operating on the mass. The production of a force by a field potential does not appear to be something that occurs by means of the rearrangements of microscopic parts. It appears to be more fundamental and almost *sui generis*. It appears that *field potentials, force* and *action* form a set of multiple generative levels. This situation is in need of philosophical inspection.

Admittedly, many physicists and philosophers often manifest here a tendency to say that '*only* potential energy is real', or conversely perhaps that '*only* forces are real', or even that '*only* motion is real', and that in each case the other physical quantities are simply calculational devices for predicting whichever is declared to be real. Please apply a contrary tendency

[1] Cartwright, *How the laws of physics lie.*

and resist this conclusion. In Section 6.4 I will evaluate such reductionist strategies and discuss the comparative roles of mathematical laws and dispositional properties within a possible dispositional essentialism.

Sequences or levels?

We normally think of energy, force and acceleration as the sequential stages of a process. However, in nature, there is still energy even after a force has been produced, and forces continue to play their roles both during and after accelerations. This means that energy does not finish when force begins, and force does not finish when acceleration begins, but, in a more complicated structure, all three continue to exist even while producing their respective derivative dispositions. The best way I can find to explain this more complicated structure is that of a set of 'multiple generative levels'. We can think of a 'level of energy' as persisting even while it produces forces. Since we take forces as existing even while they produce accelerations, we must allow ourselves to talk of a 'level of forces' as existing continuously. The idea of a 'level' is a spatial metaphor for what is not itself spatial, but the metaphor still serves to illustrate my argument.

5.3 Physical derivative dispositions

5.3.1 *Hamiltonians, wave functions and measurements*

In quantum physics, energy (the total of the kinetic and potential energies) is represented by the Hamiltonian operator . This operator enters into the Schrödinger wave equation which governs the time-dependence of all quantum wave forms. It thus generates all time evolution and all fields of probabilities for measurement outcomes, as discussed in Section 4.7. The principal dynamics in quantum physics are specified by knowing what the initial state is and what the Hamiltonian operator is. This applies to quantum mechanics as it is practised, by using Born's statistical interpretation and then naively saying that the quantum state changes after a measurement to one of the eigenstates of the measurement operator. (This is the much discussed 'reduction of the wave packet', which we can agree at least *appears* to occur.)

We may consider quantum physics in the following 'realistic' way. We have the Hamiltonian which has to do with total energy. It is somehow 'active' since it is an *operator* which operates on the wave function and changes it. The Schrödinger equation is the rule for how the Hamiltonian operator produces the wave function. This wave function is a probabilistic disposition (a propensity) for action, since its squared modulus gives a probability for different macroscopic outcomes of experiments, and since the wave function changes according to the specific outcome.

Such is the structure of quantum physics as it is practised, and we may observe a sequence of derivative dispositions in operation:

- **Hamiltonian operator:** the fixed disposition to generate the wave function by evolving it in time,

- **wave function:** the probabilistic disposition (a 'propensity wave') for selecting measurement outcomes, and

- **measurement outcome:** the final result.

We may draw this generative structure as

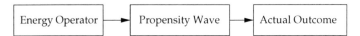

It appears again that we have multiple generative levels with the set of *Hamiltonian, wave function* and *selection event*. Note also that the final result is the weakest kind of minimal disposition, which influences merely by selection, because it *is* a selection. It appears as the last of a sequence of derivative dispositions, as a kind of 'bottom line' if we want to include it within the framework of multiple generative levels.

Admittedly, reductionist tendencies may be applied. It may be denied that there are distinct measurement outcomes in any ontological sense and that they may only be approximately defined within a coarse-grained 'decoherent history'. Advocates of the Many Worlds Interpretation or Decoherence theories take this view. Others such as Bohr take the opposite view: he holds that only the measurement outcome is real and that the Hamiltonian and wave function are calculational devices and nothing real. These conflicting views will be discussed in Section 6.4.

5.3.2 *Virtual and actual processes*

Taking a broader view of contemporary physics and its frontiers, we may further say that the 'Hamiltonians, wave functions and measurements' from above describe just the dispositions for a class of 'actual processes'. The Hamiltonian is the operator for the total energy. It contains both kinetic and potential energy terms. However, we know from Quantum Field Theory (QFT) that, for example, the Coulomb potential is composed 'in some way' by the exchange of virtual photons. Similarly, we also know from QFT that the mass in the kinetic energy part is not of a 'bare mass', but is of a 'dressed mass' arising (in some way) also from many virtual processes. This reiterates my theme: the Hamiltonian is not a simple disposition, but in fact is *itself* derivative from some prior generative level. This generative level could be called that of 'virtual processes' in contrast to that of 'actual processes'.

The class of *virtual* processes, as described by QFT, has many properties that are opposite to those of *actual* processes of measurement outcomes. Virtual events are at points (not selections between macroscopic alternatives), are interactions (not selections), are continuous (not discrete), are deterministic (not probabilistic), and have intrinsic group structures (e.g. gauge invariance, renormalisation) as distinct from the branching tree structure of actual outcomes. These contrasts suggest that virtual processes should be distinguished from actual events. The guiding principles have different forms. Virtual processes are commonly described by a fixed Lagrangian subject to a variational principle in a Fock space of variable particle numbers, whereas actual processes deal with the energies of specific observable objects leading to definite measurement outcomes. We may draw these levels, in combination with the previous three levels of ordinary quantum mechanics, as

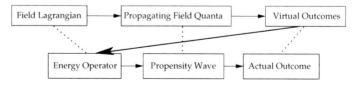

The dotted lines here show some similarities between the corresponding parts of the two main generative levels and will be discussed more in Chapter 24.

It is clear in physics that virtual processes form simultaneous 'levels' in addition to the 'level' of Hamiltonians, propensities and measurements. This is because virtual processes are clearly occurring perpetually and simultaneously with Hamiltonian evolution, as they are necessary to continually 'prepare and form' the 'dressed' masses and potentials in the Hamiltonian. Dressed masses and potentials persist during Hamiltonian evolution. In atoms and molecules, virtual processes such as photon exchanges to generate the Coulomb potentials exist continuously as a kind of background for observable processes.

5.3.3 *Pregeometry and the generation of spacetime*

Field theories such as QFT still use a geometric background of spacetime, and there is currently much speculative work in quantum gravity research to determine how this spacetime arises. Wheeler[2] started interest in 'pregeometry': the attempt to formulate theories of causal processes which do not *presuppose* a differentiable manifold for spacetime. His aim was to encourage speculation as to how spacetime might arise. The task has been taken as showing how spacetime may turn out to be a 'statistical approximation' in some limit of large numbers of hypothetical pregeometric processes. Proposals have involved spinors by Penrose and Rindler[3]; 'loop quantum gravity' as described, for example, in Rovelli[4]; and 'causal sets' according to Bombelli et al.[5] and Brightwell et al.[6].

If some pregeometry could be identified, I would speculate that a good way of understanding it would be as a distinct pregeometric level within a structure of derivative dispositions. That is, instead of spacetime being a statistical approximation (in the way thermodynamics is a statistical approximation to molecular gas theories), it could be better imagined that spacetime is an aspect of derivative dispositions that have been generated by 'prior' pregeometric dispositions. It is in keeping with Wheeler's use of the word 'arising'. This is speculative, but it does follow the pattern of some current research. I use it as an example of how the philosophical analysis of dispositions may interact fruitfully with modern physics. This

---

[2] Wheeler, "Quantum gravity."
[3] Penrose and Rindler, *Spinors and space-time. volume 1.*
[4] Rovelli, "Loop quantum gravity."
[5] Bombelli et al., "Space-time as a causal set."
[6] Brightwell et al., "'Observables' in causal set cosmology."

appears to be useful particularly since the very aim of 'deriving spacetime' has itself been called into question by Meschini[7].

5.4 Psychological derivative dispositions

There are many examples of apparent derivative dispositions in everyday life, in psychology, and in particular in cognitive processes. Such dispositions are involved whenever the accomplishment of a given disposition requires the operation of successive steps and where these are of kinds different from the overall step. The original disposition on its operation generates the 'derived dispositions' for the intermediate steps which are means to the end. An original 'disposition to learn', for example, can generate the derived 'disposition to read books', which can generate further 'dispositions to search for books'. These dispositions would then generate dispositions to move one's body, which in turn would lead ultimately to one's limbs having (physical) dispositions to move. These successively generated dispositions are all *derived* from the original disposition to learn, varying according to the specific situations.

Another example of sequential and derivative dispositions is the ability to learn. To say that someone is easy to teach or that they are musical, for example, does not mean that there is any specific action that they are capable of doing. Rather, it means that they well disposed to learn new skills (whether of a musical or of a general kind) and that it is these new skills which are the dispositions that lead to specific actions.

In this I follow the observations first in Broad[8] and then in Broad[9], where he argues

We must begin by distinguishing between dispositions of various orders. A disposition to think of a certain object may be called a disposition "of the first order". A disposition to form a disposition of the first order may be called a disposition "of the second order" And so on. No baby is born with the power to talk. But practically all babies are born with the power to acquire the power to talk.

This is the beginning of the theory of multiple levels or orders of causal influence. We might allow that particular dispositions or intentions are

---

[7] Meschini, "A metageometric enquiry concerning time, space, and quantum physics."
[8] Broad, *The mind and its place in nature*.
[9] Broad, *McTaggart's philosophy*.

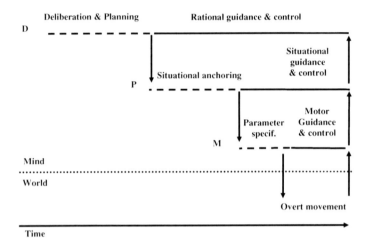

Figure 5.1 The intentional cascade of distal (D) intentions for deliberation and planning; proximal (P) intentions adapted to the present situation, and motor (M) intentions for following through with controlled movements, from Pacherie ("The phenomenology of action"), Fig. 1. Copyright (2008), with permission from Elsevier.

best regarded not as the most fundamental causes but as 'intermediate stages' in the operation of more persistent desires and motivations. The intention to find a book, for example, could be the product or derivative of some more persistent 'desire for reading' and need only be produced in the appropriate circumstances. We may say that the derived dispositions were the *realization* of the underlying dispositions. These are called 'levels' rather than simply 'sequences' because the underlying motivation still exists during the production of later levels. It operates simultaneously with the derivative dispositions. It is not the case that desire for reading ceases during the act of reading, for it is rather then at its strongest and in fulfillment.

Such ideas have been advocated by Bratman[10], who distinguishes a sequence consisting of 'future-directed' intentions, 'present-directed' intentions, and 'motor' intentions, such that a fully human action involves a progressive sequence of these three levels of intentions. Pacherie[11] sees the first two kinds more generally as 'distal' and 'proximate intentions.

[10] Bratman, *Intention, plans, and practical reason.*
[11] Pacherie, "The phenomenology of action."

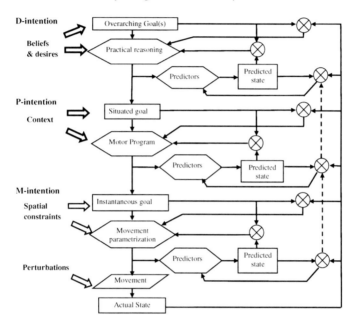

Figure 5.2 A hierarchical model of action specification, as proposed by Pacherie ("The phenomenology of action") (Fig. 2), with the three levels of intention and control. The ⊗ symbols indicate the comparison of their two input streams and generate a difference measure as an output. Copyright (2008), with permission from Elsevier.

She conceives their relation as "not merely one of co-existence", but as one where "they form an intentional cascade, with distal intentions causally generating proximate intentions and proximate intentions causally generating in turn motor intentions," as shown in Fig. 5.1. The important idea here is that of an 'intentional cascade' as describing the relation between the levels.[12] In all cases the cascade mainly proceeds 'downstream', but there are still some 'feedback' processes that allow upstream desires to be influenced by downstream circumstances such as whether the outcomes are as desired or are in error. Furthermore, she notes that "intentions at each level were assigned a specific role in, respectively, the rational, situational and motor guidance and control of the action. This implies that a D-intention does not cease to exist and play a role once it has given

---

[12] Riva et al. ("From intention to action") has reviewed these and similar ideas from several psychological theorists.

rise to a corresponding P-intention and similarly a P-intention does not go away once the corresponding M-intention has been generated. Rather, all three levels of intentions coexist, each exerting its own form of control over the action." Fig. 5.2 sketches in more detail some of the various initiation, monitoring, comparison and control processes that must be present for multi-level actions.

We want to understand and explain how all these kinds of influences exist and function in practice, and we claim that this is best modeled in terms of the simultaneous operation of multiple levels of intention and control.

5.5 Analysis of generative sequences

Because generative sequences of derivative dispositions appear in a wide variety of contexts in both physics and psychology, let us formulate some concepts for the manner of their general operation. The first general idea is that 'multiple generative levels' are a sequence $\{A \rightarrow B \rightarrow C \rightarrow ..\}$ in which A 'generates' or 'produces' new forms of B using the present form of B as a precondition. We say that B derives from A as its manifestation. Then B generates C in the same way. This sequence may perhaps continue until an end Z, say, where the only activity is 'selection'.

This rough scheme does not tell us, however, how A, B, etc might be *changed* as a result of the operation. Presumably this occurs often, as, for example, in naive quantum theory, when a wave function is changed after it generates a particular measurement outcome. It would be good to consider the philosophy for a general scheme to explain the (apparently mysterious) logic of the 'reduction of the wave packet'. Let us extract some guidelines from our example derivative dispositions listed previously. To do this, we will need to distinguish the concepts of principal from instrumental and occasional causes.

5.5.1 *Principal, Instrumental and Occasional causes*

Davidson[13] argues that causality is a two-place relation between individual events. Thus causal relations are not just implications from the descrip-

---

[13] Davidson, "Causal relations."

tion of the first event to that of the second event but are something more real. The reality of causality, however, does not automatically include such components as dispositions and propensities, although Steiner[14] wants to extend Davidson's ideas in this direction. Here, I want to allow *both* dispositions *and* previous events to be causes, although in different senses.

I recommend that distinctions be made between all of the following:

- the 'principal cause': that disposition which operates,
- the 'occasional cause': that circumstance that selects which disposition operates,
- the 'instrumental cause': the origin of the occasional cause, which is therefore another cause by means of which the principal cause operates.

The overall pattern is that 'principal causes operate according to occasional causes, which arise from instrumental causes'. This is the terminology traditionally used to describe something like multi-level causality.

All three kinds of causes appear to be necessary for any event in nature. For example, when a·stone is let fall: the principal cause is the earth's gravitational attraction, the occasional cause is our *act* of letting go, and the instrumental cause is the muscle movements in our finger releasing the stone. Its hitting the ground is thus caused by our letting go but only as an instrumental and then occasional cause. Many common uses of 'cause' (including that of Davidson[15]) refer to occasional causes rather than principal causes, as it is only in this occasional sense that events can be said to be causes. Previous events cannot be efficacious causes, Emmet[16] points out, in the sense of producing or giving rise to their effects, since events *per se* are not powers, but clearly they do make some difference when they happen. This is because events are the changes in powers, but change itself is not a power but rather the property of powers. The instrumental cause *is* a genuine causal contributor, and it may be said to set the stage by making suitable conditions (namely, the occasional cause) for selecting the operation of the principal cause.

I acknowledge that using the phrase 'occasional cause' brings in a certain amount of philosophical debate, but I see essentially the same questions occurring in many situations. We need some generic concept to refer

---

[14] Steiner, "Events and causality."
[15] Davidson, "Causal relations."
[16] Emmet, *The effectiveness of causes.*

to the circumstances, conditions, or occasions that must obtain in order for a disposition to manifest itself.

5.5.2 Causal sequences in physics

Consider now an electron of fixed charge and mass moving in an electrostatic potential according to classical electrostatics. At a given place x, the derivative of the potential $V(x)$ gives the force, and the force gives the acceleration which in turn changes the velocity of the electron, and it moves to a new place. In our framework of derivative dispositions, we see that the potential is one disposition which generates another, namely the force. It does so according to the place of the electron. The electrostatic potential is therefore the principal cause of the force, and the place of the electron is the occasional cause. A place or any other spatiotemporal property *by itself* is never an efficacious cause, but it can be said to be the circumstance by means of which the potential generates the force. When we include magnetism and radiation, such properties will include velocities and accelerations.

Note that we never have forces causing potentials to exist where they did not before, nor do we have places causing forces to occur where they did not already exist. Let us generalize by surmising a set of generative levels {Potential → Force → Places}, such that the *principal* causation is always in the direction of the arrow, and the only 'backward' causation is by selection with an *occasional* cause. The only feedback 'back up the sequence' is with the conditional aspect of certain occasions. The specific operation of prior dispositions does not happen continually or indiscriminately. Operations of dispositions need to be selected from among all those that are possible, and thus there is an essential role for 'particular occasions' as preconditions.

Consider also the quantum mechanical evolution of a system from some initial time, such that it is subject to measurement selections at various later times. The quantum mechanical story is as follows. The initial quantum wave function is evolved according to the Schrödinger equation by a Hamiltonian operator up to the time of the first measurement. Any particular measurement implies a set of possible outcomes, and after the measurement, the wave function is changed immediately to one of those outcomes. The probability of each particular outcome is determined by Born's law, namely that the probability is the square modulus of the overlap of the initial wave function with the possible resulting wave functions. The system then evolves according to the Schrödinger equation up to the time of the following measurement.

Seen in terms of derivative dispositions, the Hamiltonian is the disposition to evolve an initial state to new times, generating a new wave function according to the Schrödinger equation which contains that Hamiltonian operator. The new wave function is itself another disposition, namely a propensity to produce measurement outcomes with the various probabilities given by Born's law. The final results are the discrete selection events at the times of measurement. These discrete events have only the minimal causal powers as they influence the future evolutions of the wave function. In that sense, they are just the 'occasional causes' according to which other dispositions may operate. The principal dispositions are first the Hamiltonian operator that starts the whole process and then the wave functions considered as fields of propensity for different selection events.

Summarizing the quantum mechanical case, we see that here again, the principal causes act forwards down a set of multiple generative levels whose range of actions at any time is selected from all those presently possible, as constrained by past events. Those events thereby become occasional causes. Because the wave functions before a measurement event are the cause of that event, those wave functions are the instrumental cause of the new wave functions after the measurement.

5.5.3 *Conditional Forward Causation*

We may generalize that all the principal causation is 'down' the sequence of multiple generative levels $\{A \rightarrow B \rightarrow ...\}$, and that the only effect back up the sequence is the way principal causes depend on previous events or occasions to *select* their range of operation. Let us adopt as universal this asymmetric relationship between multiple generative levels: *dispositions act forwards in a way conditional on certain things already existing at the later levels*. This is a simple initial hypothesis, and we will have to observe whether all dispositions taken as existing in nature can be interpreted as following this pattern.

We may therefore surmise that A, the first in the sequence, is the 'deepest underlying principle', 'source', or 'power' that is fixed through all the subsequent changes to B, C, etc. Conditional Forward Causation, the pattern we saw from physics, would imply that changes to B come from *subsequent* operations of A, and not from C, D,.. acting in reverse up the chain. We surmise, rather, that the *subsequent* operations of A are now conditioned on the results in B, C, D, etc. The operations of A are therefore the *principal causes*, whereas the dependence of those operations on the previous state of B is via *instrumental causation*, and the dependence on the results in C, D,... is via *occasional causation*. I suggest that this is a universal pattern for the operation of a class of dispositions in nature, namely those that do not follow from the rearrangement of parts of an aggregate object.

The terminology suggests that only forward causation occurs, so, for example, gravity affects objects on earth, but objects on earth do not affect gravity. Certainly that is the principal direction of causation. But note also the conditional or occasional part of the scheme, which describes how subsequent effects may *yet* have some effects on principal causes. How this works in mental stages will be discussed in Chapter 22, and its operation concerning gravity will be discussed in Section 24.5.

6

A Dynamic Ontology

THE PREVIOUS two chapters investigated what kind of ontology is needed to describe general dynamical processes, where we include both physical and psychological activities. Chapter 4 established a 'dynamic ontology' that sees substances not as self-sufficient beings but as essentially dynamical and process-oriented. Chapter 5 showed how a 'multi-level dynamic ontology' must be allowed whenever the action of a disposition is to produce another disposition (as distinct from producing final events which themselves have no power apart from the fact of their existence).

This chapter reflects on these proposals in a more general way and comes back to some of the basic philosophical principles that are needed. We compare the new theory to historical proposed ontologies. We also see how it is related to a number of contemporary issues concerning natural laws, identity of objects, reductionism and simplicity.

This Part II is independent of the theism to be presented later but is designed to provide the necessary ontological foundation for understanding theism as well as the natural world. Part II could stand as a thesis in its own right, but it needs to be presented here because such concepts are not sufficiently widely known.

6.1 Dispositions as units of understanding

Dispositional essentialism asserts that that each object has some properties that are inherently dispositional. These include the causal base properties that enter into scientific laws. However, this basic dispositional essentialism by itself, we saw in Chapter 4, leaves unanswered two important questions. The first question is whether all, or only some, of an object's properties are dispositional. The second question concerns ontology.

If we want to know what *exists*, then philosophy has traditionally pointed to the concept of *substance*. But what properties does a substance have? And what do these properties *do*? Traditional definitions of substance have been based on one or more of the following requirements:

1. Endurance over time and survival of changes,

2. Independence, as being capable of existing independently and requiring no external cause for its existence, and

3. Underlying substratum for properties, so properties can be *of* some substance.

The difficulty is that none of these three requirements gives a good idea of active power or of causation. There is something like active power in the ideas of Aristotle and in the ideas of the corpuscular physicists when they talked about solidity and rigidity as primary qualities.

Chapter 4 described a simple pragmatic or Eleatic approach to ontology whereby what is necessary and sufficient for the dispositional causation of events is interpreted realistically and postulated to exist. We identify propensities or powers with substance-stuff, so that particular objects are unions of dispositional powers and categorical forms. This development, following on from dispositional essentialism, leads to a general concept of substance, Aristotle's underlying matter, as being *constituted* by dispositions and not just being the bare subject for those dispositions. We see how to understand objects as made of propensity-substance in the form of some structure or field, so that things in the world may consistently be bearers of both dispositional and formal properties.

No longer are substances defined by endurance, independence or as what underlies: none of these three definitions points in any way to the causal powers that we know are held by substances. Instead of those three, our 'unit of understanding' is the concept of *disposition*. An understanding of the theses of this book has as its prerequisite the concept of disposition, also known as potentialities, powers, or propensities. The history of this concept will be briefly discussed in Section 6.2 below.

6.1.1 *Generation + selection as a pattern*

The operation of a disposition A is conditional on some circumstance being sufficient and, after it does operate, some new effect is generated. This effect may be an event (like a fragile vase breaking), or it may be the existence of another disposition B (such as a force being produced by an electric potential). We always have this pattern of *generation + selection*, and that pattern is fundamental to dispositions: our unit of understanding.

The fact that we can have a pattern of generation + selection between two kinds of existing things (A, B) is an important philosophical step in our understanding of ontology. By our dispositional-substance ontology, A and B are two distinct kinds of objects, so this means that distinct kinds of objects can exist but still be related in law-like ways. It cannot be the case that a 'sharp metaphysical distinction' between two kinds of objects forbids there to be causal relations between them. In the cases examined so far, we find that the causal relations are not symmetric: it is not the case that A causes effects of B, and B causes effects in A in the same manner. Rather, it appears that these causal relations between metaphysically distinct kinds of objects are asymmetric and are described by the pattern of generation followed by selection, which I denote by 'generation + selection'. This means that A causes effects of B by generation, and that, in a distinguishable manner, B causes effects in A only by selection. In both cases, the active dispositional powers are ascribed to A only, and the ability of B to influence by selection resides entirely in the fact that the configurations of B provide the sufficient circumstances for the conditional operation of A.

6.1.2 *Mentality as desire–thought–action*

In Section 4.8 we asked what could be the 'true mental dispositions' that constitute our mental life, especially those which do so in a 'more fundamental' manner. The answer to this question is needed now because whatever turns out to be the most fundamental disposition will be the actual substance of which minds are formed.

In the light of Section 5.4, we must consider the possible role of derivative dispositions in our mental life and whether there are multiple generative levels within minds. In order to do this, we must see whether there are multiple patterns of generation + selection within psychological activities. The complete proposal for psychology will be presented in Chapters 11 and 22. For now it is most useful to just examine the relations between desires, thoughts and actions in mental life, to see whether they may be ordered as generative levels linked by operations of generation + selection.

We note first, following the analysis of Ryle[1], that minds as a whole are akin to dispositions, and hence the actions of a person are the effects of those dispositions. This implies that our minds and our actions may be seen as forming two generative levels. They are linked by generation, as our minds generate our actions, and also linked by selection, as our thinking is constrained by what we actually choose to do.

We should also consider the relation, within the mind, between desires and thought. That relation should be the same as that between willing and understanding, since we generally think that willing is in accordance with our desires and with our loves and motivations: we will by means of desires. We also generally think that our understanding is in accordance with our thought: we understand by means of our thoughts and ideas.

But does desire generate thought, or thought generate desire, or neither? There is room for debate on this, but there are psychological, philosophical and theological arguments to lead to the conclusion that it is desire which generates thought, rather than the opposite.

The psychological evidence stems from the fact that persons tend to think about what they want: their desires lead their dreaming, thinking, planning and eventually acting to get what they want. This suggests that desires generate the streams of thought that occur in the understanding, rather than that our thinking dictates what we want, love, or desire. Thought may influence what we desire but only by selection. Our thoughts select which desires can be feasibly brought nearer satisfaction.

Some will disagree, saying that it is primarily thought that makes our desire, and that we tend to desire things that we have thought up. This is true, but what is the causal determiner of what we think up? Thoughts seem to pop into our heads, and thoughts about what we desire are much more likely to do so! We interfere at this point sometimes and reject thoughts as unsuitable, but that rejection itself also requires motivation or desire. We do not clearly see our desires in our consciousness, but only

---

[1] Ryle, *The concept of mind.*

our thoughts and actions, so we tend to forget about the essential role of dispositions and desires.[2]

Philosophically, we could argue from the Aristotelian view that thought is the entertaining of the forms of things. Then, since forms themselves have no causal power, we could say that all the power must belong to whatever is doing the thinking and not to the thoughts themselves. This implies that thoughts themselves are not dispositions. The honor of being dispositions belongs to desires or loves. Desires are more similar to dispositions than are thoughts.

A related theological issue is that it is more fundamental to say that God is love rather than that God is thought. Aristotle believed that the Unmoved Mover, as pure intellect or Logos, consisted of pure contemplation, but the theistic traditions have asserted a more fundamental role to love than to intellection. These issues, as they relate to theism, will be addressed again later, especially in Section 11.3.

6.2 History of substance

To clarify the content and consequences of the new ideas about substances given in the previous two chapters, we examine a short list of historical comparisons and contrasts.

The Pythagoreans held that the principles of mathematics are the principles of all things. In other words, the basic structure of Being is mathematical. We find it difficult to understand how a mathematical object (a form) could constitute the entirety of a physical object that is concrete and changeable. The Pythagoreans had not taken into account the *powers* of objects, and they therefore lacked a concept of concrete underlying substance.

Aristotle used the name *hyle* (matter) for the underlying stuff of which objects are formed, in the way that a statue is formed of clay. He recognized that the resulting objects had potentialities for changing themselves or others, but unfortunately he attributed that ability to added form rather than to substance.

This neglect of underlying powers became more critical in Thomism,

---

[2] How many times have we seen people, seeming to themselves to be rational, being driven by desires which they hardly acknowledge existing?

when *hyle* (matter) was reduced to only 'pure potency': that which is only capable of receiving forms. Non-trivial or active powers or dispositions were not attributed to matter, but only to the added forms. This mistake has long persisted and is only now, with the revival of interest in dispositions and powers, being remedied. Today the underlying matter or substance is recognized for its more active role in nature. We insist that mere forms, *qua form*, have themselves no active powers or dispositions. Indeed, they can never exist by themselves in nature.

A different philosophical idea of substance was held by Spinoza and Leibniz. They defined substance as 'that whose nature requires its separate existence'. In this view, substances are self-sufficient beings that contain within themselves the complete source of all their changes. Leibniz claimed that all natural changes of his monads come from within, as "an external cause can have no influence upon its inner being" (G. W. Leibniz, *Monadology*, para. 11). The difficulty then, as Kant realized, is that on this account "it is not necessary for [a substance's] existence that it stand in relation to other things" (Immanuel Kant, "Kant's inaugural dissertation," Section 7). It is then puzzling that substances have positional relations, such as those which enable the acting of one substance on another. The possibility of *interactions* of substances can only be regained by denying that substances are self-sufficient beings. They persist, not autonomously, but for interactions.

Descartes is famous for his dualism of two substances: the mental that is essentially rational and the material that is essentially extension. In this view of nature as that which is extended, extensiveness is a geometrical *form*. Descartes is known in mathematics for his new coordinate analyses of geometry. But something is missing, we now realize. There is no component of power and hence no idea of *natural* substance.

Boyle, Locke and Newton, in contrast, had both the necessary ingredients. Their 'solid corpuscular substances' had both form (spherical or other shapes) and powers (hardness, impenetrability, mobility, and inertia of parts, according to Bk. III of Newton's *Principia*). This union of form and power enabled complete explanations in the sense of Section 4.5 above. Their explanations were logically coherent by my proposal. However, Newton's postulated existence of universal gravity, with its action at a distance, was still puzzling. Did the corpuscles have power at distances where they had no substance? That seemed to violate some principle, but which? I say that it is because we have an intuitive understanding of the deep connection between power and substance that we are uneasy when objects have powers at a distance, namely where their substance is not.

These difficulties became more severe with the further discoveries of magnetism, electric fields and (astonishingly) propagating electromagnetic waves. Boscovich wanted to accept that substances had powers extended away from a mass point in space, but Faraday argued that these fields were real in their own way—just as real as atoms. They must have some kind of 'substance' of their own since they have persisting powers. This is just as I now argue in general.

The puzzle about the substantiality of electromagnetic fields is resolved in modern physics. According to quantum field theory, these fields are composed of propagating photons. These photons carry momentum and energy, so, according to the relativistic $E = mc^2$, they have gravitational mass as well. There can be no objection to identifying them as substances. The only problem is the probabilistic nature of virtual photons and their quantum behavior, as discussed in Subsection 5.3.1. Other fields (nuclear and gravitational) are posited to be composed of their own field quantum particles (gluons and gravitons, respectively).

The philosophical implications of modern physics are still being assimilated. At the start of the twentieth century there was a denial of 'substance' altogether and of any sense of continued identity, in favor of pure process. They had a purely event or flux philosophy. Reasons for this repudiation varied. Sometimes it was the alleged unknowability of the real constitution of substances. At other times it was a preference for 'flux' or 'creativity' as against the 'Parmenidean influence' that was seen to pervade much of Western philosophy. Hume and Whitehead were the two most prominent influences here. Between the World Wars last century, an ontology of 'events' became popular, especially with the influence of a common interpretation of relativity theory and a positivistic approach to metaphysics. Russell's *The Analysis of Matter* (1927) was a good presentation of this position, wherein events are fixed in space and time. Paradoxically, they then became like fixed substances, and the understanding of event as *change* faded.

After the Second World War, Rescher[3] noted that there was a general reaction to such an extreme event-and-no-continuant ontology, and many

---

[3] Rescher, "The revolt against process."

writers repudiated 'events' in favor of substances and their relations. A very uncritical idea of 'substance' was accepted, practically identical with 'material object'. This had the result that there could be no very precise understanding of either the fact or the dynamics of real change. Recent work on powers and dispositions is on the way to remedying these failures. The program of dispositional essentialism should take its next step and discover how it can reconstitute a good account of substance based on dispositions.

6.3 Natural laws?

There are two ontological approaches to the question of natural laws, as we first saw in Chapter 4. The first is to regard all behavior of objects as governed by universal laws. In physics, for example, such universal laws are often written mathematically, and it is claimed that all changes must be in accordance with these laws. Any deviation from the predictions of the laws would indicate either that the initial conditions used in the prediction were not correct or that the laws could not have been correct. Maybe some influence was present that was not allowed for in the law, in which case it was not universal after all, and another (more) universal principle would have to be found.

A second dispositionalist approach is to consider that objects and people are constituted of propensities and desires respectively. Then, how these behave in the future is just a consequence of their particular kinds of propensities and desires, along with the forms and circumstances in which they find themselves. In this second approach there is no need for any natural law over and above the responses generated by the dispositional natures of things.

It is this dispositionalist approach which is advocated in this book. In the contemporary literature in the philosophy of science, it has been explored extensively in books by Mumford[4], Molnar[5], and Bird[6] within the framework of what they call 'dispositional essentialism'. This was the essentialism introduced at the start of Chapter 4, and I owe much to the expositions of those three authors as well as to the other authors listed in

---

[4] Mumford, "Ellis and Lierse on dispositional essentialism."
[5] Molnar, *Powers*.
[6] Bird, *Nature's metaphysics*.

Section 4.3. This impetus to regard the dispositional properties of objects as ontologically prior to any universal laws which might appear to describe their behavior can be traced back to a kind of Aristotelian approach to natural ontology. It contrasts with a Platonic approach wherein universal principles are viewed as somehow more real than the objects which they govern.

In this second approach, now adopted, if a deviation from predictions is found, then we look for new circumstances for the manifestations of existing dispositions. If that does not explain events sufficiently, then we consider the existence of a new disposition of the participating objects. We are able to consider objects with new and distinct dispositions. We can consider influences of new objects with unforeseen propensities if we cannot explain those dispositions in terms of the internal structure of micro-dispositions. There are no 'rigid universal laws' which prohibit novel events by rendering them logically impossible within the framework of a universal theory.

In practice, however, science looks for classes of dispositional properties such as of mass, charge, spin, etc., so the differences with analyses based on natural laws are not always dramatic. Nearly all of the existing scientific principles can be adopted into a dispositional ontology with only a very slight loss of predictive capabilities. This adoption is beneficial because there is generally an increase in explanatory capabilities. We now see how the behavior of objects follows from their own being or substance since that substance is identified as its set of fundamental dispositions.

6.4 Philosophy of levels

There are some who doubt that we need a philosophy of generative degrees. In all the apparent examples of multiple generative levels given so far, many physicists and philosophers of physics will assert the particular reality of one of the levels and say that the prior levels are only mathematical devices for predicting the behavior of their chosen real level.

For example, some assert in electromagnetic theory that only the field tensors (incorporating the electric and magnetic vector fields) are real and that the vector potential (incorporating the electrostatic potential) is a calculational device with no reality. They note the gauge uncertainties in the vector potential, which for electrostatics is the arbitrariness in setting the level of zero potential energy. Against this, many have said that the scattering of electrons in the Bohm-Aharonov experiment is most succinctly explained in terms of the vector potential, not the field tensor. It turns out that it is loop integrals of the vector potential which carry physical significance. I conclude that there are non-trivial physical and philosophical questions about the relative 'reality' of potentials and forces which require, not immediate preferences, but considered responses.

We saw how reductionist tendencies may be manifest in quantum theories. 'Decoherent history' accounts of quantum mechanics want to keep the wave function according to the Schrödinger equation. Such accounts deny that macroscopic outcomes occur in reality but only allow them to be approximate appearances. The founders of quantum theory such as Bohr and Wheeler, however, took the opposite view, saying that an electron is only real when it is being observed—when it makes the flash of light at a particular place—not while it is traveling. In their view, the Hamiltonian and wave function are calculational devices and nothing real, having only mathematical reality as portrayed by the mathematical name 'wave function'.

The views which make prior or later levels into mere mathematical tricks can be critiqued from the point of view of dispositional essentialism. This view encourages us to *not* invoke arbitrarily mathematical rules for the laws of nature, but, as suggested above, to *replace* the role of laws with that of the dispositional properties of particular objects. To apply Occam's criterion, the question is whether it is simpler to have multiple kinds of objects existing (even within multiple generative levels), each with simple dispositions, or simpler to have fewer kinds of existing objects but with more complicated laws governing their operation.

The previous chapter showed many examples of multiple generative levels, each composed of derivative dispositions. The questions of simplicity and adequacy will have to be examined in these cases as well. My conclusion is that the concepts introduced here enable us to take a more comprehensive and universal view of physical dispositions (such as those of potentials and forces or of Hamiltonians and wave functions) that appear to be *ad hoc* when taken individually. Furthermore, the logic of multiple generative levels is sufficiently general, such that it can be applied to wide range of processes. We can even consider applying it to God.

6.5 Identity, change and essence

A perennial problem in philosophy has been to find a concept of 'substance' as that which persists through change. A similar problem is to define the 'essence' of an object: that which defines the characteristics of an object that must be kept through all changes in order for the object to be the 'same'. In both cases we want to consider living organisms and humans. What is the essential part of a person that remains with him unchanged through his entire life? Is there such a part to define his identity? Philosophers have debated whether it is some kind of mental being which does this, such as a soul, or whether it is done by the existence of memories, or whether personal identity should be based on the continuity of bodily existence. Many of the same questions occur in physics and psychology. They come to the fore when we consider non-trivial changes such as brain transplants, body transplants, and especially when trying to understand post-mortem survival and the 'resurrection of the body'. This section confines itself to the simple question of how we recognize the essence of a particular substance or being and how it might retain (or not) its identity through change. Applications to psychology and theology will be deferred to Chapter 20.

We are able to extract a first sense of identity when we base our analysis on the concepts from Chapter 4 where the substance of a thing is simply its fundamental dispositions. This is a *strict identity*, where a substance keeps exactly the same properties for a non-zero duration of time. The finite duration of a disposition before another event was how we first identified it as a candidate for what a substance might be. At the moment we do not know, for a given substance, whether this duration is a nanosecond or a millisecond. That will require empirical investigations. All we have established is that it is logically possible that there is some kind of identity over a non-zero time interval.

A second kind of identity, over a larger interval, one that includes multiple events, may also be possible, if the disposition itself does not change. We are referring to changes in the disposition itself that are not relations between it and something else. We are talking about the disposition in its internal character or essence. The exact nature of that internal essence will have to be clarified empirically. For now we only observe that it is logically possible that a disposition can act, and yet itself be not internally changed by the acting, *qua* disposition. A charged electron can repel another, for example, without the electron being changed in the sum of its fundamental dispositions. Other properties (e.g. recoil velocity) may still change, but the charge-disposition itself does *not need* to change. If this pattern is instantiated in the real world, then we have a longer duration of identity which can be established for objects. Identity may be obtained if objects exist continuously for that duration and do not change the nature or measure of any of their underlying dispositions, namely the fundamental dispositions that constitute the substance of that being. What are excluded in that duration are changes which do modify those fundamental dispositions. An electron colliding with a positron, when both charges disappear and are replaced by two photons, would be an example of such a change (even a termination) of identity.

The first sense of identity is very strict, and the second is not so strict, but neither is adequate to determine the continued identity of a composite object, where this might be an atom, a molecule, an organism, or a person. There does seem to be a continued sense of identity for some of those beings, a sense of 'numerical identity' that persists through the many changes that organisms and people undergo while growing and living their lives. We claim that for people there should be such a generalized sense of identity. Hume was skeptical about the existence of any such sense, but we intuit that we do remain ourselves and do not become another. Is there a further generalized sense of identity which may be possible in our dynamic ontology?

With the concept of generative levels, there is indeed a new kind of identity relation that we might find relevant to persons. Consider the possibility of an organism B that is part of a structure of generative levels, such that disposition A is that which generates the powers and capabilities of B. When the organism acts, these powers produce effects C, which we may for simplicity consider the final definite actions in the world. The $\{A \to B \to C\}$ are thus multiple generative levels in the sense of Chapter 5.

Suppose now that level A experiences many fewer changes than does B, so that it is a comparatively long time between changes that change the substantial dispositions of A. Further consider the fact that, within generative levels, the level A is the cause of all the dispositions that B has and may indeed be called 'responsible' for B. The details of B depend entirely on A itself and on the details of the circumstances that occasion the operations of the dispositions of A and B. In this case, an argument can be made that there is a 'true persistent identity' that can be ascribed to B, namely the prior degree A itself. There is a sense, therefore, in which A can be considered the 'true nature' or the 'source of activity' of B and hence its true underlying identity. This underlying identity will last as long as the 'comparatively long time' (mentioned above) between the substantial changes of A.

Therefore there exists a third sense of underlying identity which can be given to objects that exist as one of a set of multiple generative levels. Any of the prior degrees could be identified as the 'true underlying identity' of that object. In a loose sense, the words 'essence' or 'true nature' could be extended in meaning to one of the prior degrees, as could the word 'soul' in Plato's sense as the 'source of motion' of an object. We will see later that such descriptions make sense within a context of theism. Theism is therefore the next subject to be discussed.

Part III

A Scientific Theism

7

Plan of Approach

THAT THERE IS a God, and that God is One, are the primary assumptions of a rational monotheism:

Postulate 1 *God exists.*

Postulate 2 *God is One.*

These are the postulates needed for further constructive work in theistic research.[1] Such a pair of postulates is not enough to generate deductions and is hence nowhere near enough to produce all the explanations that we seek. We need to combine it with further postulates. Each of the chapters in Part III will deal with one or two additional postulates. Each chapter will then build up deductions with the help of all previous chapters.

Discussions with friends have shown me that there are many differences and uncertainties concerning theism. Even within theology the question of the powers of natural objects has been commonly divorced from the question of how God sustains those objects in existence. Because I understand that the behavior of objects does depend on the details of theism and on how they are sustained in existence, I will now present expositions (from here through to Chapter 16) to elucidate the needed principles of theism. The primary function of these short chapters is to outline the core principles that will be needed as foundations for the later scientific theorizing. The postulates listed in subsequent chapters are not arbitrary but were

---

[1] Not everyone may be willing to make such assumptions. The a-theist, for example, assumes that God does *not* exist. He or she is free to do that, to make that hypothesis, to see what further ideas follow, and to see what explanations may be produced. In our investigation, however, we begin with the theistic postulates above. May the best explanation win.

carefully chosen from what I think of as 'vanilla theism'. These are the core beliefs of the main theistic religions of the world: Judaism, Christianity and Islam. Those are the three 'Religions of the Book'.[2]

The core beliefs of philosophical theism are typically that God is eternal, infinite, necessary, one, immutable, impassible, transcendent and immanent. Then, for religious purposes at least, we add that God is good, loving, a divine person, worthy of worship, worthy of praise, righteous, just, awe-inspiring, and always merciful and forgiving. However, it is not entirely clear how these last attributes are related together or even how they follow from the first (philosophical) group of attributes. A difficulty for many people is that the philosophical attributes above hardly allow that God be living. That is because it is doubtful that an 'immutable, impassible One' can be loving and merciful. God may well be both, we believe, but the rational understanding of the connection is weak.

The coming postulates are chosen, therefore, to emphasize the life and loving nature of God. They assert that God is eternal, infinite and transcendent, but insist, in addition, that God is living and that God is loving. These postulates about life and love are certainly not known *a priori*. The philosophical proofs of the existence of God never conclude by proving those particular hypotheses about the living nature of God. Nevertheless, they are core and central beliefs of religious theism. I strongly believe that they come come from revelations from God. I believe that God's input into the religious books over the last several thousand years has lead to a general awareness that God is living and loving. He is living and loving in his Divine way, a way that we forever struggle to understand.

I am not going to discuss particular revelations or particular books because I believe that the core claims I make in this book can be distilled from religious thought. Let us therefore continue with introducing the core theistic postulates to see what can thereby be derived as a basis for the principles of our world.[3]

Here are some clarifications of terminology and approach. The first concerns the meaning of 'natural' and 'physical'.

---

[2] Those religions often make further additional assumptions that are not shared by all. Sometimes I may append brief mentions of the content of those additional ideas, but I do not have the space in this book to explore all their separate consequences.

[3] There are many philosophical issues that I do not deal with here, such as those about the nature of universals, the nature of truth-makers in the world, and all questions of epistemology and justification. These questions have to be reconsidered in the light of theism. This book is just a beginning.

We rightly think that everything has a nature, namely a description of its substance and of all its essential properties and powers. In agreement with this general sense of the word 'nature', the original Greek meaning[4] of 'physical' is 'that which has its source of change within itself'. This is to distinguish it from what is artificial, which are those things that have sources of change outside themselves.[5] If theism is true and God is the source of our life and therefore the only thing with life in itself, then, strictly speaking, only God is physical! All of the the rest of us beings are therefore 'artificial' (in some sense).[6]

However, this is not the everyday use of these terms. Since we commonly use the word 'naturalistic' or 'physical' to describe the basic sciences of today, we need to invent a new name such as 'generalized-natural' or 'generalized-physical' for the above sense of everything with a source of change within itself. A 'generalized physics' would be the study of those things, and, when theism is assumed true, it will coincide with our theistic science. Both will be the study of everything that has a causal influence on the things in our world. In another variation on definitions, some philosophers[7] define "physical things [as] those things that are postulated by a complete physics." Theists claim that this must refer to the generalized sense of 'physical' which includes minds and even God. Most often, however, I am *not* going to use such a generalized terminology, delightful though it may be.

This book therefore is going to use 'nature' to refer to what is currently known as physical, including all material things and also whatever virtual or pre-geometric processes may be surmised in quantum gravity. Then, everything natural may be taken as itself dead and not living, however active or 'subtle' it may be. We will later see that natural things are energized and enlivened by something spiritual within them, but we will never need to *identify* spiritual as the 'inmost of the physical' and hence itself essential natural. The term physical, as I and most people use it, excludes what is mental or spiritual.[8]

---

[4] Aristotle, Physics 192[b]13-15

[5] Aristotle, Physics 192[b]30-31

[6] It is indeed common to view the world as an artificial tool or instrument of God, like a musical instrument which God plays to make music (us). I do not take this view, however, since I do not believe that anything artificial can love and return love reciprocally.

[7] Most recently Brown ("Deprioritizing the a priori arguments against physicalism").

[8] Such things could be called 'supernatural', but that word comes with so many associations that I will try to avoid using it.

Can we know the nature of God? There is one well-established religious tradition—apophatic or 'negative theology'—that refuses to make positive statements about Divinity. Aquinas uses this approach in part when he says that common terms such as 'life', 'wisdom', even 'existence' can only be applied to God analogically. According to him, God does not have wisdom but has something analogous to wisdom. This would make establishing a theistic science difficult. None of the terms we might want to use in our arguments actually refers properly to God under this tradition. I, therefore, do not follow it. I will instead attempt to form a cataphatic or positive theology. I want to *start* with whatever can be truly attributed to God and then use well-specified analogies and similarities to deduce what attributes can *then* be truthfully attributed to *us*. I believe we have sufficient concepts given to us via revelation that we can make statements about God that are mostly true. We do not, of course, claim to make statements about *all* of an infinite God. We only claim that our terms do properly refer to God and at least approximately describe the nature of God.

8

The 'I am'

8.1 Being itself

WE WILL now establish some basic facts about who and what exists. We use a third primary postulate of theism:

Postulate 3 *God is Being Itself.*

This postulate immediately puts God in a different ontological status compared with us. We are beings, but we are not being itself. That God has that special status is distilled from Judaism in the saying that God is "I Am",[1] and, from Christianity, in similar statements by Jesus.[2] This distillation has long been part of classical theism. God is Necessary in comparison to us mortals who are contingent. God can thus be the necessarily-existing original cause of any finite thing that comes into being.

8.2 Assertions that 'God is X itself'

Postulate 3 is the first in a series of claims that God is *X* itself. Here *X* is 'being', while other features (such as 'love', 'life' and 'wisdom') will be attributed in later chapters. Such assertions have important roles in theistic metaphysics, and these roles need to be defined explicitly.

Consider a generic assertion of the form "Object *G* is *X* itself". It first implies that, if *G* exists, it has description *X* necessarily. It is then part of its nature that *G* does not merely have description *X*, but that it does so at

[1] Exodus 3:14
[2] John 8:58

all times and in all counterfactual circumstances originating at any time. This does not imply immutable or fixed existence, only that property X is attributed at all times. That is a minimal requirement for any kind of eternal existence, though the actual manner or form of existence could be variable or fluctuating as long as it is always present.

A second component is to state that such a G is not an X exactly like other objects which are Xs, but that G is still essentially involved in the way they are Xs. Here, for example, God is not a 'being' precisely like the rest of us are beings, yet (as being itself) God is intimately involved in the way we are beings. God is still a being and still exists but in a different way then we.

From the existence of X-itself, we may deduce that every instance of X is either (a) identical to X-itself, or (b) dependent on X-itself. We conclude that if an object with property X exists completely independently (or 'in itself'), then it must be identical to X-itself, since (by construction) it cannot be dependent on anything apart from itself. The present case, with X=being and God as being itself, implies that any existing object is either identical to God or dependent on God. If anything exists at all, we could conclude that God exists, but we already postulated that in Postulate 1. What this postulate adds is that God exists eternally and necessarily.

You may dispute these kinds of arguments. You could ask: since this stone is brown, does that mean that brownness-itself exists? Does redness-itself exist? Or evil-itself, since there are many things thought to be evil? And if redness-itself did not exist, why is being-itself treated differently in theism? Theists reply that our argument for X-itself existing is not valid for every X. The argument depends on Postulate 3 for X=being and on later postulates for other Xs. These Postulates are not logically necessary for every possible X.

Alternatively, you could argue that since this stone is a being, and since God is being itself, we should conclude that this stone is God. Theists do not deny the validity of an argument like this. They insist only that it proceeds if the stone is in fact being, itself. That is: the argument is only valid if stones exist independently, eternally and necessarily, since *being itself* is eternal and necessary. Theists agree that *if* atoms in the world exist eternally and immutably then they could be said to have or be being itself. In that case, on the basis of Postulate 3 at least, they could be identified with

God. This is the sense in which the atomic materialist makes atoms into his God.[3]

Finally, a claimant such as myself has still, with assertions like this, the responsibility of showing that God identified in such a way is identical with the traditional God of the theistic religions. From the religious point of view, it would be a failure if God turned out to be identical to eternal and immutable atoms! Strictly speaking, logically if not theologically, that would be consistent with what has been asserted so far. In that case we could still *define* God in the manner of this chapter, even though God would not be a single being, and God would be distributed around all the individual atoms that somehow 'participate' in being itself. Individual atoms would have, say, instances of 'being itself' within themselves and hence be part of God. Further assertions may discount this possibility, but that will have to be the subject of discussion. Any 'proof of God', therefore, is not complete until we are satisfied that it is 'our' God who we are talking about and not other things such as microscopic atom(s). This is usually the non-trivial part of the argument. It will have to contain a demonstration of how God can be a One and yet multiple objects exist in the world.

8.3 The Argument from Being

We want to know the basic principles that operate *now*, which govern all connections between God and the individual finite beings that are us.

We will use one of the standard arguments of philosophical theism: the Argument from Being. This argument uses Postulate 3 above, and proceeds as follows:

1. God is Being itself (Postulate 3)
2. We (as individuals) have being (as, we exist).
3. Therefore, our being *either* is, *or* depends on (derives from), God (Being itself).

This argument uses the metaphysical principle that being can only come

---

[3] It is often observed that a-theists still adhere to Postulate 3, and effectively declare to be divine whatever it is that they think exists unconditionally or with being in itself. They find a new Absolute Principle to order their world, and this often functions as a new 'divinity' that takes the intellectual place of God by virtue of its unconditional nature.

from being and not from non-being (which is nothing). It uses the empirical fact that individuals in the world do exist. At least *I* exist, Descartes would claim. That is, there are some objects that are being in existence, so that we say that they 'have being'. Then, since God has just been defined as 'being itself', we say that God must have some role in our existence. Simply put, we say that "We are, because God is."

This argument establishes an ontological dependence of us individuals on God. We appear to be beings; God is Being itself; therefore we appear to depend on God. Some essence of our being (namely Being itself) is identical to God. A corollary of this argument is: we cannot have our existence separately from God or derived originally from anything other than God. If we had some other kind of being, then we would still have being itself, which is God. Postulate 3 establishes that just by existing, we are dependent on God.

Of course, this does not explain the manner in which we depend on God. I state an alternative formulation ('derives from') in the conclusion above but do not explain that. It will come later and is indeed a major aim of this book.

8.4 Consequences

The Argument from Being does not establish that we are *distinct* from God at all. If we were somehow identical to God, then our being would be being itself, and our continued existing would be obvious. This argument, by itself, can lead to several non-theistic accounts of the manner in which we depend on God. For now, I only explain what these other accounts are. Then at the end of the chapter, after the next Argument, will we have the logical means to discriminate between the other accounts and core theism.

The first non-theistic account says that all things of creation—all of us finite individuals—are in fact equal to God. This appears to solve the problem *if* all of us really are God (or Gods) though we simply never knew it. This is pantheism: that everything is God. An equivalent formulation is to say that "God is All That Is." Every smallest atom, every last bacterium, every planet, every galaxy, would then in fact be God. Religious life would then consist of learning (or remembering) this fact, which on the face of it is not obvious. It might be justified by Jesus saying that "the Kingdom of God is in you"[4] or Sankara saying that "everyone is in fact Divine."[5] Certain mystical experiences, such as those arising in nature mysticism, certainly appear to show that the Divine is present in all of nature, and these can be used to support pantheism. In the next chapter I will dispute pantheistic belief. Here I only note that its simplicity seems attractive intellectually. However, most of us, on practical reflection concerning our state in the world, cannot bring ourselves to believe that we are identical with God. Our everyday world certainly seems to be far from God.

A second non-theistic account states that the everyday world is an illusion: a false appearance produced by imperfect perceptions. Reality—if only we realized it—is actually the Infinite glorious God and *only* that God. This account is called non-dualism, and asserts that our everyday world is *maya*, a veil or an illusion. There *appears* to be a duality between the Eternal Brahman and the world of finite creatures, but reality is actually non-dual. Only Brahman exists, and the religious task is to acknowledge that in our souls.

There are further accounts which develop some kind of monism about what exists. In Idealism, God is taken as some kind of thought (or thinker) that includes all our individual ideas that appear to make us separate. There is even a way to bring in materialism, if we take energy as eternally existing and therefore divine. In that case, God (as being itself) is identified with energy, and then, according to our Argument from Being, is the being itself of everything that exists. We see that it is sometimes strangely difficult to distinguish pantheism from materialism.

---

[4] Luke 17:21
[5] The "I am Brahman" of Sankara (Sankaracharya).

9

God is Not Us

WE NEED to determine whether what exists is one or whether it is many. Having postulated *that* God exists, and that he exists as the being itself that we individuals have, we next need to know whether we form many beings or just one large being. We may conceivably be creatures who are continuous extensions of the divine being. Such creatures would be wondrous beings and feel wonderful, but it does not appear that we are that kind of creature. Why? Is there any *reason* why we should be distinct from God?

9.1 Unselfish love

To answer that question, we need to understand another component of core theism. This component is not something obvious from the philosophical point of view, but is, rather, very personal:

Postulate 4 *God loves us unselfishly.*

To understand this, we need to know what 'love' means, and what 'unselfish' means. These will be discussed in more detail later, but for now let us just remember some of the basic facts about these two matters.[1]

Some may think that love is merely a warm sticky emotion in the presence or touch of loved ones such as babies or kittens with big eyes. Others may think it is the persistant feeling of longing for the beloved. Others

---

[1] You may think they are obvious and that everyone knows these things, but in my experience intellectuals frequently make mistakes on such simple points. So this book begins at the very beginning.

(more scientifically oriented) may think it is a byproduct of the neuro-chemical and/or information-handling processes in the brain. Here, we are going to distinguish four things, all connected to love:

1. *Love*, as the underlying motivation or disposition that generates all relevant intentions and actions,
2. *Desire*, as the presence of love in our intentions,
3. *Delights*, as the sensations and joy which are the final manifestation of loving actions, and
4. *Affections*, as the feeling of persistent loves and desires that arise after experiencing delights.

For a given person and given motivation, these four things are all related. For now, we are going to focus on the love (1.), namely the underlying motivation for our actions.[2] I am using the word 'love' in a very general sense here, to refer not just to what we think of as good loves but also to the underlying motivations in all our activities. In this general sense I include each of the varied motivations for survival, such as sex, competition, and selfishness, as being different kinds of loves.

To love unselfishly means to love another person equally to or more than oneself. Its opposite is selfish love, which means to love oneself more than others. This may seem a too-quantitative definition, referring to 'more than' with respect to love, when love is well known for being difficult to quantify! I am trying here to explain 'unselfishness' without using the word again in the explanation. We certainly have in our loving a kind of ordering of priorities. What we love more takes priority, precedence and time over what we love less (especially when we are free of constraints). We prioritize from the *delight* we feel about that activity. In Chapter 11, I will discuss how we might come to know about our loves. In that coming to know there is also a coming to know of ordering, priority, and relative delightfulness.

That God loves us unselfishly, and that we should love each other unselfishly, is the import of the most basic religious injunctions, including those of theistic religions:

• Judaism: "the LORD your God is God, he is the faithful God, keeping

---

[2] To find out what that is for ourselves, imagine that we are completely free to do whatever we like with no repercussions or oversight by others: what would our imagination show us then? We would see where the underlying loves lead us if they were unconstrained. See Section 11.3 for further discussion.

his covenant of love" (Deuteronomy 7:9); "The Lord is good to all; he has compassion on all he has made." (Psalm 145:9)

- Christianity: "God so loved the world" (John 3:16); "Love your neighbour as yourself" (Matthew 22:37-39)
- Islam: "No one of you is a believer until he desires for his brother that which he desires for himself." (Sunnah)

The love of *others* makes you want to give them what you have, to make them happy and enjoy their life. An unselfish love, such as we attribute to God, promotes our being happy as much and as long as possible, and delights if we delight in our life.[3]

Such unselfish loves are to be contrasted with selfish loves. There are many other names for them, but here note only that our selfish loves want others to delight in what pleases us. We can imagine a good king who is happy because of the fact that his subjects are enjoying their life. He can be contrasted with a tyrant, who has his own ideas about what is delightful (probably involving much slave labor by others), and who wants others to become happy by making him happy. Unselfish love has the essential characteristic of wanting to give to others what *they* find delightful. Most of us agree that is good to be unselfish, even if we do not always ourselves live up to this standard.[4]

9.2 Selflessness and personal unselfishness

One way of understanding the postulated unselfishness of God would be to imagine that God is a universal being who does not have a proper sense of self to start with. In this scenario God would have more 'self-less-ness' than unselfishness, since the boundary between God and the world could not then be rigorously defined. This comes from pantheistic inclinations and in it God is not a full person. This is an impersonal view of God.

We will see however, that the God we are talking about *does* have the existence and properties needed to be a person. I am not referring to a person like us and existing among us, such that we might possibly exist without him because such a God would not be metaphysically necessary.

---

[3] Note that the qualifications 'as much and as long as possible' mean that considerable wisdom is needed to know *how* to love like God does. Ideally, we should take an eternal perspective, whereby we can anticipate possible future effects even when making decisions now.

[4] Even more of us call it good for *others* to be unselfish, but that is not quite the same thing.

Instead, I am referring to God as Being itself, and also as Love and Wisdom themselves. These together are sufficient to make God a person, with a sense of self and a sense of consciousness as a particular person. Then we can say that God loves us unselfishly and not just self-less-ly in an impersonal manner.

Some theologians dislike this view because they formulate their postulates differently. Postulate 3, for example, is taken by Paul Tillich[5] to imply that God is therefore not himself a 'being', since he is more the prerequisite or condition of possibility for any entity to exist. If God is not in fact a being, this has the consequence that God is incommensurate with human experience and cannot act in creation and hence not even love us in a way we would recognize as love. Such a view is rejected in the theism postulated in this book. I argue that Postulate 3, that God is being itself, has a strict positive sense, and that it *implies* that God is the ground of all being, while still keeping God a necessary being and a person.

9.3 God is good

The basis of declaring that God is good has been controversial within philosophical theology. It has often been simply declared as an attribute on the basis of the assumed benevolence of God. Many of us wonder, however, what sort of benevolence God could have, in view of all the difficulties which exist in the world. To declare the goodness of God, we have to understand God's strategies in more detail and see whether we would call his strategies good in terms of the sense of our sense of 'good'. This is not a trivial issue and will be continually debated in society.

On the basis of the postulates here in Part III we argue that God is a personal being who loves us unselfishly, in the sense of wanting the best for us. He wants us to be happy as much and as long as possible, even if that means less for him. In particular, he loves us all individually and intensely, whatever decisions we may make in our lives that take us away from or nearer to him. Whether, on this basis, we can accept that God is good is something that we have to decide individually, in the light of our knowledge of the world, of God's ways, and of what good is. This judgement will depend on our understanding of the possibilities open to God in managing the world. That is a topic on which I say a great deal later.

---

[5] Tillich, *Systematic theology.*

We will come back to the question of God's goodness at the end of the book when discussing the problem of evil. In the meantime, I return to the implications of God loving us unselfishly.

9.4 The Argument from Love

We are now in the position to frame the Argument from Love:

1. God loves us unselfishly (from Postulate 3),
2. Unselfish loves cannot love only themselves,
3. Therefore, we must be separate from God in some ways: God is not us.

This Argument from Love has a number of important consequences. From an essential aspect of core theism, we see that there must be an irreducible distinctness between us and God. This must be an absolute distinctness, not just an apparent one, because it must be a difference which appears so to God, who presumably sees things as they really are and not just as they appear.

This need for an 'otherness' between God and all those loved by God has long been recognized as essential to theism, but it is rarely given a logical justification. It is usually assumed by religious writers that creating independent and freely-choosing humans is a 'great good' which justifies many other things. Now we have gone back one step in the logic and can see that there is a reason for some kind of independence. That reason stems directly from the kind of love that God has for us.

Another consequence is that, though God could conceivably create those creatures I mentioned at the start of the chapter—those creatures who are continuous extensions of his divine being—there would be no point in his doing so. God could not love those creatures unselfishly, since they would be entirely part of himself. It may not be that God is lacking in omnipotence, but that there are consequences of the nature of God that directly limit what is *good* to do. Think how cruel it would be to make a creature who could not be loved by God!

This otherness is dramatically expressed in the writings of many theists, especially those who have had spiritual or mystical experiences. God is like a mighty brilliant sun—it is as if God is brighter by millions than the noon-day sun—and we are minor creatures walking on the face of the earth. Others have described how the numinous sight of God induces fear and trembling, and a feeling of great humility arises from the enormous differences immediately apparent.[6]

To deny this otherness is a serious mistake from the theistic point of view. However often mystics may experience temporary oneness with God, they are still distinct and lovable-by-God creatures, and, as such, they return to their individual consciousness afterwards. Others may want to deny this absolute distinction and want to become 'as God'. The Judaic bible in Genesis chapter 3 has a story of creatures wanting to become as God. They suffer badly because they want what is impossible.

We see that the Argument from Love has direct consequences concerning the systems of pantheism, nonduality and idealism. The necessity, if love is to function, of a deep division between divinity and us beloved beings is not allowed in pantheism. According to pantheism, we are all and entirely part of God, and that cannot be true if God is to love us unselfishly.

The problem with strict nonduality is even simpler. If God is to love us, we have to exist. This requires that our finite existence have some reality, and that it not be an illusion like *maya*. It can *not* be that our soul (Atman) is actually identical with the divine being itself (Brahman), no matter what the sages may have written. There must be some relation between them, but not one of identity.

9.5 Combining the Arguments from Being and Love

We now look at the consequences of combining the Arguments from Being and from Love. The first concluded that all our being is because of God's being. The second concluded that we are distinct from God. There is a *prima facie* problem here. How can we share God's being if we are necessarily distinct from Him? If we are other than God, it would appear that we are separate beings. How can that be true, if the essence of our being (namely being itself) is identical to God?

The resolution of this paradox is the key to understanding theism from the philosophical point of view. We can verbally affirm both Arguments, but if they contradict each other, then we have a logical set of statements

---

[6] To what exact extent such people have seen God, who in himself is infinite, remains to be determined. Religions with an incarnate deity do make it easier to see God, as then such differences are moderated.

containing a contradiction. From such a set any statement could be derived, and we understand nothing. Our task here is to offer a resolution to this paradox. This paradox is particularly poignant because it is one that God himself had to resolve before he could create anything. How could he create beings whom he could love? It is a real problem, not just ours, so we look at how God solved the problem.

Part of the solution will be to find a way that we can be close enough to God, without becoming identical with him. This talk of being 'close enough' is in fact a spatial metaphor, and such metaphors may not strictly apply in reality. However, as an aid to understanding, we can give several more visual metaphors which begin to suggest how a solution may be possible, indeed implemented, in our world.

We may imagine that we are 'adjacent' to God and maybe even 'touching' him. This equates to our not being continuous with God, but rather contiguous. There must be very close connections between God and us, connections sufficient to transplant being from God to ourselves but with still enough differences remaining that we are not part of God.

Another metaphor is that 'God is within us,' but this is a metaphor often open to multiple interpretations because of multiple meanings of the word 'in'. My own favorite here is to think of us creatures (all of the finite world, in fact) as 'hollow inside', and as God filling up that hollow in a way that keeps him distinct from us. This is again a touching metaphor, but is now restricted to an interior space which is only vaguely conceived. The concept of interior spaces is one which will recur in later chapters.

Whatever spatial metaphor we use to picture our relation to God, it must include that, despite our existence being distinct from God, we are still in some way connected with the divine. This is possible if God *sustains* our being, even though we have some separation. What is the meaning of 'sustain'? Is this something that God does once at the start of the universe or something that happens all the time? And is it something that God does automatically just by existing, or does it require some continual active contributions from God? Does it require contributions from us?

9.6 Analogical and literal language

The previous section has presented some analogies for how we might be related to the divine. In some traditions of religious philosophy, such as that of Aquinas, this is all that can be given. According to him, we talk about love with humans and love with God, but these are not strictly the same thing. Rather, God has something that is *like* the love that we know. It is sufficiently like love that we do call it love, but it is strictly distinct. Terms in his theology are not univocal, but analogous. This is not the same as the apophatic theology mentioned in Chapter 7, but it would mean that any theistic science would be difficult, since the terms we would use would not properly refer to God.

Duns Scotus (1265-1308) was one opponent of Aquinas on this issue. Scotus holds that 'being' is a *univocal* notion applicable to everything that exists without restriction. This to return to the position of Parmenides, for whom being is the central concept. According to Scotus, we should be able to unequivocally describe God with terms such as being, love and wisdom. Scotus' view has become the dominant view in later Western history, and we will need it within theistic science. We should try to avoid using analogies at the most fundamental level of explanation. That should not blind us, however, to the crucial role of analogies in learning new ideas concerning nature and divinity.

In fact, some analogies are so important that they link not just our ideas, but also nature and divinity themselves. We call these relations *correspondences*. Part IV will explain how such relations are more than analogies and how they are important descriptions of structures and dynamics within theism. And, using theistic science, we will unequivocally describe things related by such correspondences and then see *why* the various analogies do hold. In this way we will have the univocal language of Scotus, while simultaneously agreeing with Aquinas that particular analogies are essential to understanding the relations between divinity and created things.

10

Images of God

W E NOW HAVE to establish principles that make connections between what God is and what we are. In Chapter 8, we saw that we do share 'being' . Now we look for more detailed relations that govern our interior constitution. The first thing to establish is whether there is any such detailed relation. Is there a principle in core theism which affords connections between Divinity and the mundane world? Certainly, if God continually sustains our existence, then we would expect that there must be something about ourselves, and continue to be that something, that allows these acts of sustaining to have their effects. In Judaism and Christianity, humans are made 'in the image of God, in His likeness.'[1] This *imageo dei* appears to tell us something about humans, and, perhaps, something about God. This is generally interpreted to mean that humans are rational or have a rational soul because God is in some sense the Logos, the first principle of rationality. In this view, animals are not images of God and neither are plants or inorganic material.

Apart from our rationality, we can see that we have many similarities with animals. The internal functions of our bodies are almost all mirrored in simpler forms in some animal or another. Even plants have nutritional functions within their physiology that are simpler forms of the biological functions that go on within our human bodies. Moreover, within the Bible story of creation, the processes leading up to the creation of man suggest that plants and animals were partial contributions to this making, not to mention that they can both be food for humans.[2] There are a great many internal similarities of plants and animals with humans. Such similarities

---

[1] Genesis 1:26

[2] Note that I am not asserting that Genesis chapters 1-11 are literally true, only that they portray true theistic principles if the meanings of those chapters can be properly understood.

remain even though animals have sensation and locomotion that plants do not and even though humans have a rationality that animals do not.

All these similarities cannot be about size or shape since there is an enormous range of sizes from the smallest plant cells to the largest mammals. Instead, we must be talking of similarities of *internal forms and functions*. If the similarities concern the systemic organization of living organisms, then there are indeed similarities between cells and mammals, starting from metabolic, genetic and sensory structures. Even nonliving things have their own patterns of nuclear, atomic, molecular and chemical structures, which everything in the world is conceivably able to share in some way.

Humans themselves are, of course, more than just their rationality. It is common to say that a human is a whole and unified person which consists of one body-mind combination and to try in this way to obviate the problems of conceiving minds and bodies together without a 'dreaded' dualism. Our own theistic view of the unity of humans will be derived later, in Chapter 20; for now we only insist that humans contain not just rationality in the soul, but also sensations, loves, affections, actions—and that all these have effects in the body as well as in the mind and/or soul.[3]

Let us take a broader view of the constitution of humanity and of the structure and materials of which our bodies are formed. We should give a generalized formulation of the way in which we, with all the world, are images of God. This is to assert

Postulate 5 *All the world, and each of its parts, is a kind of image of God.*

This formulation still allows that the rationality of humans is a special kind of image of God, namely a more complete image. To be a 'likeness' seems to imply a closer and more complete relationship than an 'image'. This generalized principle implies that plants and animals are also in the image of God but to a lesser extent. The challenge to theistic science is to elucidate in each case what kind of image of God is involved and what 'lesser extent' is implied in connection with plants, or even conceivably, with minerals, etc.

We observe that present-day humans are not angelic in everyday life and that some fail to show even normal humanity, let alone glimpses or

---

[3] We will later find a non-reductive account of humanity in which all of these things can exist simultaneously, in their own manner, without any being reduced to another.

pictures of divinity. In such cases, the generalized principle, which allows for lesser images, seems entirely appropriate.[4]

The possibility, even widespread likelihood, of lesser images of God is in agreement with the eternity of God.[5] That eternity implies that God is constant while the world varies. That is, variations in the ways that creatures are sustained must reflect the variations in those individual beings, not in God himself.[6]

Since organic and inorganic non-living materials have extensive similarities in their atomic structures to living materials, we may conclude that physical materials are, in a weak sense, also made in the image of God.

The postulate of theism, that all things in the world (all the human and inhuman, all the good and the barely good) are each a 'kind of image of God', allows us to make significant progress in theistic science. The properties of God must be conceived in such a way that our being such images is a sensible claim. The non-trivial question is then to determine *what kind* of lesser image should be envisaged in each case. The following chapters will describe the structures of the world in such a way that they can be images of the divine. This is the heart of theistic science, which describes general structures for mental and physical objects. In Part IV our task will be to identify the specific parts of this structure. This is easier since fortunately many of them have already been discovered by science.

We note that the principle of *imageo dei* is often criticized as anthropomorphic, as if God were (to much amusement) the ideal creature of each group of humans or animals. However, we are proceeding in the other direction: we are starting from basic features of God and seeing how the world might be constituted and might function in the presence of such a God. In a genuine theism, this is not at all the anthropomorphic 'God in the image of man', but rather 'theomorphic': man in the image of God.[7]

---

[4] We should also note that the 'image and likeness' comes at the *end* of a creation story, and hence that such similarities are more like the culmination than the starting point of our religious and spiritual life. It may therefore be that the creation story describes, by images and likenesses, the stages of spiritual regeneration in religious life, rather than of stars, planets, plants and animals.

[5] To be discussed in Section 15.4.

[6] Similar conclusions are indicated by Matt. 5:45: "He causes his sun to rise on the evil and the good, and sends rain on the righteous and the unrighteous".

[7] There is here a similarity also to the principle of 'As above, so below', that is advocated in certain non-theistic groups. It could be true in pantheism, since then 'the above' = 'the below', as all is divine. It is still proclaimed in nondualism, but there it can not actually be true, since 'the above' is the infinite eternal godhead, and 'the below' is illusory and transient appearances, and no things more different could be imagined.

11

God is Love

ALL THE THEISTIC RELIGIONS teach that God loves the believers, who are those who follow his commands and love him in return. They also teach that God is continually producing goods and trying to give them to believers and unbelievers alike. This strongly suggests that God loves them all, in the sense of desiring good for them all. This love persists whatever may have been the reason for the unbelief and, hence, whether or not the love is even accepted or reciprocated by the person. God offers a 'covenant of love' to all.

11.1 Love Itself

It is another step now to assert not only that 'God loves all' but that God is Love Itself. This is certainly not an *a priori* or obvious truth, and it is most explicit in Christianity.[1] Many now seem to have gotten the message, and the identification of God with Love is now one of the central tenets of theism. We therefore adopt

Postulate 6 *God is Love.*

To say that God is Love, is to say that God's inmost nature is to be loving, however it may initially appear to us with recalcitrant wills and limited vision. If God's inmost nature is Love, then, because he is being itself, that being must also be Love itself. As discussed in Chapter 9, this Love that is God is not a mere emotional state of attraction or feeling good but rather a burning desire to give all of his own to be used by finite beings, for their

---

[1] Notably in 1 John 4:16

delight for a long as possible. It is an unconditional love and is not based on feelings or emotions. God loves us all because God is love.

The idea that God is Love is not traditionally recognized in philosophical theology. It was not present in Aristotle's concept of an Unmoved Mover who kept the world in motion. Aquinas allows that 'in God there is Love', but makes God's loving to be unlike ours: to be an act rather than a 'passion of the appetitive soul'. Most systematic theology starts by defining God as the omniscient and omnipotent being, and the connection between such and a God of Love takes a while to construct. Now, however, the identification of God with Love Itself is taken as one of the primary postulates of our theism. Pope Benedict XVI published "Deus Caritas Est" ("God is Love") in 2005, asserting in its first sentence that "these words .. express with remarkable clarity the heart of the Christian faith."

11.2 Love and substance

We now apply the ontological analyses of Chapter 4 to the case of God. In that chapter, we saw how the underlying power or propensity of a being could be identified as the *substance* of that being. That chapter dealt with physical dispositions since it was based on generalizing how science analyzes causes. Once we allow that non-physical beings can exist, exactly the same logic follows for mental, spiritual and divine beings.[2] We therefore argue:

1. The underlying power or propensity is the true substance of that being.
2. The underlying power or propensity of God is love.
3. Therefore, love is the true substance of God.

This is to conclude that divine Love is the substance of God. It is the substratum in terms of which he exists and is the subject of all his properties. We are not saying that 'God was formed out of this substance (love)', because there was *never such a forming event* in the past. Rather, God is love itself and always has been. We say that we can intellectually distinguish (in God's present being) the Love that is the basis or substance of that being.[3]

---

[2] You may perhaps feel qualms at using the same logic for all cases including that of God, but this is justified when we follow from the previous chapter that we are an image of God and hence have some functional and structural similarities. More of this later.

[3] We are not deducing this *a priori* but assembling it from what God has been telling us over the centuries. The processes of intellection will be discussed in more detail in Chapter 14.

Then, because created objects are a kind of image of God, we can conclude that something like love is the substance of all things in the world. In a nutshell, 'Love makes the World go Around.' This is not to say that love is the direct mover of every natural object and the immediate instigator of every natural event. Rather that *something like* love does these things. For minds, the 'something like love' can be loves, desires and motivations that we know are significant in human life. For physics, the 'something like love' could be deepest principles of energy, force and propensity that keep the physical world moving. These are grand claims: that desires, propensities and energies are 'images of love', and that they respectively are the substance of humans as well as of all animate and inanimate objects. Fleshing out and understanding the details of these claims, especially concerning the relations between the mental and the physical, is the task of theistic science.

11.3 Love and thought

Although we have not discussed thinking and thoughts in this chapter, we can here usefully remind the reader of some of the important differences between love and thought following the discussion of Section 6.1.2. This will help to elucidate the claim of this chapter that love (not thought) is the fundamental substance.

We first note that in introspection it is thoughts and perceptions which are immediately apparent, rather than loves. Loves provide a kind of background tenor to our conscious life, where this includes thinking as well as feeling. A second level of interior inspection reveals our feelings and emotions to us, especially if we have sufficient emotional self-awareness or emotional literacy.

Neither thoughts nor feelings, however, are the loves themselves that lead us to do and enjoy what we do. The loves are the underlying motivations that exist even before we act. Feelings and emotions tend to be the affections generated according to whether or not our loves are successful. It is thus difficult to discern our own loves.

To see our loves, we have to follow similar methods to those used in the sciences to discover dispositions. The relation between loves and thoughts is analogous to the relation between dispositions and structures: loves and

dispositions determine what we would do, whereas thoughts and structures show what we *are now*. The loves are that which determine what we
would do in various situations, just as are the dispositions and potentialities of physics.

Our loves may thus be discerned by one of the following procedures:

1. Seeing what we have done,
2. Seeing what we do now, especially when free,
3. Seeing what appears to us to be good,
4. Seeing our bodily and affective tone and responsiveness when various
   courses of action are considered,
5. Seeing where our desires take us when they are given free reign, and
6. Seeing where our imagination leads us when it is free to wander.

All these methods are like scientific experiments, in that they require us
to infer from events (real or imagined) back to their causes. In our mental life, we are fortunate to have available the last three non-destructive
methods.[4] It is interesting to reflect on the role of freedom in the above
procedures, whether freedom of action or freedom of imagination. Some
kind of freedom often turns out to be necessary if we are to discern even
our own loves.

Another analogy to help distinguish love from thoughts is to think of
loves as being like heat or energy and thoughts as being like light or illumination. There is a long history of seeing 'light' as a metaphor for thinking and 'insight' as referring to understanding. Remember, there is also
energy, which we cannot see, though (as heat) it produces light. The sun
produces both heat and light, or energy and illumination, which, though
carried by the one set of particles (photons) may be intellectually distinguished. This is because the energy of light is not itself visible *qua* energy.

The constitutive role of love has been controversial in philosophical history. It was traditionally recognized by the importance of the *will* in mental
life, but the relative importance of will and understanding (where love and
thought are considered to reside, respectively) has fluctuated. Descartes
was prominent in defining the essence of the human soul to be rational
thought. According to Descartes, the will was defined as the *actions* of the
soul, which, as effects, are rather different from the view in theism of love

---

[4] I call them non-destructive (an engineering term) because no human or living being need be harmed
in the investigations. They could be called 'thought experiments' but not in the common meaning,
because they are experiments we carry out in the thoughts of our own minds.

as the *cause*. The view of mind being developed here is very non-Cartesian, because of the substantial role being given to love rather than to rational thought. Descartes was never able to say what was the substance of the soul other than that rational thought was an essential activity. F.W.J. Schelling extended dualism somewhat along the lines of theism, or, we should say, consistently with the logic that we need in theism. According to Schelling, the world consists of 'will and representation': the will has the part of love, as substance, and representation has the part of form, as features of that substance.

11.4 Summary

We conclude in theism that divine love is the substance of divinity. The being of God is therefore Love itself. This love is the father of all creation, in the sense that all non-divine objects are reduced images (or likenesses) of that Love. All the world's objects are forms of love. The specific loves of objects (and of ourselves) are not immediately visible. They are only obvious when their effects are seen in real or in thought experiments. Exactly what we mean by 'reduced images and likenesses' or 'reduced forms' has still to be determined.

A detailed account along these lines will have to address the problem of evil. How can evil exist and persist in a world governed by a God of Love? Because many specific questions have to addressed first, that discussion is deferred to Chapter 29.

12

God is Life Itself

W E ARE going to generalize the previous chapter and say that theism affirms that not only is love the substance of God, but that *life itself* is also identical to God. For this, the concept of 'life' will be defined. We will show in theistic science how this is connected with the Love that is God. That is a long demonstration that depends on many pieces of theory and evidence and will only be fully sketched out by the end of Part IV. For now, we simply affirm the central point:[1]

Postulate 7 *God is Life Itself.*

12.1 Life

We have to understand in practical terms what life means here. Modern science has been progressively reducing the idea of anything specific that can be called life. In our new context, we want a general concept which can be used for all psychological, biological and physical processes. I acknowledge that physical objects are not normally taken as 'living' in the normal sense, and elsewhere in this book I have stressed that they are 'dead'. Yet here a particularly inclusive concept is required. We will therefore define

Definition 1 *Life of an object is the most fundamental (or: original, deepest) disposition: whatever it is that gives rise to its actions and capacities for interactions.*

---

[1] This is claimed by Christianity in John 5:26: "For as the Father has life in himself, so he has granted the Son to have life in himself."

An object's life is therefore that from which all of its behavior is derived, given its environment. In God's case, the life consists of the divine Love as postulated in the previous chapter. In the case of other objects, persons, etc., we have yet to work out what the most fundamental dispositions are, but whatever they are, that is their life. When we talk of 'derivation' of capacities from the 'most fundamental dispositions', we must allow ourselves to use the theory of 'derived dispositions' within multiple generative levels, as described in Chapter 5.

Core theism asserts that, remarkably, God *is* that life itself. This means that the behavior of all objects derives from God. We have yet to see *how* this is done and how a single God can be the life itself of multiple living creatures. And, of interest to us humans, we would especially like to know who is in control at each stage. Who decides the course our life?

The task of science is to explain the dispositions and causal powers of all objects and to understand what is the life of humans, animals and plants, etc. The materialist view is that all these have a life which is reduced entirely (and only) to that of the fundamental dispositions of the composing atoms and molecules, and that these constituent particles have the powers as discovered by physics. If this were true and were combined with theism, we would have to conclude that atoms and molecules were divine. In that case, it would follow that the fundamental particles would be divine and would be indestructible and eternal since they have life in themselves and 'live' from themselves. If it is not the particles themselves that are divine, then perhaps it is the energy from which they are produced. This line of thought has indeed been followed by many atomic philosophers, from Democritus into the twentieth century.

A non-reductionist view is also possible. Such a view says that we have some kind of life—whether vital, mental, or spiritual—that does not derive from that of our constituent atoms but has a different origination. Most of us sense that this might or ought to be true, as we have reasons to believe that our spiritual and rational lives do not originally spring from physical causes. We may have difficulty, though, maintaining such a view in a way that is coherent with the conclusions of modern science. The view of scientific theism is even more divergent, as it insists that *all* our life is non-reductionist, since it originates from God. Even the fundamental powers of elementary particles come from that source, a theist insists. Our challenge is to make detailed sense of these claims, while avoiding a pantheism whereby we (or atoms) are part of God or whereby God is part of us.

12.2 Life of created beings

One essential corollary of Postulate 7 concerns the sort of things that God can create given his nature determined by this and previous postulates. Theism says that all life originates from God. From this, we have the Argument from Life Itself, which concludes that created beings cannot have entirely their own life in themselves. God cannot make created beings to have life in themselves. Suppose that it were possible that

1. God did create something that lived from itself.
   Then
2. That thing would have as one of its attributes life itself.
   So
3. That thing would have as one if its attributes God.
   Then, since
4. God is One (by Postulate 2),
   we should conclude:
5. That thing would not be distinct from God.

We saw in Chapter 9 that God cannot create lovable beings that are not distinct from himself. The logic here, again, is that he can certainly create beings that live from themselves but there is no point in it apart from them as tools, because they would not be loved by him since they would be an essential part of himself. His love is unselfish and cannot love only itself.

Applying this logic to the Christian quotation of the footnote at the beginning of this chapter, we would have to conclude that Jesus, since he has life in himself, is therefore not distinct from God. That he is of the same substance as God is the orthodox position in that religion.

This above *reductio* argument implies that created beings do not, and cannot, have life in themselves. There is no elementary particle and no fundamental energy that is its own source of capacities for change. From the previous chapters, we conclude that finite objects do not have being in themselves nor do they have love in themselves. In theism, these conclusions are not independent claims after all, since God's being is love, and that love is life itself.

12.3 But we *do* appear to live!

But do we not appear to have our own lives? As sure as we are of anything, do we not live? In fact, animals and plants in the world all seem to be living in their many ways. Does it not seem strange for theists to insist that this life is not really their own, but someone else's? Even if the someone else is God, it still is a hard teaching to accept.

The theistic reply is *yes*, we *do* indeed appear to ourselves to live. More accurately, we have the *appearance* of life from God. Every moment of every day, the Life of God is living in us, but in such a way that it appears to ourselves, and to everyone, that we are living from ourselves. The way God does this, is to *give us* his life. He provides us with life, and after he has provided it, we *think* it is our own life. All along, he is closer to us than our heartbeat, closer even than our life-vein.[2] Our own life comes *from* God, and we live *as if* from ourselves.[3] This 'as if' will prove to be an important phrase in many contexts of scientific theism, including:

Postulate 8 *We all live from God's life, as if from ourselves.*

This issue of appearance does *not* refer to the fact that we exist, that there really are thoughts, feelings, actions in ourselves, or that the physical world really exists. All of these things exist unequivocally: not at all like the *maya* of non-dualist philosophy, where all of these things are held to be an illusion and just an appearance. In theism, the only thing that is an appearance is the *attribution* of the life that gives rise to these thoughts and feelings. What theism is saying is that our originating life does not belong to us. It does not come from our own nature. Rather, our life, as the deepest originating source of our capacities, is life itself, namely God. It just *appears* that it comes from ourselves.

You may wonder *why* God gives us our life in this indirect manner. The

---

[2] Qu'ran 50:16.

[3] Kant also has an 'as if' in his philosophy (*als ob*), but its role is different. According to Kant, we may not be sure there is a God, but we should behave 'as if' there is. For this reason, he says, we should follow universal moral laws. With theism, however, we know (or assume) that there is an objective God, but we should behave 'as if' there is not. For this reason, we appear to have our life as from ourselves and do not simply wait in silence to God to act for us.

answer should already be obvious: we cannot have being, or love, or life, in ourselves; yet God loves us unselfishly and wants to give us all those things which belong to himself. Moreover, he wants us to delight in all of these. The important thing is that we only delight in the love and life we receive from God if we take it *as if* our own. If we regarded that life all the time as forever belonging to God and not to us, we would regard it as external and imposed from without. It would then generate good feelings, but they would not be our good feelings!

12.4 Appropriating life

Another way of stating the theistic claim is that we have to 'appropriate', 'assimilate', 'receive' or 'take' the love from God into our own lives. Even though God has all the life and power in the universe, there still has to be an act of acceptance on our part. Put bluntly, since we have to accept life, we have to eat and swallow it and then digest it. Only then can it contribute to our internal welfare. It can also be thought of as drinking.[4] Whatever images are used, appropriation requires a balance between giver and receiver if it is to work at all well.

Let us look at the ways in which we might appropriate God's loves 'as if' our own. We might, among other things,

1. act from *loves*, urges which creep up on us and then appear to be our own,
2. think from *ideas* which 'suddenly occur to us', and which henceforth we are very proud of,
3. feel *delight* from those actions resulting from decisions which appear to be own own, and
4. *change* in new and unpredictable ways as the result of our previous actions.

If we reflect on inputs to our minds in the light of our own experience, we remember that loves and ideas have often come to us unbidden. We are used to being given new desires and ideas. Often we say that "an idea just came to me". Ideas are the most likely things to arrive this way, as our imagination is perpetually giving us new ideas, images and dreams.

---

[4] Or even, 'buy without money and without cost.' (Isaiah 55:1)

New urges come infrequently and slowly. We observe that received loves can never feel impelled or imposed. Rather, changes can only be gradually insinuated if we are to gradually modify our loves. Here there are interesting questions of personal identity. How can we identify a person over time? Is it based on memories or on bodily continuities, as philosophers have debated, or is it based on our loves?[5]

What about making decisions and then acting on them? Is there any phenomenology of decisions being given to us? I think not. Rather, decisions and actions and delights are the things which we most surely regard as our very own! Aspirations and ideas may come to us from 'elsewhere', but what we decide to do is our very own.[6] We may acknowledge that we receive life from God before or after our actions but never *during* our acting: that stage of our mental life is our most private and individual. So we support:

Postulate 9 *Our actions (what we actually do) are our own.*

This means that if the life from God is to be regarded by us as our own, it must be what leads to our actions. Only then can it become embedded into our lives and appropriated from God into our own derived being.[8] The results of our actions must therefore select that life we receive from God, in the same way that appropriate circumstances select for the particular operation of a disposition, to use the schemes of Chapter 4. This can be seen as in agreement with the way that the character of an occasional cause selects the operation of a principal cause, to use the schemes of Chapter 5. This selection can be phrased as the important principle:

Postulate 10 *The life we have from God is in accordance with what we have actually done.*

It can be generalized to all living and non-living objects, by means what I have called[9] 'Divine Dispositional Immanence:' that *the dispositions of an object are those derivatives of Divine Life that accord with what is actual about*

---

[5] Perhaps some love in us is fixed and could be the basis for defining our identity? This will be discussed in later chapters; here we just note that, if there are some fixed loves, then those loves must have been received only once in our lifetime and then never changed.

[6] This emphasis on the individuating nature of our own actions is reminiscent of Existentialism. Sartre[7] says that we are the 'ensemble of our acts." He says also we are "nothing more than this", but I do not agree.

[8] We will examine later the method of this 'embedding' and 'deriving'.

[9] Thompson[10]

that object. Here, we are taking definite historical actions or interactions as 'what is actual' about an object. In this way we talk universally of natural, living and human beings.

This postulate ensures that Postulate 8 holds—that we appear to live as if from ourselves—and that we enjoy doing so. Whatever life we have, it must act in such a way that the consequential delights are felt by us as our own and never imposed upon us. That this happens is my guiding principle within theism, and God's bringing this about must be one of the overall purposes of creation. We will see in later chapters more of what contributes to our feeling delights as our own.

Note that God is not different for different creatures. The divine is equally present everywhere. What is different is us. Consider two analogies. God provides life as the sun shines on the earth. The sun shining on the earth is constant, but the energy received by the earth varies by days and seasons. We know that this variation is according to the earth's distance and orientation: according to something actual about the earth and not because of variations in the sun. A second analogy is that God provides life as we are provided with food. Consider the way animals consume food in order to live. What an animal is capable of doing after eating depends on its digestive system and how it has assimilated the food. Different species will respond quite differently to the same food, according to how they are constituted.

Postulate 10 means that the loves which we can accept and retain may be a very small fraction of the loves that we need from God in order to live properly. Depending on our own nature, we may or may not be able to accept all the 'good loves' that we need from God. Our lives might not be lived in the most enjoyable and most useful way they could be, since we might not govern them properly with wise and unselfish loves. Unless we become aware of what is happening here, we will start along a path that diverges from what is good and hence develop selfish or other not-good loves. It seems possible that unwholesome actions in our past lead us to only be able to live with loves that cannot all be classified as good, even if they originated by the partial reception of some initial good love.

After all of our actions, when they have already been (at least partially) appropriated, is the right time to reflect on the general process of reception. It is time for us to *acknowledge* that the life is not really or originally our own but in fact comes from God. We should at least acknowledge that fact, according to theism. Most religions advise giving thanks to God for this his grace and mercy. It is not accurate to think that the life with us in fact *belongs* to us. If we should think that by mistake, the theistic religions remind us, then we turn ourselves away from receiving more than a little in the future.

In concluding, we note within theism the requirement of our appropriating God's love into our own life. This places severe constraints on what God can do to us and with us. He may want to whisk us into a heaven of entirely sweet loves. We may, indeed, also want him to do that, but if we cannot appropriate to our own nature those new kinds of love, then such an experience would be at best a temporary grace, after which we would return to our normal lives. For long term projects, therefore, God has to work with the material at hand. That material is the nature of the life we have, which, according to theism, depends on the actions and loves that we have already made our own.

13

God is both Simple and Complex

TRADITIONALLY, there have been many tensions within theism. We all have an initial preference for simplicity. One tension, therefore, comes from theism asserting both that:

Postulate 11A *God is simple because he is One,*

and that:

Postulate 11B *God is complex because he is Infinite.*

Looking specifically at the above claims we see that these seem to be contradictory assertions. In this chapter we investigate these matters. We are not going to get into a discussion about the different kinds of infinity that have engaged philosophers and mathematicians over the centuries. We will focus on those aspects that address the role of God in possible new kinds of scientific explanations.

These questions are topical because there has been recent debate concerning whether science always explains what is complicated in terms of what is simple. We generally agree that the world is complicated, though still finite. Theists, such as myself, now want to use God as part of some scientific explanations of that complex world, as would seem appropriate for a being who created, sustains and interacts with that world. The question is whether an explanation in terms of God is in some sense 'good enough' for scientists. Usually, scientists say, we explain all sorts of effects in terms of a few underlying laws, and since these laws have been simpler than the effects, we have gained knowledge and understanding. We now understand, they say, why those various effects occurred, and we can make predictions with our (simple) laws for what will happen in the future, in new circumstances as well as those already well known.

Such scientists see the theistic explanations, but are not satisfied. "That is not science," they say, "because you have explained the many effects in terms of something not simpler but infinitely more complicated. Furthermore, you have not actually told us the nature of our biology, minds or thoughts, if all you have done is to explain them indirectly in terms of the mind of God. This is just the homunculus scenario all over again. By explaining the outer person in terms of an inner person, you have not really explained at all what a person is." Their reply is summarized by saying that God, since he does so many things and interacts with so many people, is clearly a complex being—infinite, indeed, theists claim—and therefore you are not explaining the complicated in terms of the simple but in terms of the even more complicated.

Theists, such as Plantinga, have replied that God is in fact *simple*, and therefore explanations in terms of God are indeed allowed within the framework of science. Others[1] have allowed God to be of intermediate complexity: not perfectly simple, but still perhaps simpler than the (rather large) complexity of one universe specified by a point in the configuration space of 10^{70} particles.

But why do theists insist that God is simple? Somehow that does not seem quite right. We readily acknowledge that God is one, especially in the sense that there is only one God. After all, that is the most central tenet of monotheism and very much emphasized by all the theistic traditions. But how do we reconcile this with God being infinite, which is also asserted? Of course, we can always *call* God infinite, since we are hardly likely to be able to prove it. If we are serious about it, however, surely God is infinite in more than name only. Would he not actually *be* infinite? Would not his love and life *be* infinite? If God is to be infinite more than nominally, surely there should be actually infinite things existing within God!

All talk of 'things within God,' however, has to be done very carefully. Whether God is one or infinite, it is clear that he is never divided. God is never made out of pieces. As Aquinas (ST 3 1) says, "God is not, like creatures, made up of parts," not least because there is no-one else to put him together. But though God is never divided, we may indeed intellectually distinguish what is within God, even though those things are never

---

[1] For example, Day[2].

actually separated. In the next chapter we are going to intellectually distinguish the wisdom of God from his love, and we are going to look at some of the components of that wisdom. We can do this, even though the divine wisdom and the divine love are never separated, and even though the components of God's wisdom never exist separately.

Our challenge in scientific theism is to give an account whereby both the simplicity and the complexity postulates can be true. This will be done by asserting the more general covering postulate:

Postulate 11 *God is a unity, in which there is an infinity of what may be intellectually distinguished, but what is not in fact separated.*

From this postulate, both the previous postulates 11A and 11B—those in apparent contradiction—can be deduced. We could discuss the (very interesting) theology here in more detail, but I want instead to return to the nature of scientific explanations, since I am trying to establish the basis of a science.

We acknowledge that explanations in terms of God can refer either to the overall simplicity of God (namely divine unity) or to the detailed complexity of what is within God (namely divine infinity) or to both. This implies that some theistic explanations do not explain the world in terms of simple postulates. Maybe the postulates can be simply stated, for example as they are written in this book, but when they are examined in more detail, we find that there are great many consequences. Endlessly many, we might imagine, if we had an eternity available to examine them all.

What is it about such explanations that might remain unsatisfying to some scientists? They cannot complain that we are not trying to tell the truth. Suppose, Sober[3] points out, that we should discover that the digestive capacities of an organism are not its own, but are actually performed by parasites in its stomach. Then that 'homunculus' account of digestion is not *ipso facto* unscientific. Why is the situation different in psychology? Matters of fact should be of paramount concern to science! Sober concludes that, "Postulating little men in the head is permissible, as long as the little men do not have the same full-blown abilities as the people they inhabit. Homunculi are all right, if they are *stupid*." (italics in the original)

It often happens in theistic explanations that the possible 'homunculi'

---

[3] Sober, "Why must homunculi be so stupid?"

are not stupid. Despite yielding many new scientific consequences, is theism unscientific just by virtue of describing non-stupid homunculi? Is it not simply telling the truth? Maybe it can be admitted as still scientific, but there is still the question of whether we have *explained* what mentality is. Do we 'really understand' mentality, if our mentality derives from the mentality of God and is not actually generated anew anywhere? How could science make predictions in that case?

The theistic reply is that we just have to bite the bullet and accept that some explanations are *not* in terms of simple things but of complicated ones. That is just the way it is. The ultimate explanation in theism is in terms of a God who (in essential ways) is infinite. That is just the way it is. I am not going to offer an explanation for why God is infinite. We just live facing the infinite God.

All is not lost concerning explanations, however. When we discuss divine wisdom in the next chapter, we will see that God does give us the means to understand his life, touched as it is by infinity. He gives us an understanding that is touched in the same way and is therefore sufficiently suited for the task of understanding life. By being suited for understanding God and divine principles, we find a science that can understand the needed causes and effects, can understand how our own minds are formed, and can know all these sufficiently well so as to make predictions about new situations. This is just what is always wanted by scientists.

The infinity of God should only be a worry in science if it gives us too much freedom to explain almost anything, as it would then really explain nothing. We will see that subsequent chapters of this book only rarely rely on an explicit infinity of God, and even then, concern only the potentiality of what God can love and can know.

14

God is Wisdom and Action

CONSIDERATIONS so far have concentrated on being, love and life. Now we come to wisdom and to how we should attribute wisdom to God. We do not *define* wisdom, or attempt to contain it, but we seek a place for it with our scientific theism. In order to do this, we have to remind ourselves of different kinds of knowing and of what constitutes wisdom.

14.1 Knowing causes and loves

There are many grades of knowing and wisdom, so first we will establish the principal gradations in the ways that we can know, or think we know, something. We can discriminate between three kinds of knowing, which concern effects, or concern causes and effects, or concern loves, causes and effects. These three are usefully named as:

Knowledge: knowing an *effect*, or the *fact* of something,
Understanding: knowing the *causes* of something,
      including knowledge,
Wisdom: knowing the *love* which leads to a thing,
      including understanding and knowledge.

It is useful to distinguish wisdom in this way because the role of love in the world has been sadly neglected, yet its supreme role with people is easily acknowledged. One of the achievements of modern science is to prize the *understanding*. Scientists want to know the causes of everything so they can make predictions and test hypotheses, etc. They also want to know the causes of thoughts and emotions, which is good. They want to know the causes more than just to describe their effects, so we say they want understanding rather than (just) knowledge.

Theism sees love and causes as widespread and leading to effects. That means that complete information about whole processes requires wisdom and not only knowledge and understanding. We will look at loves and causes in more detail in later chapters, but for we now need only recognize that Wisdom (in the sense above) should be attributed to divinity. God certainly knows everything possible about love as well as about causes and effects.

14.2 Abstract knowledge

We also need to distinguish thought about what exists from *abstract* thought. We recognize abstract thought as knowing the *forms* of things, and this is contrasted with thought of existing things, whether they be material, mental or divine. According to the Aristotelian ontology developed in Chapter 4, everything non-abstract that exists is constituted by a substance (or power) in some form. The role of abstract thought is to consider the forms of things and ignore their substance or power. We say that the form of an object is 'entertained' in the mind, and thereby known. It can be mentally compared with other forms, used to make conclusions, etc.

Mathematics is the science of forms *par excellence*, so mathematics can tell us nothing about what actually exists. Rather, it can tell us about what can *possibly* exist. It can describe the forms which may possibly be instantiated in natural or mental objects. We had a discussion in Chapter 4 about whether the physical world could be made out of forms, as, for example, Pythogoras imagined a world made out of triangles. The conclusion was that some additional component of substance was needed, as otherwise the world would be purely abstract or formal (of forms). Formal worlds do not change. Forms can be used to *describe* change, by effectively removing the temporal aspect or modeling processes as a new (changeless) spatial component or dimension that is only *called* time. A formal theory cannot describe substances (which are powers) themselves but only describe how they change. Abstract theories of causes in science describe how objects have changed, will change, and might change. They define dispositions, for example, in terms of possible changes.

Formal worlds do not change, as physical and mental worlds do. Abstraction and lack of change cannot be used to distinguish God from the world, because, though God's love and wisdom do not change, God is definitely not solely abstract.

Abstract knowledge only knows forms and only knows love according to its effects and not its essence. So abstract knowledge does not itself constitute wisdom. There is more to wisdom than abstract knowledge or abstract understanding. That extra something must come from a more intimate acquaintance with love. Only by having wisdom fully linked to love can it yield a general knowledge about the essence of love and thereby be truly wisdom. Without that link, wisdom cannot be properly said to exist.

14.3 Divine Wisdom

We accept that a theistic God must be all-knowing, all-understanding, and all-wise.[1] God understands the forms of all things actual and possible and also how they may change because of their underlying substance (powers or loves) according to the ends or purposes of that love. A proper understanding of things therefore requires the wisdom of love, or wisdom united with love. Since God is love itself, let us declare divine wisdom in the same manner as the previous postulates:

Postulate 12 *God is Wisdom Itself.*

We now take the Platonic step that there is a sense in which universals (forms) all exist in the mind of God. This is standard in theism, so we claim that *all forms are themselves part of divine Wisdom*. This Wisdom includes all possible forms and all the possible changes of objects. We can think of all those forms making a unity by imagining the combination of all possible colors into a beam, where each color (spectral distribution) corresponds to a particular form. When these are all combined, the beam is of pure, clear light.[2] This can be taken as analogous to the light of divine Wisdom. The Wisdom of God is (or at least contains) an infinite collection of forms, from which collection all objects have specific forms by selection. The collection

---

[1] Doubt in us is still advisable, of course, about our own comprehension of that wisdom.
[2] We name such a beam 'white light', though it is not actually white. It just enables us to see things which *are* white, because it is not missing anything in the spectrum or showing any bias.

does not make up the Wisdom by an aggregation of many parts, but the infinite number of forms is distinguishable within that Wisdom.[3]

14.4 Relating Love and Wisdom

In order to understand Postulate 12, we consider again how divine Wisdom is related to divine Love. We saw that wisdom contains a collection of possible forms and furthermore that it must be connected or linked to love in some essential way. In Chapter 11 we saw that love, as the underlying power or disposition, was the substance of the divine. These requirements are satisfied if love and wisdom in God are related, in one being, as the substance and as the form of that being. That is, love is the substance of God, and wisdom is the form of God.[4]

When love is the substance and wisdom is the form of God, it shows how love and wisdom are related and united together within God. The love is itself invisible (as substance), whereas the wisdom (as form) makes God known as the image of the invisible. It is only by forms that anything can be known to intellect or to perception, as discussed in Section 14.2. Everything that God does, by its very nature, requires the joint contribution of love and wisdom, as is entirely appropriate within theism.[5]

14.5 God as the source of our own understanding

We will consider how *our own* understanding and wisdom are related to those of God. According to theism, our understanding only functions because of continuous contributions by God. How might this work? Some of the details of this process will be outlined in Part IV. For now I present a pictorial image of the method. This image of our understanding uses the representation of God as a brilliant sun that shines on us and the representation of his Wisdom as clear, pure light.

---

[3] If they were not so distinguishable, there would not be any point of having them.

[4] This is not a deduction, but it fits in with everything that has been stated so far concerning core theism. What is certain, is that God has (or, is) both Love and Wisdom united together within himself. This, moreover, does not imply that this Love *equals* Wisdom, as we have above explained the distinct manners in which God is Love and in which God is Wisdom, united without confusion.

[5] There are extensive Greek traditions, adopted also by Christianity, that say wisdom is the Logos within God. According to John 1:1-3, the Logos was with God at the beginning, and through him all things came to be, and no single thing was created without him.

The basic idea is then that our own personal understanding of what is true is a kind of *perception in the light of God's Wisdom*. When we understand anything, a mathematical proof for example, when we actually see it to be true, we are seeing it as if an object in the light of God. Truths, when properly understood, are 'in plain view' of 'the light of truth.' If the light is not clear and pure, but colored, then we see things in a biased manner: some true things now appear false, and some false things appear true. Everyone thinks he sees clearly, but theism claims that clarity of vision depends also on the purity of his associated loves.

Everyday language is full of metaphors for thinking in terms of seeing and perception. Do you see my point? Do these suggestions yield any insights? Perhaps you cannot see clearly what I am presenting to view. If not, perhaps I am not casting enough light on what I want to illuminate or elucidate.

This view of personal understanding means that perceiving what is true is not a matter of calculation but of seeing with a clear mind. Illumination for our minds has many analogies with the process of light for our physical eyes. The source of light does not shine into our eyes (mind) directly, but it shines on objects which select from the clear source and reflect back limited spectra to our eyes. The source is certainly not within our own eyes. We are not the source of light, but we use light that comes from the source. We rely on its color purity for accurate perceptions.

14.6 God is Action

Love and Wisdom in God are not themselves sufficient for action, but it is essential to theism that God is able to act with power. The love and wisdom exist continually, but actions are adjusted to be suitable for each occasion. Actions from God are a kind of 'going forth' or 'proceeding' into the world, and (at least as appears to us) they vary with time. They not only have to be different at different times but also depend on the divine knowledge of our actions. That is, God has an eternal and unchanging 'core', namely his love and wisdom, which leads to a part of himself—still divine—that *is* changeable.

We will use the word 'Action' to refer to this determination to act and to its continuation into the world as long as it has life in itself and is therefore continuous with God and remains divine. We may visualize this perhaps as the 'arm' or 'hand' or 'breath' of God, because it moves to do things and is part of God. It may well influence objects that are already existing, and in doing so it carries an aspect of divine power for that influencing. This Action may also be called 'Power' or 'Energy'. In the Eastern Orthodox church it would be called the 'Divine Energy': that of God which goes forth into creation, though still remaining itself completely divine, as it has life in itself. Sometimes this is called the 'Divine Spirit' or the 'Divine Breath', especially in Christianity. I do not use the name 'Holy Spirit', however, since this has a specific meaning within the Christian Trinity.

Theism assumes that that proceeding part cannot suffer, decay or become corrupted—it has, after all, life in itself—but that it is still able to feel, respond, and experience delight. Life can certainly allow us humans to do all these things. How much more likely is that someone with life in himself can act and feel and delight? We summarise our central idea with the assertion:

Postulate 13 *God contains proceeding Actions.*

Here 'contains proceeding' means that the temporal Actions are continuous with God, and are therefore an extension of God.

These proceeding Actions could also be called Power, but they have to be distinguished from the underlying dispositions that make up the Divine Love. That is because the Love is the originating source, whereas the proceeding Action or Power is that ability generated by love acting by means of wisdom. It is generally true that correct or good actions require the proper union or marriage of love and wisdom. This is true for us—as discussed in detail later—and is certainly true of God.

14.7 A triad within God

From all of the above exposition, we see that there is a triad (triple, trinity) in God. That is because there are three components in the initiation of any action. We start from *love* choosing some end to be desired, then *wisdom* works out the correct plan and form for love to achieve this aim, and finally *actions* occur whereby love and wisdom together produce the desired result.

This pattern is within a single person, that is, within a single willing-understanding-acting unit of consciousness. It is the pattern which we (should) know within ourselves, as, in that respect, we are a kind of image of God.

We note that these ideas are similar to some conceptions of the Christian doctrine of the trinity. That doctrine asserts, as here, that all members of the trinity are of one substance which is life itself, but it goes on to make them separately responsible for love (by the Father), for wisdom (by the Logos, the Son), and for the power of action (the Spirit). How this is supposed to work, however, has been the subject of considerable and continuing discussion, and no claim has yet completely resolved the problem.

15

God is Transcendent and Immanent

OFTEN God is initially defined as that being which is transcendent, omnibenevolent, omniscient, omnipotent, and eternal. In this chapter we see how these magnificient attributes can be related to the postulates already stated. Some attributes will follow in a straightforward way, whereas others will lead to additional claims that we should identify clearly.

15.1 Transcendence

Traditionally, God is conceived as *transcending* the universe: as completely apart and distinct from us and all material objects and existing eternally and incorruptibly. God would still exist unconditionally even if he had not created a universe.

According to the theistic postulates presented so far, we see that there is a metaphysical gap between those things that have being in themselves and those things that do not. The first are divine, and the second are not but are created by the divine. This difference has to be maintained at all times in order that God's love for us may remain unselfish. This metaphysical gap implies that the being of God is completely distinct whatever kind of being we have from him and that there is hence a necessary transcendence of the world by God.

Similar forms of argument hold with respect to Love, Life and Wisdom, as God has all of these in an original sense. God is love itself, life itself, and wisdom itself. We persons are loving, living or wise only in a much weaker or derivative sense, a sense which is completely transcended by the way in which God is loving or wise. A thing with life in itself completely transcends those things which do not.

In all these forms of the argument (concerning being, love or wisdom), the same kind of conclusion is reached. This is, the nature of God completely transcends the nature of the derivatively-existing objects in the world, and this applies with respect to all objects, whether humans, animals, plants, or galaxies.

I do not draw the line here between constant and variable things, since, as we saw in the last chapter, God also contains a changeable part. Conversely, things in the world participate in mathematical (geometrical, etc.) forms which are constant. The distinction that must be drawn is between that thing which lives from itself and those things that do not.

15.2 Immanence

Traditionally, God is conceived as also *immanent* in the universe: as completely present and pervading all of us and all material objects. God can thereby see everything and know everything about the world even if we cannot see him.

Our postulates on Being, Life and Wisdom have flip sides. Although we (as created) objects do not have being in ourselves, we still have some form of being because we do exist. There must be *some* sense in which we participate in the being of God, and in *that* sense it can surely be said that God is immanent in our existence. It is a rather weak sense, however, because it relies on bridging the gap of transcendence we have just been establishing and which is clearly an absolute difference.

15.3 Omnipotence

Traditionally, God is conceived as *omnipotent*: as capable of doing everything that is logically possible. Supposedly, for example, God can unmake and remake the universe again within the blink of an eye.[1]

The extent of divine omnipotence is commonly misunderstood, and this is in part because it has the greatest number of practical consequences for

---

[1] Luke 1:37: "For God nothing will be impossible".

our life and for understanding the history and future of life on earth. Some theologians insist that God has completely unfettered infinite and absolute power, and hence that God is capable of (for example) making, changing, and/or remaking the whole universe millions of times a second.

Many theologians modify arbitrary omnipotence in various ways so that God, while omnipotent, is unable to do various things, such as to change the past that has already been formed, to sin, or to do something morally wrong. More generally, omnipotence should not mean God doing something incompatible with divinity having the essential properties it has. We can insist that God always acts consistently with his nature. If, for instance, that nature has led him to create a world with natural laws, then he is not going to abrogate those laws. Still other theologians maintain that it is a 'great good' that humans have freedom, and that since we must be able to see the regular consequences of our own actions, God does not interfere in the production of those effects of our own decisions.

According to our core theism, the degree of God's omnipotence follows from the previous postulates:

First, we saw that all power and causation arise from the life which is God himself. This implies that all power belongs to God. There is no other source of life, power, or action. Thus, we have one first and important sense of 'omnipotence,' namely that without him we can do nothing.[2] This does not tell us the limits of what God can do. It only tells us that 'all power' (omni-potence) is his.

To determine the limits of God's actions, we must distinguish 'what is logically possible' from 'what is good and useful to do,' as this distinction is not sufficiently often made in theology. We agree with the traditional claim that God only acts in agreement with his nature. But what is his nature? We remember that he is Wisdom itself, so we can conclude that God only acts in agreement with his wisdom, or (more simply) that God only acts wisely.

We also know he is Love itself, which love is unselfish. There are many things that he could do, but does not, because he would not love that result. This might be, for example, because those actions might not produce distinct persons who can be loved. There are many direct actions possible to God, such as producing persons or objects that live on their own accord,

---

[2] Cf John 15:5.

but (as we found in Chapter 12), these things would not be distinct enough from God himself. It is possible he may create such beings but only as extensions or tools, and as part of himself, not as 'others' who can be loved.

We found in the previous chapter what it takes for creatures to delight in living, namely that they have the appearance of living and appear this way even to themselves. This is the requirement that persons receive or appropriate the love from God. This again limits the omnipotence of God, not because of some restriction to his infinite power, but because the point of creation is that people can continuously enjoy some life while always feeling to be themselves. The loves of a person cannot be completely changed because our being is our love and changing all our loves would destroy us and replace us with another. Loves cannot be suddenly changed unless the old person can still appropriate the new loves into his being, which means that appropriation must be by love.[3] The range of good actions and changes that can be performed on a person is therefore limited, and this effectively reduces the extent of divine omnipotence.[4]

15.4 Eternity

The logic that we have developed so far allows the Love that is God to be unchanging but to still be the desiring and producing of actions in the world.

This is because the love is taken to be in the logical class of dispositions and also because there is no logical requirement that dispositions (themselves) need to change when they produce time-varying effects. Rather, all the time variation may arise in the circumstances, occasions, or 'triggers' for action. More formally, this is ascribing principal causation[5] to God, and only instrumental causation to people and objects. Both of these causations are required to produce an effect. There has to be a disposition existing as well as the circumstances in which it will tend to manifestation, though of course we (and God) can act unilaterally if there are no recipients involved.

There is a difference between causation by love itself and causation by other (derivative) dispositions, because love itself (namely God) is not changed when it acts, whereas other dispositions do usually change. The

---

[3] This is the old requirement about *wanting* to change.
[4] See Chapter 29 for further discussion.
[5] See Section 5.5.1 for the philosophical definition of principal and instrumental causation.

divine substance may therefore be not necessarily subject to change, according to theism. It may have existed forever in the past and may exist forever in the future.

In order, therefore, to unambiguously affirm this component of theism, let us state:

Postulate 14 *God exists eternally.*

Core theism asserts that eternal God has an immutable nature. The divine Love and the divine Wisdom, being the substance and the form of divinity, have permanent and immutable natures. The underlying love and the principles of wisdom do not change with time but are the same throughout all history. Everything, from the formation of the universe to the production of living creatures and to the making of rational persons, has been motivated by a constant Love, and has been governed by the immutable principles of Wisdom and hence of divine order. God, therefore, cannot become a better God with time or become a worse one. God can never be born (start to exist) and can never die. Our knowledge of the divine will change with time, of course, especially if revelations from God are progressive according to our abilities of comprehension, but the nature, love and wisdom of God remain constant during all eternity. Our emotional responses to God may similarly vary with time, especially if our spiritual maturity grows over multiple generations, but the love and character of God remain constant. The intrinsic nature of divine Love and divine Wisdom is clearly outside all of time. In terms of process ontology, there are no potentials within God for changing his own nature.[6]

---

[6] This argument leads the Thomists to assert that God consists of Pure Act, as excluding all potentiality. Whatever that may mean, however, it should never exclude that God can be constituted in his eternity by Love. More precisely, by Love itself, which is almost in the category of pure potentiality!

16

We Act Sequentially

16.1 Time

THE PRECEDING chapters have spelled out what is (or should be) in core theism: that there is one eternal God who is Love itself and Wisdom itself. And then, that this God is the source of all the life and understanding and powers of living beings so that they have life as if from themselves. We now come to the discussions of what we are like, we who live in this derivative fashion. Surely the facts that our life continually derives from God and that we live in his image have many important consequences for the nature of what we are and how we act. That is the basis in scientific theism upon which we will rest our case for theistic science.

Seeing how we might act as if from ourselves is to see how it is that our actions are related to the enjoyment of feeling or delight that follows from doing them. We saw in Section 12.2 that our actions are what are most our own: those things for which we are responsible. These are responsible for building up our own individual character. Theism argues, however, that all the life we have still essentially belongs to God. The question now is how God arranges it so that we think that our actions are directly linked to the delights which might suitably correspond to them. This has to be done, in order that we live as if from ourselves. This is necessary, and even more important than that we have pleasant feelings, for if we did not live apparently from ourselves we would not even be inclined to make the effort to live at all.

This problem does not arise for God himself. His loving and thinking are both eternal and constant. As life itself, God's own delights after action are automatically present. How can we be happy too? Even though we do not have life itself, how can we enjoy the delights of life? God would be much happier, as emphasized in Chapter 9, if we could be happy also.

To solve this problem, God has come up with a very clever idea: *time*. There is eternity in God by himself, but time is possible with us. The existence of time allows for two very important things which are largely responsible for us to live as if from ourselves. The first is that we can, by thinking, choose the time for action. The second is that there is a constant correlation between our actions and their resulting feelings and satisfactions.

In order to choose *when* we act, there obviously has to be the existence of time. By creating time, God allows events to be known sequentially instead of in the simultaneous or eternal way they are known by him. Given sequential processes, the order of thoughts and actions can be delegated to us. We can choose when we make our actions. As workers today know, the ability to order and pace our own work contributes enormously to our sense of freedom and individuality.

Another role of time is to allow our actions (our individual choices) and the corresponding delights (from God) to occur in a constant succession. Whenever we act, God can arrange that the feelings constantly follow. And, as David Hume has emphasized, whenever we see constant conjunctions we think that this is causation. Even if it starts as occasional causation, it is to us effectively a full, real causation. We then think that our own actions have caused or produced those feelings. We practically and hence uniformly think that we live from ourselves. That is the desired effect. *Afterwards*, as discussed in Section 12.3, we may reflect on where those feelings came from and give thanks. But this reflection is in our understanding and does not remove the feelings and delights themselves from our life.

We therefore see the reasons for God to have us acting in time, even though there is no such time essential to the eternal divine nature. Sequences require time to be present to our minds and bodies.

16.2 Foreknowledge

There is much yet to be understood concerning the nature of divine eternity and of its relation with our own existence within time. Let us reflect on the balance between divine eternity and processes of change in nature.

In Part II, we formulated a process ontology wherein there were dispositions, propensities and events. We found a way to define substances in terms of them. These concepts are very Aristotelian, and they support the idea of a world in which there are real processes that develop according to the powers within them and undergo a succession of states. Natural objects are constituted in their substance by those powers. The future is open, since nothing actually exists until it actually happens. This view suggests that God is developing with us and that God will be developing the world together with us as co-creators.

If God is eternal, he cannot himself be changing in the same way that we change. Every kind of theism asserts that God knows all that has happened, is happening, and everything that is possible to know concerning the future. One weak claim made is that God knows all possible outcomes, with their likelihoods, since that is all that can be known about a future which does not yet exist.[1] This is the claim of process theology or 'open theism': that these *possibilities* are all God knows about the future. God, in this view, has to watch the world to discover what it is actually choosing to do as time goes by. There is certainly no predestination in this view, only desires (or 'lures') on behalf of God for what he wants, and people are always absolutely free to choose any action.

According to core theism, however, the eternity of God's omniscience means that God knows not only all that has happened and is happening, but also what *will* happen.[2] God is the Alpha and the Omega, the Beginning and the End, who is and who was and who is to come.[3] God is omniscient and hence knows all these things in his foreknowledge. God has foreknowledge of all the actions that we will take in the future, whether these actions be forced or free. God foresees all our free actions that we have yet to make.

Augustine suggested that one way of picturing this foreknowledge is to think of God as 'outside time' and hence seeing all time 'at once'. With modern relativity theory, we can similarly imagine looking at all of space and time together, as space-time. We imagine God seeing, in one glance, every event from the time of the Big Bang to the end of the universe. This makes the world a kind of 'block universe', in which everything exists together. The process theorists oppose this by arguing that then nothing

---

[1] This has been called 'weak omniscience'.
[2] This has been called 'strong omniscience'.
[3] Revelation 1:8.

'actually happens' and nothing new comes into being, since all past and future events exist simultaneously in an essential sense. They say there would be predestination, since all future events in some sense already exist. Many (non-process) philosophers have advocated determinism in the block universe manner, wherein we are never, in our future actions, free 'to do otherwise from what we actually do', and there are no real possibilities in that kind of future. But there are then no possibilities for God changing the world either! Suppose God foresees some undesired future and wants to warn us. Can he do that? Not if the future is already determined,

We need a more sophisticated theory of how eternity and time are related. We need a theory more sophisticated than saying either that God is always with us in the present and does not foresee future free acts (as in process theology or open theism) or that God is outside time and viewing space-time as the block universe and is unable to change any of it. How can we have human freedom and also avoid predestination, if God knows all the future? The process theorists would argue that, if God knows the future and things *are* as God knows them (no better knowledge is possible), then our future acts are already definite, now. And if they are already definite, we cannot change them, and we are not free to act otherwise. In this case, why would we even make an effort to bring the future about, if what will happen is already is definite? The process theorists cannot see how divine foreknowledge avoids giving rise to the unpleasant doctrines of predestination or fatalism (this fact is what led them to open theism in the first place).

One clue for a resolution is to observe that the *eternity of God's love* is different from the *eternity of divine wisdom*, precisely in the way they relate to time. Love, even divine love, relates to what is present *now*. I will argue that any actions of God's are now, in the present. Recall that, in any process ontology, even one that God has created, not even God can change the past after it has been formed. I will argue, from similar principles, that God also cannot change the future directly, except by making changes in the present.[4] This means that, despite God's eternal wisdom which knows all times, God need only love and act in the present.

---

[4] To allow such direct changes in the past and future is to open all the paradoxes associated with time travel. In a theistic universe, time travel remains a science fiction rather than a science fact. It also implies that, if Einstein's general relativity is correct, there are no closed time-like curves as Gödel[5] hypothesized.

16.3 The future

In order to resolve the long-standing dispute between freedom and fore-knowledge, we have to distinguish the ways in which God's love and wisdom are related to time, even if they are perfect and divine. Secondly, we have to remember that core theism states that God is a living God, and he is free (not predetermined) in what he does and how he interacts with the world.[6]

I began above to argue that, whereas Divine Wisdom by its nature encompasses all truth eternally, Divine Love and Action are always in the present. Whatever we or God may know about the past or future, we only love what is present to us, and we only act in the present. For example, we may perhaps have a vision of our future grandchildren, but, even if that vision proves to be completely accurate, we do not *love* them until they actually exist. They certainly cannot love us until they come into existence. That occurs by being born. Even perfect foreknowledge, we conclude, does not provide objects to love.

Another approach is to consider that, in process ontology, the future does not yet exist. It has no substance. Foreknowledge of such a future could only refer to the form or shape or structural details that will (one day) become instantiated. Even perfect foreknowledge cannot know the instantiated event as an actuality, since that does not yet exist. In the terms of philosophy, perfect foreknowledge may know the *types* of future events, in some theoretical manner, but it can never be acquainted with the actual *tokens* which will instantiate those types. In a process ontology, we have always to remember that reality is not purely mathematical or formal but has an actuality at least in the present.

Our conclusion is that divine foreknowledge may be possible in a process universe with real becoming in the present. We allow this as possible only as long as that foreknowledge is confined to the formal types or forms and not to the actual tokens or substance that will instantiate those types or forms. This makes divine foreknowledge, based as it is on the wisdom of forms (as discussed in Chapter 14), an abstract knowledge rather than a concrete acquaintance of an actual being. It is not the case that 'things are

---

[6] These features of God are not emphasized in classical theism which states that God is *immutable* or changeless and is *impassible*: He cannot be affected by anything in the created order. However, classical theorists still conceive that God can make free Actions in time, even though their cause is eternal and immutable.

as God knows them', because that knowledge is knowledge of form and not of substance. Since love is the substance of things, and wisdom is the knowledge of forms or types, the ideas in the previous two paragraphs are essentially the same.

Core theism may thus consistently affirm that, while we may have a process ontology of substances being each the power to make their changes freely, God may yet have perfect foreknowledge of the form of the future but still *not* have acquaintance with the actual substance of the future. Bringing about the *substance* or actuality of the future still needs the loves and propensities to make actual things. As we cannot just sit back and wait for the future to actualize with no effort on our part, if that effort is needed to bring about the future, there is no fatalism.

You may wonder about the *reality* of those everyday loves and propensities, if knowledge of their outcome already exists. What reality can be attributed to the multiple possibilities we thought were possible at each moment if only one of those possibilities is 'really possible' according to God's foreknowledge? My answer is that the multiple possibilities *would* show up if the configuration or state of those objects were repeated identically, based on the fact that the being or substance of objects is constituted by their powers. If there were free actions of persons or random actions of quantum objects such as decaying atoms, and if an identical experiment were run in the future, then the results would be *different*. Multiple radioactive decays of nuclei, for example, should give a distribution of different results just as predicted by quantum mechanics and Born's Law. We may easily allow that God knows in advance both the common tendencies and the varying actual outcomes.

16.4 Freedom

Again we wonder: if God knows about our future free choices, what would happen if he were to tell us what these will be? Would we be bound to fulfill them? In this case, would we not be predestined to watch our future approach and not be able to do anything about it? That *would* be predestination!

The answer must be no to both questions, for the simple reason that if God tells us something, we are changed. Any acquisition of knowledge must change our state and give us the power to do something different in the future. The whole universe must now evolve differently because of that interaction, and we have to conclude that even spoken divine predictions become, *ipso facto*, not necessarily still true. We may accept the prediction, or we may rebel or repent so it is now longer true. This means that, if God is to tell us of his foreknowledge, the best he can do is to tell us where we are heading and hence what we *would* do if he did not interact with us by the telling.[7]

The preliminary ontology assumed here is that God is outside the universe. He sees all future possibilities and also knows which of these will be actualized if the universe proceeds by itself. However, God is living and hence free to interact with the universe at any time. Actions are always in the present. Those interactions change the future that starts from the time of the interaction. It may seem odd that God can change the world so it has a new future he did not see before. Cannot he see what he is going to do? And what about God's Wisdom and foreknowledge of the future: knowledge that is supposed to be eternal and timeless. How can timeless knowledge change? The answers to these questions are that since God can act, the world *must* change as a consequence and hence also his knowledge of that must change. It would be entirely illogical for God's actions to change the world and for God's knowledge not to be able to reflect those changes![8]

We should remember that this model of God being outside the universe and only intermittently interacting with it is not itself strictly true within theism. This whole book is based on the principle that the universe can never really be an autonomous system, but needs continually the life that only comes from God. Later we will see more details of that 'life that comes from God'. For now we only note that God is (almost certainly) frequently interacting with the world. I speculate that we may be often receiving information that comes from divine foreknowledge, and furthermore, that much of our inner spiritual life may in fact be based on receiving that information in a reliable manner. The resulting insights, for example, may continually inform us about where we are heading and give us means to

---

[7] In religious histories, it is well known that much prophecy has precisely this structure. On its face it is a prediction of our future, but in reality it is often a means that may enable us to escape that future.

[8] The question of whether God's Wisdom can eternally and immutably foresee all his interactions with the world and its consequent changes, is left as an exercise for the reader. Related questions are: can God tell our future to us, such that the prophecy remains true? Would that prophecy be only accidentally true, or can it be necessarily true? And can (or should) God tell our future to us, such that the prophecy becomes true when it was false beforehand?

make revisions. By God's giving us our own partial foresight, we have a means to freedom from compulsions that might otherwise be difficult to achieve.

Concerning predestination, we find that either we do not know of the projected future, in which case we still make our own life as if on our own, or else we do know of the projected future, in which case we are free to react on the basis of that knowledge. In neither case are we presented with a given future that we must inexorably see coming towards us as predestination, so fatalism would always be an irrational response. In both cases, rational life is still possible, whereby we think about possibilities and decide which of our loves to manifest in our life of action.

17

We are Composite, as Spiritual, Mental and Physical

IN THE previous chapter, we saw that God enables our sense of freedom and life by letting us act when we choose. The ability to act, not just immediately when our desire first exists, but *later when we choose*, is a necessary component of our sense of freedom.[1]

17.1 Retaining life

In order for us humans to act when we want to, at a time of our choosing, we must keep our loves and our thinking partially separate, at least until they combine to produce the desired action. There are successive stages of the operations of our loves and our understanding in producing actions. When we act there must be the separate stages of (1) desiring, (2) thinking about what to do, (3) doing it.

Our ability to have separate stages of love and thought and action, means that we have to *separately receive* love and wisdom. Once received, they have to be *separately retained* until the chosen times of deciding and acting. If we have have these separate 'stores' of retained love and wisdom within us, we are composite in a very important way. Each of those parts of us must be a discrete component.

Our being composites is like God giving us the separate ingredients for cooking. We keep the ingredients dry and available and only mix them and cook the mixture when we want the results. In our minds we have loves persisting and thoughts occurring, but when our thinking decides in conjunction with some love, *then* we act.

[1] We will see in later chapters some of the other components of that freedom.

The kinds of compositions needed in us are exactly the separate and discrete images of the love, wisdom and action in God. There is (ideally, at least) love in us because there is love in God; wisdom in us because there is wisdom in God; and effects in us because there is action in God. These are all united and continuous in God, but in us they have to be distributed over our composite parts and separated by a discreteness. Let us frame the generation of this separateness as a general postulate:

Postulate 15 *What is unified and continuous in God, is imaged as discrete distributions.*

This can be seen as a further and more detailed elaboration of Postulate 5, that we are kinds of images of God.

17.2 Spiritual, mental and physical

If we collect together the retained loves of all persons, then they may be said to form a 'realm'. Similarly, the set of all retained thoughts form another realm. Again there is a realm of all the actual effects. In this sense, creation has three realms: the first, a reduced and distributed image of divine love; the second, a reduced and distributed image of divine wisdom; and the third, a reduced and distributed image of divine power and action. More detail will come in Part IV, but I now argue that these three realms should be identified as the spiritual, the mental and the physical. So:

- The *spiritual realm* contains the separate loves in creation, including desires, loves, affections, motivations, purposes, dispositions, etc.
- The *mental realm* contains the separate carriers of wisdom, including thoughts, ideas, understandings, rationality, plans, ideologies, beliefs, etc.
- The *physical realm* deals with all the separate final actions and effects, including the entire sets of things we know from external observations and physics.

Note that, strictly speaking, since the spiritual is a part of the mind, we could talk about 'spiritual mind' or 'internal mind' as well as the 'external mind' here called the 'mental'. For simplicity I have shortened the terminology.

In this and the next chapters, I will argue that God, the spiritual, the mental, and the physical are four levels of a generative structure. Before that we must discuss what we really mean by a realm.

17.3 Realms

Let us consider what is necessary if love is to be retained in some way and if wisdom is also to be retained in a similar way. The first requirement is that what is retained be embodied in some kind of substance. The second requirement is that that substance be contained in some structure of *other* substances in order to protect and keep it until it is ready for operation. That other thing is like a cup or vessel for the first substance.

The first requirement is that love (or wisdom) be embodied in a substance. Substances, we remember from Chapter 4, are the persistent loves or dispositions for some action. The substance that can embody *love*, therefore, must be a substance that is active and preserves some particular tendency to action. Imagine this as similar to the way a hot gas preserves energy, where the high temperature entails a tendency such as pressure. Since the 'substance that is active' must (by Chapter 4) be a disposition (in this case, a love A), and since the preserved 'tendency to action' is also a disposition (in this case, another love, B say), then we have a love A for a love B.

The substance that can embody *wisdom* is similarly the love for wisdom. Wisdom, as a set of possible forms, cannot itself exist as an object, even a mental object, because it is not a substance. It can only be the form of a substance. Storage of wisdom requires a substance (which is a love) that is persistent but malleable. The love must be something that can take a form and keep it as long as needed with as little change as possible. This must be, therefore, a love for wisdom. Imagine this processes as similar to the way a white page or a blank slate may be imprinted with letter forms and preserve those forms unchanged until needed. Mentally, memory is like this, but even better would be a love that *seeks out* and assimilates forms (which are the objects of knowledge).

A substance that can embody *effects* is also needed. There has to be some kind of matrix or infrastructure of substances that can receive intentions from love and wisdom and generate a process of making permanent the effects of actions. These substances must be relatively inert, and so we will say that they are forms, not of loves but of dispositions. Dispositions in this sense are 'reduced' loves, and can be thought of as 'dead' rather than 'living' (as will be discussed in more detail in Chapter 24).

In order that these loves for love, and also the loves for wisdom and dispositions for effects, be kept available and ready for operation at a time to be chosen later, we asserted that they have to be preserved in some way and also kept separate from each other. We can think of this by analogy with many processes existing in nature. It is like our bodies keeping food until it is needed for living. The love and wisdom we receive from God are like spiritual food that is needed for our spiritual and mental lives.

Preserving and keeping these embodied loves or wisdoms separate is accomplished most easily by having 'receptacles' or 'containers.' I surmise that they interact with the retained substances in a minimal way, so as to preserve them as long as possible with minimal contamination from the outside. There are many similar processes in nature, such as blood being preserved in blood vessels or energy from the sun being preserved by photosynthesis.

Because we are now talking about possibilities for interactions and because these different possibilities have relations to each other, we have, as explained in Thompson[2], the minimal ingredients for there being some kind of *space*. A space is a set of possibilities for interactions, where the different possibilities are related to each other by some predetermined principle, namely by *extensive relations*. We are not yet making assumptions about the overall topology of these spaces or whether they are continuous or metric spaces like the three-dimensional space we are acquainted with.

Whatever the topology might be, we conclude that each realm is in a space. More precisely: a space may be constructed in each case from the different possibilities for interactions. The result is that there is a spiritual space of loves, a mental space of ideas, and a physical space of effects.

Loves (or ideas) are in some kind of space of their own. We have not yet examined the *relations* between the loves of different people, the ideas of different people, or the effects of different people. Neither have we examined the relations between the love-space, the idea-space, and the effects-space of a given person. These issues will be discussed in the next chapter.

---

[2] Thompson, *Philosophy of nature and quantum reality*.

It appears that the substances making up the containers are more inert than those being contained. The interior substances—the loves for love and for wisdom—are 'more like' the source of life. The exterior substances—the receptacles of love and of wisdom—are 'less like' that source and 'more like' the final effects which are physical. These considerations will be discussed in more detail in later chapters. For now, we just give the more familiar names. The receptacle for love-substances is what is known as our *will*. Contained in our will we have loves, desires and feelings. The receptacle for wisdom-substances is what is known as our *understanding*, so contained in our understanding we have wisdom, intelligence and thoughts. The receptacle for effect-substances is what is known as our *body*, or *nature* more generally. Therefore contained in nature we have all the physical effects in the universe.

18

We are Sustained by Influx From God, Directly and Indirectly

THE PREVIOUS chapter talked about three realms in the created world, where each realm in turn contains substances which respectively receive love, receive wisdom, and receive actions. We call these the spiritual, mental and physical realms. The three substances are exactly the loves for those three things (love, wisdom and actions), and, moreover, are in some kind of realm or space wherein they are able to interact with others of the same kind but not of different kinds. We now discuss the way that the three realms operate together, and we ascertain the relations between the different spaces.

18.1 Spiritual, mental and physical operations

The reason for these three, we saw, is that they are images of the three components of God. These components must act together if any results are to be achieved. The basic principle of operation is this: love acts by means of wisdom in order together to produce actions. They have distinct existences in the three realms, but the overall effects of operation are similar (since all of creation is an image of God).

The best way of seeing the operation of substances in the three realms is as multiple generative levels as discussed in Chapter 5. If we place them in the order shown in Table 18.1, then we have a generative sequence as we go down the list. These operations are governed by the principle of Postulate 10, where the new life being received is always in accordance with what has actually been done at each level. The successive stages of operation are:

God
Spiritual Mental Physical

Table 18.1 *Combining God with the three created realms gives a set of four generative levels.*

1. God generates first the *spiritual* realm, where there are containing-substances which appropriate and retain love. The particular existing containing-substances select which loves from God *can* be appropriated and retained (by Postulate 10).
2. The spiritual realm (of loves) acts by producing new thoughts in the *mental* realm, where there are containing-substances which appropriate and retain ideas. The particular existing containing-substances select which ideas generated by the spiritual realm *can* be appropriated and retained (by Postulate 10 again).
3. The mental realm (of ideas) acts, in conjunction with the loves from the spiritual, by producing new effects in the final *physical* realm where there are containing-substances which appropriate and retain actions. The fact that there are such containing-substances selects which actions generated by the spiritual+mental realms *can* be appropriated and retained.
4. The physical realm (of actions) is the final effect of the chain and is the 'bottom line' or termination of all the processes. The set of effects which actually occur is the ultimate selection of which results come to full achievement.

18.2 Is this occasionalism?

The scheme of the previous section may be reformulated using the terminology in Section 5.5.1 concerning principal and occasional causation. Then, at any given level, the next-higher level is the source of principal causation, and the previously-existing things at that level form the occasional cause.

Many philosophers and theologians reject the idea of occasional causes, especially as it was promulgated by Nicolas Malebranche in the seventeenth century. According to Malebranche, there are no actual powers in the world, and God is the immediate cause of all the events that occur. Previous physical events, our own minds and decisions, etc., are merely the *occasion* for God choosing to act to produce the effects we see. This view is commonly rejected because it gives no individual powers to created objects or living creatures (including humans). We are no longer our own agents of action but merely a set of excuses for God to act. Theologically, this makes God directly responsible for all actions, whether good or evil and whether in accord with God's will or not. Every act in the world, no matter how mundane, is therefore God acting and never us.

The theism being developed in this book does, at first glance, look like occasionalism. Every act of causation is the operation of a principal cause according to some previous occasion or instrumental cause. Events in the world are only instrumental causes and do not, strictly speaking, cause their effects! But, if we follow the causal philosophy of Chapter 4 then we must oppose this interpretation, for surely physical objects, as constituted by their dispositions to act, must have causal powers distinct from God. Would this not be a contradiction?

My answer is that it would indeed be a contradiction but only if there were *only two* generative levels in the world, namely God along with the ultimate level of physical effects. In this case, all events would certainly be directly caused by God, and there would be no created objects with their own powers and certainly no objects consisting of their own powers.

But in fact, the theism here has *multiple levels* of substance between God and the ultimate physical effects. The actions of God now do not produce the physical effects directly. God does not have to act directly and continually in the physical world. Rather, as we see just above in Section 18.1, the actions of God create spiritual objects which in turn create mental objects. Then both together create physical objects. The intermediate objects are not made purely of events but are themselves dispositions and, therefore, substances. These substances are therefore what usually act directly and continually in the world, and it is not necessary for God to do so. Still, we admit, all the being, powers and action of those substances are derived from God, who is therefore immanent with them.

18.3 Multiple spaces and discrete degrees

We still have to determine the relation between the spaces of the three realms. They could all be regions of one large space, or they could be three distinct spaces. By distinct spaces, I mean spaces which are logically disjoint and have no places in common. It would be a more monistic view to have all the realms existing in different parts of the same space, but theism requires that they be in different spaces. The distinction between the spaces is therefore similar to the distinction between God and all of creation as a whole. We take this as one of the core postulates of theism:

Postulate 16 *The relations between created realms is an image of the relation between God and creation.*

it can be regarded as a further extension of the *imageo deo* of Postulate 5. This new postulate is the principle of *discreteness* of the three realms. There is no continuity between them. It claims that there is no way to continuously move from one realm to another.

Postulate 16 conveys a dualism between the physical and mental and another dualism between the mental and spiritual. Both are similar to (or reduced images of) the dualism between God and creation. Such dualisms have long been argued in philosophy and theology. They have been denied by monists, who want to see all things as essentially composed of one kind of substance. Scientists have been suspicious of dualism because they cannot see the reasons for the distinction existing nor the reasons for the dynamical connections between the multiple realms. We saw in Chapter 5 that there are many distinctions already known in physics and psychology. I will later show that these are of the same essential nature as the dualisms alluded to in Postulate 16. Using our scientific theism, we can begin to learn of the general principles that link the dynamical processes in the several realms. These are essentially just the operations discussed in the previous Section 18.1.

18.4 Consequences of discreteness

One part of the well known 'hard problem of consciousness' is seeing how mental properties could ever arise within the physical world. The possibility of having distinct spaces for physical, mental and spiritual processes makes it very much easier to understand them from a scientific point of view.

It has been intuited that mental and spiritual processes are 'not in space'. Wherever we look in space we never find thoughts or feelings. Now, however, we can acknowledge that mental substances are not in *physical* space but are in a space of their own. We have yet to determine the topology and metric of 'mental space' or even whether it has a fixed topology at all. Answering this question is one task of theistic science. We might surmise that mental topology is based on a metric of 'similarity of function' (of ideas), and that spiritual topology is based on a metric of 'similarity of purpose' (of loves). Both are therefore in spaces, defined by different metrics with different topologies. Mental spaces might therefore make what psychologists call 'associative memory', which is a simple and natural activity. Physical spaces are continuous metric spaces that are mostly independent of what events happen or what objects exist at various places.[1] Mental topologies might be very different from physical topologies. They would then have quite different measures of similarity between different loves. Some kind of mental space is needed in order to distinguish multiple loves and/or ideas.

This discreteness of the realms implies a real and clear dualism between the physical and mental realms. Without knowledge of this discreteness, many thinkers have tried to characterize the mental-physical difference in other ways. Most of these other schemes end up with *continuous* gradation between the physical and the mental and not the *discrete* gradations we see in theism. They have also been used erroneously to characterize the relation of the earth to the realm of spirituality. These schemes have been many and various and have portrayed the difference as spatial ('up in the sky'), as density ('finer material' or an 'aether'), as frequency ('higher vibrations'), as dimensionality ('the fourth (or fifth) dimension'), as size ('cosmic consciousness'), as a polarity, or as an intensity, etc., etc. I will discuss these different proposals at greater length in Section 23.2. Here the basic consideration from theism is that it is impossible to continuously transform what is physical to what is mental or spiritual.

---

[1] This small dependence in physical spaces is gravitation, according to general relativity.

18.5 Direct and indirect life from God

One important consequence of Postulate 16 is that similar kinds of mechanisms are used between God and creation and between the separate degrees of creation. The later degrees are derivatives of the previous degree (as described in Section 18.1). The later degrees can also be direct derivatives from divine power. Because the differences between the degrees are similar to the differences between the degrees and God, derivative powers from either source can look the same once they are produced. Whether and how much this option is availed of by God remains to be seen. It is at least metaphysically possible that the world receives both direct life from God and also indirect life via the previous (higher) degrees. Physical bodies, for example, can be directly sustained by God and also, by essentially the same mechanisms, be indirectly sustained and controlled by the mental and the spiritual processes of the individual person. We do not have a case of overdetermination, as the actual effect of these two inputs is from their combination. They may cooperate or may be in tension. One input by itself, in such cases, can never completely override another.

18.6 Influx

All these processes of generation, retention and selection can be usefully imaged by the 'flowing' of life *from* God *into* us as receptacles that retain that life until it operates. The different discrete degrees can be imaged as successive pools in a chain of waterfalls: pools which keep the flow for a short period before it flows on down to later stages. This is the reason for waterfalls being used as the cover picture. The flow of water conveys aspects of the 'influx of life', in that the 'being' of the later degrees is dependent on the previous ones. The image of water influx is not accurate, however, when it comes to the *discreteness* of the successive degrees, since water flow is indeed continuous, and not discrete.[2] Nevertheless, we henceforth use the term 'influx' to refer to the general manner in which God sustains and enlivens the world.

The traditional view of God creating the world is different. It is by *fiat*, taking literally the commands '*fiat lux*: let there be light,' and so on. The-

---

[2] The fact that God sustains all beings by such 'influx' can be the meaning of Matthew 5:45: "He ... sends rain on the righteous and the unrighteous." Alternative imagery in the same verse refers to light rather than liquid flow: "He causes his sun to rise on the evil and the good."

ologians have usually separated the question of how God sustains the existence of things from the question of their dynamical properties. These properties are taken to give rise to secondary causation, which is assumed to be independent of whatever primary causation there is from God.

The creation of substantial objects nevertheless involves God giving them their being (since he is being itself). There can be no power without substance nor without some kind of presence. It is impossible that God sustains merely the existences of things while at the same time remaining completely absent. We discussed presence in Section 15.2. In the theism of this book, we claim the immanence of God, by which all things are sustained, is less an abstract metaphysical principle and much more the immediate and mediate re-generation of life by continual influx from God. The sustaining of being by re-generation does allow this, as long as the *beginning* of the chain is in the presence of God.

18.7 Consciousness

Since we all accept that we are conscious, the nature of conscious awareness must be an essential part of mental activities. Within our theism, there is an awareness generated when the love and the wisdom from God come together again, after having been received and retained separately in various sub-degrees. This coming together is primarily the generation of an action, so let us postulate something specific for when consciousness exists:

Postulate 17 *Whenever love acts by means of wisdom, that action is a conscious action. There is consciousness of the production of the result and also of the delight that arises from the achievement of that production.*

The awareness is of the action itself and not so much of the love and wisdom that produced the action (to be aware of these things also will require another level of consciousness at a 'prior' discrete degree within the multilevel structure). Consciousness thus arises everywhere in all levels within the mental and spiritual degrees, and also in God, but it does *not* arise within the physical degree. Natural processes are not themselves aware or conscious of the events taking place. Such awareness requires an accompanying and corresponding mental process.

19

God is Equally Present in All Subparts

W<small>E SAW</small> in Section 15.2 that God is immanent in creation since every object is capable of immediate continued existence because it is derived from divine power. Some consequences were discussed, and now we explore some further implications.

19.1 Subparts as enneads

From general immanence, it follows that God is immanent in every *part* of creation and in every *part of each part*. God must be present in every realm that influences each part and each sub-part. God must be imaged in each thing of love, and in each thing of thought, and in each physical thing, as well as in the interior realms of all of these. God's pattern is of love-wisdom-power, which we now abbreviate as L/W/P. This pattern must be within every part, which implies that we have 3 sub-parts each of love, of thought, and of effect. This is nine altogether. We talk of *enneads*, from the Greek for nine. The function of each of the original three spiritual, mental and physical degrees is itself further distributed over the nine sub-degrees that must be present, three in each. Each element of the resulting ennead has its own substance, its own quality, its own space, and its own actions, according to the way each is an image of the divine.

There is no reason to stop there. The L/W/P pattern should be recursively applied in all creation at all levels, giving rise to discrete degrees, sub-degrees, sub-sub-degrees, and so on. All these discrete (sub-)degrees will have generative and selection relations linking distinct levels. They will all be within their own spaces, in various shapes, and they will all act by contacts within the same space or level.

This scheme of nested images of God comes about because God is the same everywhere, at all scales in space and at all degrees and stages of generation. God is the same, but all these things are different, so the reception varies This scheme, moreover, is not a mechanical fragmentation of created reality. Rather, it is a source of ideas at each level which are all qualitatively as well as quantitatively completely distinct. The qualitative novelty that results is almost overwhelming. It is certainly the result of the overflowing love of God. Each step of the ladder is a new world with new dynamics. Soon we get to the end of what can be predicted *a priori* in any scientific theism. In Part IV, we will use empirical observations with a theistic science to identify some of those qualitative worlds.

19.2 Explorations

Now we have three degrees (spiritual/mental/physical), 9 sub-degrees, 27 sub-sub-degrees, and 81 sub-sub-sub-degrees, etc. As we go into the subdivisions we learn more detail, but the abundance poses some significant strain on our comprehension! Here I will sketch the 9 sub-degrees briefly. We will see that we can find some comparisons with existing theories of physics and psychology which will make it easier to understand.

We adopt a numbering system, starting with 1, 2 and 3 for the first three realms of spiritual, mental and physical, as in Table 19.1. Then 1.1, 1.2, 1.3 for the sub-degrees of 1. And 2.1, 2.2, 2.3 for the sub-degrees of 2, and so on. This gives the ninefold set, the ennead, of Table 19.2 for the 9 sub-degrees. In this second table I write first '*A* of *B*' where *A* is the part from Table 19.1, and *B* is the sub-part of that part. This '*A* of *B*' is therefore to be read as *B* being a further specification of *A*. In the final column, however, I change 'of' to 'from', since effects are more clearly like the final result than the instigator of something. For the same reasons, I have sometimes exchanged the words 'action' and 'effect'. The meanings of all these in common language will be given in the next Part.

These are written in a square since there are obvious similarities along the rows. They could also be written linearly as 1.1, 1.2, 1.3 > 2.1, 2.2, 2.3 > 3.1, 3.2, 3.3: from the beginning of creation to its end.

Creation:	1: Spiritual degree love in the spirit.	2: Mental degree thoughts in the mind.	3: Physical degree actions in the body

Table 19.1 *Summary of the first three degrees.*

1: Spiritual degree love in the spirit	2: Mental degree thoughts in mind	3: Physical degree actions in the body
love of loving: 1.1	*thoughts of loves:* 2.1	*effects from loves:* 3.1
love of thoughts: 1.2	*thoughts of thoughts:* 2.2	*effects from thoughts:* 3.2
love of actions: 1.3	*thoughts of actions:* 2.3	*effects from effects:* 3.3

Table 19.2 *The first ennead of the 9 sub-parts of the first 3 parts.*

Each of these nine sub-degrees describes substances of its own kind which act in distinct spaces. Within those spaces there can be contact between two objects of the same kind. These nine substances exist simultaneously and interpenetrate without collision. Note that 'interpenetrate without collision' is only a metaphor for the relation of the nine spaces.

Remember our discussion of Section 17.3, where we saw that when we talk, for example of 2.1 (thoughts of loves) as a substance of its own kind, we realize that only loves can be substances. Thoughts by themselves cannot be. Thoughts are merely the correspondences of different forms of the different substances of the mind. Those substances are forms of love or forms of dispositions derived from love. We should actually rewrite the above ennead table as in Table 19.3.

We cannot yet totally understand what all these different substances and 'formings' are doing. After Part IV many of this chapter's obscurities will be clarified and puzzles solved.

In the physical degree, the physical powers have passed through many stages of derived productions and have become almost the final or ulti-

1: Spiritual degree	2: Mental degree	3: Physical degree
spiritual substances forming loves:	mental substances forming thoughts:	physical substances forming effects:
spiritual substances forming *love of loving:* 1.1	mental substances forming *thoughts of loves:* 2.1	physical substances forming *effects from loves:* 3.1
spiritual substances forming *love of thoughts:* 1.2	mental substances forming *thoughts of thoughts:* 2.2	physical substances forming *effects from thoughts:* 3.2
spiritual substances forming *love of actions:* 1.3	mental substances forming *thoughts of actions:* 2.3	physical substances forming *effects from effects:* 3.3

Table 19.3 *The ennead again, showing the nine kinds of substances.*

mate effect. In the physical stage, what started out as loves are no longer living or conscious but are 'dead' (not-living) and unconscious. Instead of 'love', we should therefore talk about 'source' or 'governing principle'. Instead of 'thought', we should talk about 'cause' because cause is the middle between the love and the effect. Instead of 'action', we should talk of 'effect' or 'events'. The physical sub-degrees and sub-sub-degrees can therefore be redescribed as in Table 19.4.

3: Physical degree actions in body		
Effects from ends: 3.1		
Effects from ends of ends: 3.11	Effects from ends of causes: 3.12	Effects from ends of actions: 3.13
Effects from causes 2.2		
Effects from causes of ends: 3.21	Effects from causes of causes: 3.22	Effects from causes of effects: 3.23
Effects from actions: 2.3		
Effects from actions of ends: 3.31	Effects from actions of causes: 3.32	Effects from effects of actions: 3.33

Table 19.4 *An ennead again, showing the nine kinds of substances in all the sub-sub-degrees within just the physical degree.*

20

The Theistic Universe

W E WILL NOW review the kind of universe to be expected under theism by summarizing the results of the previous chapters. Later on we will proceed to detailed scientific theorizing.

20.1 Support for the dynamic ontology

The assertions in the theism being developed have been made on the basis of the dynamic ontology developed in Part II. They are in accord with the principles developed there. We follow the slogan 'No process without structure, no structure without substance, no substance without power, no power without process,' even as it applies not only to temporal beings, but also to God. We follow the ontology of substance and form. We do not need to resort to exotic ontologies that make, for example, information basic. We do not have to understand how act may be an attribute that applies at all levels including in pureness even to God.[1] All of us, as well as God, follow the basic principles of causation by interaction. The past is definite and never retrospectively changeable. Even God, who always works in the present by means of an eternal view of the future, does not change the past once it exists. As images of God, at least in our rational capacities, we are given abilities to understand what we need to know about the substance and operation of the universe, both physical and mental. These are not essentially or perpetually impossible to understand. The details may be difficult to comprehend, but the means and the perseverance are available

---

[1] This is the view of Aquinas, who also starts from an Aristotelean natural point of view in trying to understand theism. However, he takes God as the limit of 'pure act' and 'pure form'. This unfortunately deprives his theology of taking loves as the substance of minds, spirits and God, but (strangely) insists that these are purely form and also purely act.

to let us understand at least some of the ways God and the universe are organized in relation to each other.

20.2 Life from God

We have in scientific theism the principle that all our life, love and being derive from God. He has all these things in himself and, indeed, as himself. From this it follows that God exists whenever any life, love or being exist, The dispute with the materialists is whether God is the transcendent and benevolent One of theism or (as they claim) the multiple eternally-existing energies of the universe. My aim is to provide sufficient theoretical detail and consistency for the God of traditional theism.

This life from God is that which infills and enlivens all living beings and non-living things: all conscious creatures and all non-conscious objects. It infills and enlivens according to the outermost forms of those beings, creatures and objects. According to Postulate 10 that outermost form of a being is composed of the previous actions that it has performed.

Between God and us, theism implies that we have multiple generative degrees—of spirituality, mentality and physicality—each with internal complexities that we have only begun to explore. What I know about them will be presented in Part III. We will see many of the mental and physical processes that we have already come to know and love in the sciences. Now they are being put together within a new theoretical framework. Much of the individual phenomena of the sciences can be carried over unchanged. What will change are the kinds of *causes* that are supposed to produce those changes. This will be particularly interesting in psychology and biology, especially concerning origins and evolution. Neurophysiology will be revised, in at least its theoretical component. At present, it looks for 'neural correlates of consciousness' and maybe finds some. Instead, the actual causal relations between consciousness and its neural correlates will have to be established in a non-reductive manner.

The final effects of all loves and dispositions are the physical actions that we perform. These actions, which are kinds of choices, are the bottom line of theistic theory. They are the final and definite effects whose occurrences are the basic foundation for the existence of a particular created world. The temporal world is most certainly never *maya* (either as a game or as an illusion) because the production of particular acts in the physical world is what in turn provides the occasions for the operation of all prior loves and dispositions. God cannot create permanent beings that are fully formed, except insofar as there are prior physical events that form the foundation and outer framework for the dispositions of the new being. What God can immediately create are physical events themselves. Everything else takes somewhat longer.[2] There are no instant adults.

20.3 Mirrored functions as correspondences

Consider the multiple generative levels implied within creation according to the principles outlined in Chapter 5. There will be detailed constituent events in both of a pair of prior and produced degrees. Because of these microscopic events, there will be successive generative influxes from the prior degree reciprocating with sequential selections by the produced degree. This alternation will repeat itself longest if the *patterns* of the constituent events are most similar in the two degrees and they do not get out of step. By a sort of survival of the fittest, this gives rise to *correspondences of function* between adjacent degrees. We may conversely say that the functions in distinct degrees sustain each other in a kind of 'mirror' or 'resonance' when they are most similar in the patterns of their constituent events. We could speculate, for example, that our minds and brains sustain each other by influx and selection when psychological and neural processes are most nearly isomorphic to each other in their functional description. There is much detail here to be learned by derivation and observation, not just in mind-brain functioning but throughout living organisms. The different discrete degrees are never of one continuous substance that makes both. They have functional relations that make them 'contiguously intertwined' at all stages and at all levels of detail at each stage. These will be discussed further in Section 25.3.

20.4 Persons and their identity

The system of discrete degrees that comes from an analysis of theism suggests a possible solution to the problem of continued personal identity. In

---

[2] What is surprising to me is how much longer is needed (over 10^{10} years).

Section 6.5 we saw that, within an ontology of multiple generative levels, there was a sense in which the continued identity of a person could be attributed to some prior degree, especially if this prior degree were relatively unchanging. So, if the prior degree were strictly unchanging during a person's lifetime, then we would have a means of identifying our personal identity both during our growth and changes in this life and possibly also after the death of our physical bodies. There would then be a core in us that would be the basis of our continued existence, and that could said to be our 'true self'.

This core, according to our basic theism, is our most fundamental love. For God this core is the divine love. That is clearly his core and the basis of his continued divine identity. For us, it is the love that is the most prior generative degree that can be said to be 'us' rather than 'someone else'. That love is the most constant underlying disposition in our life. It is like Plato's 'self-moving soul.'[3] Let us call this most constant underlying disposition our *principal love*. Because the principal love produces our life, it is recognizable by its effect of producing a 'theme of our life'. We agree with Hume that this identity is not immediately apparent to our introspection, but that does not make it any less real. Along with dispositions in general, our principal love can be tested by examining skills, character, and performances when there are few or no external constraints, by examining affections in action and in the voice, and so on. Just as physicists test dispositions by experiments and not by mere inspection, so our own identities could be inferred by examining all our characteristic actions more easily than by introspection.

This concept of personal identity as principal love would be most useful to psychology and theology if that love were completely unchanged during our lifetime: from birth to death and even after bodily death. This would require it to keep all the same intrinsic properties even though its effects and relations may vary. Its relation to us will certainly vary as we grow up and later die. It would also be most useful if we could assume that no two people had the same principal love. Then we could be sure not to confuse any two people. Theistic religions claim that we have some kind of continued identity that survives bodily death. I offer the concept of principal love as a candidate for the needed kind of identity.

---

[3] Plato, *Phaedrus*. According to Plato, our soul is the source of all our motion. However, within theism a soul is not actually *self*-moving, since only God is strictly self-moving. Only God is life itself.

20.5 Intentionality

There is a clear intentionality of mind implied by the fact that desires, intentions and ideas are always *about* things. This does not seem possible for physical objects.

This intentionality of the mental does not arise from a spatial aspect of mentality and the way in which it may be a model or map of reality. Rather, it arises from the fact that ideas are always being generated from loves, since loves are part of intentions for specific results. Ideas are the entertainment by the mind of forms of things, and therefore those ideas refer to the objects of which we are considering the form.[4] Intentionality of loves and thoughts comes about because they both arise from God's love. That love is the love of *others*. Intentionality is part of the very nature of God. The resulting psychology will be discussed in Chapters 22 and 27 and will include outlines of many other aspects of mentality.

20.6 Law and divine intervention

It is often assumed that religion should become accommodated to modern science, that the best that can be hoped for from theology is evidence that God created the world, and that the governing constants of the physical world are fine tuned to make life probable. On this basis, we hope that we can come to know that 'we are wanted', and that there exists a 'plan for our lives'. In such a theology, divine intervention into the world is not strictly necessary and may even be said to be poor management, as if God could not have set up the world to behave properly. Such modern believers might even admit that miracles were once necessary, for example at the beginning of a religion in order to convince by means of miracles. However, now 'we are mature adults' and miracles are no longer necessary. They do not think divine intervention occurs in modern times, so they can follow with a clear conscience the principles and findings of those sciences which specify the causal closure of the physical world. This amounts to deism as distinct from theism.

Such a view misses the point of creation. We are not made for God ei-

---

[4] This is a combination of Aristotelean perception (the mind accepting the forms of objects) and a representational view (the mind containing ideas or percepts which represent external objects). Here the representation occurs between ideas and objects which have some forms in common. The object has that form for its own substance, and the mind has that form to make up an idea.

ther to 'intervene' or 'not intervene' in the world. We are made for God to *reside* in the world in order that we may live. The physical world provides the framework in which God can place his life and infill and enliven us with the *life* (spiritual and mental) that comes *only* from God. It is as senseless as asking a resident: are you going to intervene in your house or not intervene? Or asking a person, are you going to intervene in the world around you or not intervene? In theism, it is not a question of intervention but of presence and residence. What is residence and presence but constant contact? How can there be constant contact except by persistent and bilateral causal connections? The purpose of the world, in theism by comparison with deism, is not just that we are in God's plan, but that we are present and enlivened by God's love. Presence in reality, rather than only in thought, is an essential part of our dynamic ontology. As proposed in Chapter 4, we follow the Eleatic Principle: existence should only be ascribed to that which has causal power. We lose nothing by applying this also to the divine. We only have to then to reconsider science at the same time as theology because science (especially empirical science) is concerned with whatever has effects in the world.

The reciprocal causation in theism is not equal on both sides. Rather, it follows the generation + selection pattern described in subsection 6.1.1. On the side of God it is generation, and on our side it is selection. The result of this asymmetric conjunction is a workable whole. It yields an effective bilateral cooperation between God and the world. In this bilateral cooperation, both sides have important roles to play. God's role is to produce and govern all the loves and life that come from him. Our role is to select by our actions those loves and life that we wish to become permanent within our own persons. There are many intermediate stages in this process, as will be explored in the next Part.

We might ask about the role of physical laws in describing the processes that occur in the physical world and on whether the actions of God in that world might not be described as 'divine intervention'. Do occasional interventions suspend or even violate the laws of physics? Think of conservation of energy and momentum in closed systems. Are those conservation laws broken by God when what some would call miracles occur?

To answer this we note that the *true* law that governs the world of theism describes the multiple generative levels that start from God. They eventually end up with the definite physical actions that beings perform in the world. Any so-called miracle that occurred or occurs must follow that true law.[5] If anything appears to be inexplicably miraculous, it means that we do not understand the true laws of the universe or the true intentions of the persons (including God) who may be acting within the structure of those laws (or both). Even with that understanding, however, we still might not understand the occasion or speed of operation of those laws.[6]

The remaining paradox comes because much of modern science is built on the assumption that physical laws (such as the conservation of energy) hold universally and without exception. However, according to theism, this is not correct. Rather, these apparently universal laws are held only locally and approximately within those physical systems whose *purpose* within theism is to provide an overall container or enduring structure that can persistently select a rather complicated set of internal dispositions. In theism we expect that there are complex organic bodies with a large amount of 'physical autonomy'. The bodies are never entirely autonomous within theism. The bodies have the purpose of sustaining (by corresponding generation + selection relations) equally-complex internal mental and spiritual bodies. The existence and dynamics of these internal bodies will be discussed in the next Part IV. Each kind of body (physical, mental or spiritual) is *nearly* autonomous, and purely-physical laws are nearly but not completely universal. That is the pattern expected within a theistic universe.

---

[5] The logical possibility of something does not mean that we should not neutrally (and perhaps skeptically) examine the evidence for an alleged occurrence.
[6] I suspect that most of the miracles of the New Testament in Christianity, for example, are representations by correspondences of the processes of spiritual regeneration appearing much more quickly than we would ever expect in normal life.

Part IV

Theistic Science

21

Methods

21.1 Beginning theistic science

W E HAVE in Part III deduced a formal structure for a universe within theism. We defined it in terms of images of the Love, Wisdom and Action of God. It is a multilevel generative structure with many parts arranged together in non-trivial ways. But what exactly are all these discrete degrees and sub-degrees? Do we know them? And, how do we find out the details of these arrangements and how they function together? What sorts of spatial configurations exist at each level?

I propose that we now combine our deductive method with empirical investigations. All of us already have practical experience concerning the way that physical and mental processes are organized and related. The many sciences of today have extended our everyday concepts into more detailed theories. So, by 'empirical investigations' I will refer to results of the sciences that already exist.

The first steps here will therefore examine the components of the structures derived in Part III to see whether we can identify them with any of the structures postulated by contemporary science, in particular by contemporary psychology or physics. Maybe in the future theistic science will get better at predicting the details at each stage. In this book we are just *beginning* theistic science, and so we will accept any help that might be available.

We will not just accept all existing theories uncritically. A theory may be wrong. It may involve structures which are not directly visible and hence open to revision. Even if the structures are correct, the causes attributed to the structured objects may not be conformable with our proposed theistic science. This last possibility will frequently be the case because existing sciences hardly recognize the idea of multiple generative levels. Instead they think that the objects under investigation simply cause all the observed behavior. They neglect to recognize the causal inputs from *prior* or *upstream* generative degrees. Occasionally, in psychology for example, they will also not recognize the selection constraints from *later* or *downstream* generative degrees. The process of unifying existing theories will result in changes to those theories.

The logical basis of theistic science is very different from the logical basis of the scientific theism presented so far. Part III attempted to deduce a formal structure and, as long as the Postulates are true and as long as I have not made a mistake, the consequences will rigorously follow.[1] Part IV is on a much weaker logical foundation. Unlike a set of deductions from postulates, it is much more likely to be in need of revision. In fact, it is just like today's science, consisting as it does of hypotheses and inductions suggested by experiments. To put it bluntly, this Part consists of speculation, and it can only be justified by comparison with observations and experiments. The accuracy of what is said depends on my understanding of contemporary physics and contemporary psychology along with further suggestions based on the overall structure of theistic science.

The connections and identifications to be proposed in this Part are therefore *logically contingent* rather than logically necessary, even given the truth of our Postulates. It is on the basis of this fact that we accept Hume's dictum that there are no necessary connections between particular objects apart from God. It means that everything I say from now on can and should be examined carefully and persistently to make sure that it is not mistaken. Changing some of these proposals does not mean the end of theistic science, since this will be the normal process of revision of scientific hypotheses because of theoretical arguments or empirical observations. What I next propose is falsifiable. Trying to falsify is one of the ongoing jobs of scientists. This work is no longer deduction from theistic premises. Now I call on meanings in ordinary languages and in the sciences. These will have historical and contemporary overtones that certainly cannot be called deductive conclusions!

---

[1] As was pointed out in Chapter 17, the identification of spiritual, mental and physical degrees should, strictly speaking, be part of the theistic science here and not part of the previous deductive theism.

21.2 Methodology of levels

Now I will attempt to identify and characterize all the different levels within the set of multiple generative levels. Let us sketch out some of the generic methodological steps that might be commonly used in this kind of scientific investigation, a sketch that tries to illuminate degrees and sub-degrees.

To begin with, we try to understand the overall nature of each degree, whether in psychology or physics. We investigate what overall function that degree has within the theistic universe. We focus on that particular degree or sub-degree and first examine that level by itself. It is important to determine whether its function is aided by the interaction of parts arranged in some space. Any such parts should be found and investigated.

Functions may be accomplished not only by the interaction of spatially-arranged parts but also by internal sub-degrees, especially if different sub-steps involve distinct and successive qualities that might be arranged as derivative dispositions. Science is, on the whole, rather good at investigating the detailed spatial and temporal sub-processes needed to fulfill particular functions: everything from structures of atoms through structures of cells to structures of planets. This feature of modern science is fortunate. The deductive procedures of the scientific theism of Part III are (as yet) poor at making suggestions for spatial multiplicity and temporal sequences. They are more oriented to probing the 'deep structures' of individual causes and effects.

To investigate (within theistic science) any structure at any level, we have to examine also the surrounding levels within the overall generative structure of the universe. In the end we cannot avoid this. The behavior of a given degree will necessarily depend, to some extent, on deriving dispositions from prior degrees and on constraining selections from what has already happened at later degrees. Theistic science is always able to put a given level within broader context. It is able to provide a broader set of reasons and consequences for its operation. This broader context is needed not just to understand the abstract 'why questions' but also to answer specific questions of cause and effect.

Various simplifications may be advisable in order to (temporarily!) remove that broader context. It will often be a fruitful method to 'bracket off' nearby or distinct degrees. This removal is always intellectually possible and sometimes useful for methodological reasons. A consequence of this bracketing-off is that scientists may (and do!) spend their entire life focusing on just one level and hence learn a great deal about just one particular sub-degree. With the existence (by Chapter 19) of sub-sub-degrees of that level, there is always a great deal to learn. The world is a wonderfully complicated place and is comprehensible only gradually. Within an overall theistic science, such bracketting will never be a long-term solution.

22

Discrete Degrees in the Mind

NOW COME the investigations that are part of science and use the structure from Part III as a template. We are continuing the identification work begun in Chapter 19. We begin with a focus on the *mental degree*. It is the second of the three main degrees that exist in all persons. Table 22.1 shows again how this degree fits in with the other two degrees. The spiritual degree comes first in this order, and the physical degree comes afterwards. Normally these three degrees are considered separately in science. However, now we have them as part of a single overall scheme, and we hope to generate theories about how the three are related. Here we explore the mental degree by itself. In Chapter 25 I will give more detail on how the degrees are related.

This mental degree has the overall function of enabling loves to find suitable ways of producing results in the world, in order to achieve what that love wants to bring about. This degree is an image of Divine Wisdom. Wisdom has the same function with respect to the Divine Love in God as minds do to loves in persons.

Creation:	1: Spiritual degree love in the spirit.	2: Mental degree thoughts in the mind.	3: Physical degree actions in the body

Table 22.1 *Summary of the first three degrees, from Table 19.1*

22.1 Minds

The contents of the mental degree are *thoughts*, along with the *affections* that motivate and accompany those thoughts. The collection of all the thoughts and affections of a given person is that person's mind. Usually a mind contains many thoughts and affections. Each thought is a particular mental object, and such objects exist together in some appropriate kind of space: a different space (with different metric and topology) for each degree or sub-degree. Each object persists for some time before fading away. While existing, it interacts with other thoughts, often resulting in the creation of new thoughts. This is what we call thinking.

We do not yet know the topologies or metrics of those mental spaces, but scientific investigations should be able to make theories on that subject and test them by observing cognitive activities and products of thinking organisms (animals as well as humans). I speculate that the spaces are of an 'associative' nature, in which objects that have some similar meanings are 'closer together' and hence more likely to interact.

On the grounds of theism given in Chapter 17, we further expect that our ideas, in their space, are contained within some overall frame or body, just as our body is a framework for containing our physiological activities. We could call the 'body' for the mind our 'mental body'. It lasts much longer than the more ephemeral ideas that exist within it.[1]

22.2 Microscopic mentality

In order to see how thinking could be attributed to the existence and activity of ideas as substantial objects within the space of our mental body, I now begin to show how those activities can be in agreement with what we already know about thinking in our minds.

At the 'microscopic' level, every idea is an object within a larger structure of multiple generative levels. If we focus on a specific level or degree Q, say, then we must recognize that there are prior generative dispositions P (prior), and also subsequent dispositions R (results). The level P

---

[1] If you want an image of this mental body, you could think of cells in the biological body or neurons in the brain. These are contained by an overall membrane to make a more lasting structure. Another possible image is that of the multiple alveoli, the small air sacs within the lungs. In this case, the various ideas could be imaged as the different air masses and the different sounds as we speak.

dispositions produce the level Q dispositions conditionally on what is already existing at Q. Similarly, the level Q dispositions produce the level R dispositions conditionally on what is already existing at R. There will be other higher dispositions O, and other derivative dispositions S that may sometimes be relevant. All these dispositions are in fact some kind of love that determines what its effects are. Furthermore, they have some form or internal structure that contributes to the nature of the idea.

I envisage that a mind consists of a small set of mental objects existing within the mental body. Each object is a perception or an idea. Its meaning or content is given in part by its internal form and in part by its relation to other ideas that are in the mind or in memory. The internal content consists of the particular dispositional-substances that make up the idea and of the structure of those substances within the idea. The ability of an idea or perception to *represent* something else (in the mind or in the world) depends on that particular structure. The ability of an idea or perception to enter into dynamical processes with other ideas depends on the nature of its dispositional-substances. One example of a 'dynamical process' is the process of logical thinking, but there are many other processes which also occur, from imagination to planning to perceiving to accomplishing tasks in the world. The extent to which ideas enter into such dynamical processes of the mind will vary from idea to idea and from time to time. We may attribute some kind of 'activation level' to each idea in this way, measuring how much each idea is disposed to have strong effects on others.[2] We say that strongly activated ideas are in the forefront of our consciousness, or in our short term memory, or in the 'global workspace' of Baars[3].

Each level of ideas Q exists in its own space, with its own metric and topology. This is *not* a physical space but a space of its own kind for each level. Spaces, in general, are sets of possibilities of interactions: this is a definition equally valid for physical and mental spaces. I envisage that the precise details of mental spaces depend on the particular previous operation of prior levels O, P, in ways to be investigated. I only note that this means that, just as with physical space according to general relativity, the metric and topology are not necessarily constant but might well (and often do) change with time according to to the specific processes which have taken place. As a result of these considerations, the metric of mental spaces

---

[2] This activation level is a kind of 'energy'. In Chapter 24, however, we will see that this is not physical energy but only something similar to physical energy. It is therefore better to keep the idea of loves as the underlying substances.

[3] Baars, *A cognitive theory of consciousness*.

is expected to make them *associative spaces*, in which similarity of content implies that the objects are more likely to interact and hence that they are closer together in mental space. It remains to be determined whether similarity should be measured in terms of agreement of *all* aspects of an idea's meaning or in terms of the strong agreement of just a *few* aspects of meaning. The later option would enable ideas with just a few similar components of meaning to be more likely to interact with each other: that seems to be what is observed in minds.

There is an enormous amount of detail to be discovered in the operation of minds, and consequently there is already a very extensive psychological literature discussing the nature and modeling of human mental processes. In this section, I can only hint at a few of the necessary ingredients that allow us to think correctly about minds within our theistic and generative framework and hence get these models started on a realistic basis. Up to now, the basis of mental activity has been obscure. Some researchers prefer to model in terms of beliefs, desires and actions. Others prefer explanations in terms of the processing of symbolic information. Still others try to explain mentality in terms of networks of connections, whether or not the meaning resides entirely in terms of the relational context. In the theory of this book, each idea does have its own symbolic content, but ideas can also be arranged in networks according to how they cause other ideas' activation levels to vary with time. Let me begin by discussing the simple ingredients for the processes of reflective awareness, mental associations, production rules, and memory.

As laid out above, all ideas Q are produced as derivative dispositions from some prior (upstream) level P, and in turn produce lower (downstream) levels R as results. When a new idea Q_1 first exists, for example, it may well provide the circumstance for some previously-dormant prior degree P_1 to operate. This is the minimal scenario for us to say that the higher level P_1 'sees' the new idea Q_1. Chapter 25 will discuss perception more generally and give the reasons why this process is called seeing or perception and why multiple levels need to be involved for seeing. This particular perception at prior level P_1 can also be called the *reflective awareness* of processes at level Q.

If the activated higher-level idea P_1 operates, it will produce new idea Q_2 in the same level as Q_1. If we were not aware of multiple levels, it would appear that Q_1 produces Q_2 directly, by a kind of direct 'associative reflex', but life is not that simple. In general there is a sequence $Q_1 \rightarrow P_1 \rightarrow Q_2$, where the first arrow is a conditional activation, and the second arrow is a derivative generation. The P_1 idea is in fact necessary for the associative reflex to act in a regular manner, and it can well be called a *rule* for generating Q_2 whenever Q_1 appears. This pattern can be taken as the basis for much more complex and flexible production rules, detailed planning, and general modular functions in the mind. Each prior degree can be regarded as a set of rules for processing patterns of activated ideas in lower-level degrees. The ability to have *functions* existing in the mental architecture has long been assumed by those who model in terms of symbol processing but is difficult to achieve in a general way within purely connectionist networks.[4] The rules here, it should be noted, are sensitive not only to the overall structure of the input ideas but also to their internal dispositional content and hence to all aspects of their meaning. This means that the new rules are not purely syntactic but are sensitive to the semantic content of the initial ideas that start the operation of the rule.

Ideas enter into *long-term memory* if they were sufficiently activated at some earlier time. This memory must consist of declarative as well as procedural memories, which in our context means that ideas Q as well as production rules P can be remembered. Memory is generally considered to result from the production of permanent effects or traces in some downstream (lower) substratum S, such that later processes involving that substratum may lead to the activation of new ideas Q' or P' that are sufficiently similar to the initial mental contents. In our multilevel generative framework, much mental content eventually produces effects at lower levels R and S, first in the mind, then in the brain, and hence finally as effects in the physical world. That is their overall purpose. Memory traces will therefore exist if the effects in those lower levels are permanently stored. It remains a topic of research, though, to find out which levels in particular are used for this storage process. Once the traces are formed, wherever they might be, then retrieval will occur in the future when the traces are the precondition for the operation of some prior degree P. If the operation of parts of that degree is conditional on the traces in memory, this leads to the re-formation of the remembered Q', etc.

This is a barely-adequate sketch of the process: memory retrieval is most commonly driven by particular associations which retrieve memories with

---

[4] For an early discussion of a possible multilevel network structure, see Thompson[5].

some semantic features in common. If this is to happen, then something about the memories, some 'weakly activated' idea q, say, must continue to exist at the level Q in order that its position in the associative space at that level lead it to be retrieved on the basis of possible associations.

There are many more mental processes, including symbols themselves, language, grammar, etc., that should soon be addressed in the framework of this book. Languages, for example, seem to have their own self-contained generative modules for their semantic, syntactic and phonetic generation of spoken content. There is also the ability to make *names* that can be associated with almost any other idea in the mind with only limited reference to that idea's actual content. There are whole research programs waiting here.

22.3 Whole-person mentality

Let us now consider mentality not at its finest scale but in its overall position within the whole person. In a person, we place thoughts in the middle between love and effects, as shown in Table 22.2. Of course our minds can think also about love and about effects. The claim of our scientific theism is that there are specific parts of our mind that are specialized for these three tasks. Each degree is an image of God in its own way and therefore has three sub-degrees in the same way that God has degrees of Love, Wisdom and Action. This implies, as we already saw in Chapter 19, that we have the sub-degrees shown in the Table 22.2.

The sub-degree 2.3 is specifically the thoughts of actions and effects. Within modern psychology this would be called a sensory system or module. Within stage theories of cognition it would be called the sensorimotor

1: Spiritual degree love in the spirit	2: Mental degree thoughts in mind	3: Physical degree actions in the body
love	thoughts of loves: 2.1 thoughts of thoughts: 2.2 thoughts of actions: 2.3	effects

Table 22.2 *The 3 sub-parts of the mental degree. This is a simplified version of Table 19.2.*

1: Spiritual degree	2: Mental degree	3: Physical degree
love in the spirit	thoughts in mind	actions in the body
	higher rational: 2.1	
love	scientific rational: 2.2	effects
	external mind: 2.3	

Table 22.3 *The 3 sub-parts of the mental degree. This is a rewritten version of Table 22.2.*

degree, especially since it contains the 'external interface' with outer actions, which, when actually produced, are physical actions in the body. There is much more than sensation and motor activity in sub-degree 2.3 in humans, since language to describe actions is also present along with the affections and motivations for activities concerning actions in the world and talk about those actions. In this sub-degree, I intend to include all the mental activities of children in the first decade of their lives. Let us call this sub-degree the 'external mind'.

The sub-degree 2.2 is specifically the thoughts of thoughts. This is not intended as self-reflexive but simply as a way to portray the fact that mental, logical and mathematical structures in the mind can *themselves* be the objects of further thought. Children from the second decade of their lives can consider operations as such and consider, for example, whether operations are reversible or how they can be concatenated. Later comes the mental ability to consider formal structures as such, even without thoughts of concrete objects necessarily being present. This sub-degree must also include the ability to look at systems of thought as wholes and so to consider how a paradigm or system of thought may be replaced by another system of thought. Much of scientific activity is conducted within this 2.2 sub-degree. Let us call this sub-degree the 'scientific rational'.

The sub-degree 2.1 is specifically the thoughts of love. Love involves and produces all the things of one's life so this sub-degree enables us to reflect on our life as whole. The thought in this sub-degree is (or ought to be) able to determine the loves which are active in the life of the person, by first observing the actions freely performed and then inferring back from this to the originating loves (as discussed before). This sub-degree, again, ought to be able to decide whether those loves are good and useful or selfish and dominating. All these kinds of thoughts, when present in adult life, indicate intellectual and emotional maturity. Let us call this sub-degree the 'higher rational'. With these new names, Table 22.2 is rewritten as Table 22.3.

22.4 Order of production vs order of growth

We have talked of multiple generative levels in the mind. Table 22.2 shows that there is a process where the higher rational acts to produce (as a derivative disposition) the scientific rational, and it in turn acts to produce (as a derivative disposition) the external mind. This is the *order of production* and should be that operating in mature adults. But this is not the order we see during human growth. From childhood into adolescence we see exactly the opposite order. The *order of growth* starts with the final effects within this mental degree and works back towards the source, towards the most prior degree. The order of growth is the order of cognitive and emotional development in our lives, from birth to maturity.

There is a good reason within scientific theism for this: for why human development starts at the outermost effect and works back towards the source, coming via thoughts up toward mature loves. That is because, as argued by means of Postulate 9 on page 115, it is our actions which are most specifically our own. If we are to build our own lives, or at least a life that retains the loves which we think of as our own, then, according to our scientific theism, we need to build up a history of actions. God cannot do this for us—not even God can invent or change history—so we need to begin our lives by mental activities which are directly involved with actions and physical effects. Being born in the physical world is the way God requires us to start, if we are to one day attain and retain the spiritual life of loves that God wants to give to us.

This same pattern, of growth beginning with outermost actions, applies at every level and at every degree and sub-degree. Before more mature loves or deeper thoughts can be retained we have to develop an 'external structure' or framework of actions at an outer degree in order to be able to keep those desired loves and thoughts. We may simplistically think of it as us needing to make ourself be a good container before it can be filled with life.

The process of mental growth here appears to be a kind of emergence.

It appears that we begin with sensorimotor thoughts in the external mind, and then, after we become proficient with these, there somehow *emerges* the next-higher sub-degree of the scientific rational, and so on.[6] This might be the case *if* the scientific rational could be constructed from configurations in the external mind, and if, say, it could then develop a self-sustaining life of its own. However, this cannot be the case in our scientific theism. That is because it is the scientific rational which is the disposition that can derivatively produce the external mind, *not* the other way around. This same argument applies with any adjacent pair of degrees: from external to internal, we only ever have constraints and selections.

We might wonder how the scientific rational can begin, since it is not already existing or implicit within the developmentally-prior external mind. The answer is that we do have some initial mentality to start the process of learning a new sub-degree and therefore a ready supply of new ideas and feelings on new levels. This initial mentality and supply of new content is always with God and from God, and later with other intermediate minds. In either case, the problem with learning a new sub-degree is not the supply of new thought, but the ability of the newly-developed mental degree to *retain* any of these new thoughts. This is a general law for all growth into new degrees: God is always and everywhere present in fullness, and it is only our ability to receive and retain which varies.

This means that growth into new sub-degrees is a patchwork to start with. It depends on specific knowledge, skills and patterns of actions being already established in any one of many cognitive domains. It is only rarely that the transition to a new sub-degree will be simultaneous across all cognitive domains.

22.5 Substructures

Much work in developmental psychology provides good evidence for sub-degrees that are the external mind, the scientific rational, and the higher rational and also for intermediate levels within each of those. Our scientific theism predicts that there will be *three* sub-sub-degrees in each case, and that eventually we will see evidence for three sub-sub-sub-degrees of each of the sub-sub-degrees. Let us begin with the first claim.

---

[6] As advocated, for example, in Feldman[7].

The early observations of Inhelder and Piaget[8] led to a theory in which children go through four stages of cognitive growth: the sensorimotor stage (0–2 years) and the pre-operational stage (approx. 2–6 years), followed by the concrete-operations stage (approx. 6–12 years) and the formal-operations stage (12–18 years and beyond). Comparison with the three sub-degrees defined above indicates that the sensorimotor and pre-operational stages are part of the 'external mind', and that the concrete and formal operations stages occur successively within the 'scientific mind'. However, there are only two stages within each sub-degree, not three as predicted. Furthermore, Piaget's stages were taken as rather sudden system-wide transitions within the mind over all cognitive domains, but Goswami[9] and others have shown that there is often evidence for there being precursors to higher-degree cognitive functioning even at much earlier ages than Piaget would allow. Brainerd[10] asks whether there is any independent evidence for a causal basis of Piaget's stages, because, if not, the stage labels would be merely descriptions of successive kinds of behaviors and not themselves explanatory.

The missing third substage within the scientific-mind degree was found by those developmental theorists examining post-formal stages: stages beyond Piaget's formal-operations degree. Commons[11] makes a hierarchical classification of task complexity following the proposals of Fischer[12] and indicates evidence for a 'systematic' stage after the formal degree of complexity. Commons also has a later 'paradigmatic degree', but that does not map easily into the beginning of the 'higher rational' proposed above.

The case of the missing substage within the external mind is more complicated. In fact, Commons[13] has six degrees in the external mind whereas Piaget has only two. Commons groups his degrees in pairs in order to compare with Piaget's stages. In that case, the Commons theory does postulate the required number: three sub-degrees in the external mind. He calls these the 'sensory or motor' sub-degree, followed by a 'nominal' and a 'sentential' sub-degree, all of which are pre-operational in Piaget's sense. We will talk of degrees or levels rather than stages when they refer to clas-

[8] Inhelder and Piaget, *The growth of logical thinking*.
[9] Goswami, "Cognitive development: No stages please—we're British."
[10] Brainerd, "The stage question in cognitive-developmental theory."
[11] Commons, "Introduction to the model of hierarchical complexity and its relationship to postformal action."
[12] Fischer, "A theory of cognitive development."
[13] Commons, "Introduction to the model of hierarchical complexity and its relationship to postformal action."

sifications of interior mental content or refer to the tasks performed by that content. We use 'stages' to refer to historical eras or periods in the development of individual persons.

More work is needed here to confirm or refute my claim that these sub-degrees have the relationships to each other predicted by our theism. In our theory, the three sub-degrees should be related (in developmental order) as images of effects, thoughts, and intentions (more generally, as images of action, wisdom and love). The fact that Commons[14] has two (rather than three) sub-sub-degrees suggests to me that a third such sub-sub-degree should one day be found. Further empirical investigations are required to confirm or deny this hypothesis and also to fill in many missing details.

22.6 Stages of emotional development

There must be appropriate loves and emotions in every cognitive stage in order to provide the purpose and motivation for thinking through all those cognitive details. Supporting evidence for the general validity of the theistic structure is therefore available when *emotional* as well as cognitive stages are structured in suitable way. Such emotional development is always directly related to the various loves which are in the foreground of operations at each stage. We are not like computers, driven to think without feeling or consciousness. In our minds, even the very smallest processes require the combined contributions of love and wisdom. Equivalently, we require emotions and thoughts. Or equivalently again, we require substance and form.[15] Let us consider emotional development in more detail.

The most useful classification of emotional development is that of Erik Erikson[16] as displayed in Table 22.4. I now argue, with his widow Joan Serson Erikson (in Erikson and Erikson[17]), for a ninth stage (old age), along with moving forward the years of young-adulthood to 19-25, middle-

---

[14] Commons, "Introduction to the model of hierarchical complexity and its relationship to postformal action."

[15] This is a repetition of the reasoning which also led up to formulating all the degrees as shown in Table 19.3.

[16] Erikson, *Problem of ego identity.*

[17] Erikson and Erikson, *The life cycle completed.*

1. Oral- Sensory	Birth to 12 to 18 months	Trust vs. Mistrust	Feeding	The infant must form a first loving, trusting relationship with the care- giver, or develop a sense of mis- trust.
2. Muscular- Anal	18 months to 3 years	Autonomy vs. Shame / Doubt	Toilet training	The child's energies are directed to- ward the development of physical skills, including walking, grasping, and sphincter control.
3. Locomotor	3 to 6 years	Initiative vs. Guilt	Independence	The child continues to become more assertive and to take more initiative, but may be too forceful, leading to guilt feelings.
4. Latency	6 to 12 years	Industry vs. Inferiority	School	The child must deal with demands to learn new skills or risk a sense of inferiority, failure and incompe- tence.
5. Adolescence	12 to 18 years	Identity vs. Role Confusion	Peer relation- ships	The teenager must achieve a sense of identity in occupation, sex roles, politics, and religion.
6. Young Adulthood	19 to 40 years	Intimacy vs. Isolation	Love relationships	The young adult must develop in- timate relationships or suffer feel- ings of isolation.
7. Middle Adulthood	40 to 65 years	Generativity vs. Stagnation	Parenting	Each adult must find some way to satisfy and support the next gener- ation.
8. Maturity	65 to death	Ego Integrity vs. Despair	Reflection on & acceptance of one's life	The culmination is a sense of one- self as one is, and of feeling ful- filled.

Table 22.4 *Eight stages of psychosocial development, according to Erikson* (Problem of ego identity).

adulthood to 25-40, and maturity to 40-65, leaving old age for years 65 and beyond.

I agree with the observation of Gowan[18] that these (now) nine stages can be usefully arranged in a 3-by-3 grid, as in Table 22.5. Let us examine separately the columns and rows of this new ennead and see what is common within the elements of these. The third column, labeled 'latency', is clearly concerned with actions in the world. The middle column is labeled 'identity' but is in all rows concerned with thinking and preparation of means. The first column, labeled 'creativity', is in all rows concerned with love, purpose and initiative. The three rows can again be readily identified with the three stages of mentality as displayed in Table 22.3. The lowest row concerns the outermost actions in the world, the middle row concerns the development of thought and autonomy, and the first row concerns the application of wisdom and love in our life. This suggests that Table 22.5

---

[18] Gowan, *Development of the creative individual*.

		CREATIVITY 2 thou THE OTHER	IDENTITY 1 I, me THE EGO	LATENCY 3 it, they THE WORLD
ADULT	Erikson Erikson Age	9 (AGAPE-LOVE) old age	8 EGO-INTEGRITY Renunciation-wisdom 40 - 65	7 GENERATIVITY Production-care 26-40 (?)
YOUTH	Erikson Piaget Erikson Age	6 INTIMACY (Creativity) Love-affiliation 18-25	5 IDENTITY Formal operations Devotion-fidelity 13-17	4 INDUSTRY Concrete operations Method-competence 7-12
INFANT	Erikson Piaget Erikson Age	3 INITIATIVE Intuitive Direction-purpose 4-6	2 AUTONOMY Pre-operational Self-control-willpower 2-3	1 TRUST Sensorimotor Drive-hope 0-1

Table 22.5 *The nine extended Erikson stages of psychosocial development, arranged in a 3-by-3 grid, after Gowan (*Development of the creative individual.*). The ages are only approximate and descriptive.*

		LOVE 2 thou THE WILL	THOUGHT 1 I, me THE INTELLECT	ACTION 3 it, they THE WORLD
HIGHER RATIONAL	Erikson Erikson	2.11 AGAPE-LOVE	2.12 EGO-INTEGRITY Renunciation-wisdom	2.13 GENERATIVITY Production-care
SCIENTIFIC RATIONAL	Erikson Piaget Erikson	2.21 INTIMACY Systematic Love-affiliation	2.22 IDENTITY Formal operations Devotion-fidelity	2.23 INDUSTRY Concrete operations Method-competence
EXTERNAL MIND	Erikson Piaget Erikson	2.31 INITIATIVE Intuitive Direction-purpose	2.32 AUTONOMY Pre-operational Self-control-willpower	2.33 TRUST Sensorimotor Drive-hope

Table 22.6 *A renaming for theistic science of the nine (extended) Erikson levels of psychosocial development, by a modification of Table 22.5. The cognitive content of level 6 has been changed from 'creativity' as suggested by Gowan, to 'systematic' as proposed by Commons ("Introduction to the model of hierarchical complexity and its relationship to postformal action"). The numerical labels have been changed to the decimal system used in this book to describe sub-parts of degrees.*

should, within our theistic science, be rewritten as the levels of Table 22.6. Here, the cognitive content of level 6 has been changed from 'creativity' as (suggested by Gowan[19]), to 'systematic' (as proposed by Commons[20]) and the numerical labels have been changed to the decimal system used in this book to describe sub-parts of degrees. I claim that the excellent agreement of this new version with what should be expected within theistic science is good evidential support for the project of theistic science (noting, of course, that evidence is best taken from specific observations).

[19] Gowan, *Development of the creative individual.*
[20] Commons, "Introduction to the model of hierarchical complexity and its relationship to postformal action."

23

Spiritual Discrete Degrees

23.1 What is the spiritual?

THERE MUST be a first degree in all creatures according to the triadic structure outlined in Chapter 17, and that degree is here identified as the *spiritual*. There has been debate over the centuries concerning what it is which constitutes or characterizes the spiritual. Is it contemplation of pure forms (Plato), or is it purest intellectual thought (Aristotle)? In our theistic science, the spiritual is that concerned with *love* and in particular with that fundamental or principal love of our life which comes from God, permeates our entire being, and defines the nature and purpose of our life's work. This love is contained in our spiritual being, in something that may be called our soul.

Spiritual love is placed as the highest degree, over thinking in the mental degree, because our ontology makes love the substance of which thought is a property and thinking an activity. We do not follow Aquinas, in making the intellectual form a supreme aspect of our existence. Neither do we follow Descartes, who made the essence of our soul rational thought and not love. In fact, Descartes made the same mistake concerning both mind and physical natures: if their essences were to be rationality and extension, respectively, then they would be correspondingly missing exactly love and substance! Something whose essence is extension would be pure form and no substance. Similarly, a mind whose essence is rationality would be pure form and no substance. But minds do have substance, namely love. We therefore do not subscribe to Cartesian dualism.

According to theism, love is the first degree since it is that part of our mind which receives the love of God and is hence the image of God. This image holds first in the way that spiritual love is related to our mentality and physicality, in the same way that God's Love is related to his Wisdom and Action. The image also holds in that, since God is present as a whole in all parts, the spiritual degree will itself have sub-degrees that repeat the same triadic relation of love, wisdom and action. The function of the spiritual degree, as indicated in the first paragraph, is to provide the initial substance of our being and to motivate all our thoughts and actions. Love therefore is something that influences what thoughts are most favorably considered. In turn, the thoughts in our mind are able to guide the actions that produce the effects originally desired by our loves.

Another practical reason for the importance of spirituality comes from the great number of people generating reports of 'peak experiences', including those called visionary, mystical, out-of-body, near-death, heavenly, and spiritual. On the basis of the repeated evidence presented in these reports and in the absence of visible intentions to deceive, I am convinced that there does indeed exist a realm about which we are normally unaware. I claim that this is the spiritual realm being discussed in this chapter. The actual content of this realm remains to be carefully determined, especially since the manifest thoughts and visible contents in our mind are influenced by our loves, sometimes very strongly and very thoroughly. Despite the frequent lack of visibly deceptive intentions, investigators of the spiritual realm must always consider the principle and underlying loves of the various observers since these necessarily influence the nature of their reports.

23.2 Common misconceptions

Many people are not sure what spirituality is. Theistic science gives a specific answer to this question, but our previous conceptions and prejudices need to be directly addressed. Here they influence even the first understanding of what theistic science is saying. This section is strictly a digression from the main thesis but is necessary in order to clear up some misconceptions.

One common idea, especially with those who consider themselves down-to-earth, practical, and oriented to their actions in the world, is that the spiritual is 'merely spiritual', and hence something weak and ineffectual. 'Spiritualizing a parable', they say, is to rob it of its immediate force and effectiveness. I agree that this would be true if the spiritual had no (or could have no) mental or physical effects, but I insist instead that the spiritual is the whole means of one of the essential stages for producing all other kinds of results. Nothing significant can exist if it has no effects. The spiritual degree does certainly have effects. It is our first recipient of love, and love is the primary or principal substance of all things. The spiritual is in fact extremely powerful. Used in the right way, it can move mountains of ideas. We know how difficult it is to persuade someone to change their thinking, especially if their loves are attached to particular conceptions. These are the mountains[1] that spiritual love can move.

Some people are aware of the importance of spiritual power and love, but, lacking the concepts of discrete degrees and multiple generative levels, they imagine spiritual things to be properties, previously undiscovered, of physical nature. They have a sense that the spiritual is significantly different from the physical world but are not sure how. Those with near-death experiences feel that they have been touched by spirituality in some way but have trouble forming a consistent understanding of their experience. Many wonderful proposals have been made to this end, as we will see. The most important criterion in theistic science for judging such proposals is that spirituality is a *discrete* degree distinct from the physical. Therefore the properties of any spiritual object *cannot be continuously transformed* to or from the physical.

It is difficult to have a proper idea of discrete degrees, especially starting from our senses and logic, but it is not impossible. Our initial desires and the kinds of knowledge we can accept are all based on ideas that we can obtain from our senses, and, in our 'scientific rational', from logical reasonings derived from sensual ideas. Most of our starting ideas, therefore, are based on images obtained from sensations of space and time, and these spatial and temporal images attach themselves to many of our attempts to think about discrete degrees. One purpose of this section is to show how spatial ideas attach themselves to ideas of discrete degrees and hence of ideas of what is spiritual. We will see how spatial images may correspond to discrete degrees but be not identical with them.

Let us look at some ideas that have been used to describe discrete degrees. We will examine each in turn to see whether it is discrete or contin-

---

[1] Matthew 17:20—"Because you have so little faith I tell you the truth. if you have faith as small as a mustard seed, you can say to this mountain, 'Move from here to there' and it will move. Nothing will be impossible for you."

uous and whether it is a means for understanding what is spiritual. First we consider

Concepts derived from space:

1. Natural things with discrete units include such things as a ladder, a multi-storied house, even the earth with plants and animals and the sky, etc. Religious scriptures use such images, but only for illustration. We may picture the body, with head, neck, torso, legs, and feet, as representing or illustrating different discrete degrees by correspondence, but from looking at human bodies, as from biology alone, we do not thereby understand what spiritual degrees are.

2. Similarly, the whole and its parts may be imagined as discrete degrees. The cells, nerves, muscles, skin and whole body of a person may be discrete degrees. However, the whole body, while controlled by the spiritual degree, is itself an aggregation of its parts.[2] It is therefore not itself of a different degree from its parts.

3. Sometimes the spiritual is thought of as expanded consciousness such as 'cosmic consciousness' in contrast to everyday 'contracted' or 'narrow' awareness, so the basic dynamics of consciousness are expansion and contraction. But size is a continuous property. Expanding one's consciousness to include all stars and galaxies, whether in imagination or in reality, does not thereby give spiritual awareness.

4. Sometimes the spiritual is thought to be raised consciousness such as 'high levels of consciousness', in contrast to everyday 'myopic' or 'low-level' awareness, as if the basic dynamics of consciousness were elevation and depression. However, while height is used on earth and in religious scriptures to represent degrees of spiritual condition, height on earth does not confer any spiritual advantages. Neither size nor height is a discrete degree.

5. We may think of discrete degrees as another dimension such as the fourth (or fifth) dimension of space and time. It is true that dimensions can be counted and so are discrete in some sense, but they can still be continuously transformed into each other, for example by rotations. It is clear that rotating or expanding does not, by that fact, take one to a new spiritual discrete degree.

6. Infinite space, or Space Itself. Spinoza, for example, saw matter and

---

[2] I am referring here to the normal scientific view that all the properties of an aggregate are determined by its structure of parts and their individual properties and dispositional natures. This touches on all the current philosophical discussions concerning reductionism, supervenience and emergence.

space as the twin aspects of an infinite divinity from which matter and space are themselves infinite in their details and in their extents. However, physical space is the product of creation and is in a discrete degree distinct from all divine and spiritual degrees.

Concepts derived from time:

7. We may think of discrete degrees as new frequencies of vibration. Entering the spiritual world has been called 'entering a new vibrational level'. However, frequencies can also be continuously transformed into each other, since time in nature is on a continuous numerical scale. It is clear that vibrating faster does not take you to a new spiritual discrete degree. Neither does vibrating more slowly.

8. Some natural objects have discrete harmonic modes of operation. A guitar or cello string has fundamental and harmonic vibrational modes, and these resonate among themselves. Electrons in atoms have discrete levels of different energies. However, if we look in detail, we see that all intermediate vibrations and energies are still possible, in all combinations and for varying durations. I have already discussed the possible roles of different frequencies, and in physics, vibrational energy is proportional to frequency.

9. Series of successive processes, such as waterfalls or other emanations, are often used to represent 'successive discrete degrees'.[3] Theistic science often describes discrete degrees as 'successive degrees' when we talk, for example, of prior or later (upstream and downstream) degrees. We should be aware that this is just another representation based on time. Discrete degrees (such as spiritual and natural) exist concurrently and so are still 'simultaneous' in an essential manner.

10. Infinite time, or the denial of time, is taken to be eternity. Encompassing all time is sometimes seen as a degree above all of us time bound individuals. However, the eternity of God is the source of all life and activity and is certainly not the freezing of time. Divine wisdom does see all time together (past, present and future) in an eternity. The accomplishments of his love require enacting that time successively.

Concepts derived from natural states:

11. Solids, liquids and gases are discrete phases of many substances in nature. Ice, water and steam are discrete manifestations of the one chemi-

---

[3] Even on the cover of this book!

cal H_2O. However, these multiple phases of water can be continuously transformed one into another and back again, so they are not discrete degrees.

12. A related suggestion is to use the classic quartet of earth, water, air and fire, and, especially, to identify a spiritual degree as fire.

13. Sometimes, spirituality is experienced as extremely intense light, of an intensity and detail unimaginable to us on earth. However, intensity is a continuous degree, so, unless some discrete differences are also essential, intense light by itself is not a discrete degree. Only by comparison with the impossibility of light ('thick darkness') is it discretely different.

14. Sometimes we imagine the spiritual as a fine or subtle substance that pervades and influences 'coarse matter' as Epicurus and Lucretius suggested. Something like this may be true, but unless we have an independent idea of the spiritual degree, we cannot properly describe it merely from the idea of 'fineness' or 'subtlety'.

15. Various polarities in nature, such as positive and negative in electric charges or male and female in biology, may be taken as indicating spiritual in contrast to nature. Opposite electric charges, such as of electrons and its antiparticle the positron, however, are exact mirror images at exactly the same natural level. Male and female organisms, in contrast, have internal complexities that are very similar and meet at the same level. We cannot say, for example, that only positive charges or only females or their opposites are connected to what is spiritual.

Concepts derived from Inside and Outside:

16. We may think of discrete degrees as the internal and the external of bodies or of persons. The inmost, inner, and outer may be the discrete degrees we are trying to describe. Certainly we can use these adjectives to contrast spiritual with mental and natural things. However, if we examine the specific meanings of these words, we see that they are essentially spatial images that must be interpreted metaphorically if they are to indicate spiritual, mental and natural as distinct discrete degrees.

17. Connected with the previous suggestion, sometimes the spiritual degree is seen as the 'first person' inside view of nature, so that physical matter is the outside or 'third person' view. This is a popular belief among those trying to reconcile science and spirituality, but it does not help, for example, in trying to understand life after the death of the physical body. How can there be a life from a coherent inside view if the outside view is of matter broken into pieces?

18. A recent suggestion is based on chaos theory where we see self-similarity: a similarity of behavior patterns when we compare the whole and the parts. Again this is an image of Divine operation, according to Chapter 19, but self-similarity does not by itself require that operation.

I hope not too many of your favorite images have been singled out here!

Many of the above distinctions have been adopted in popular culture as sufficient for defining the distinctness of degrees that lead to the spiritual, and some gain satisfaction, for example, with understanding the spiritual in terms of higher resonant states in higher dimensions of reality as yet undiscovered in physics. However, all the above classifications are continuous, not discrete. The desires for continuous spiritual degrees, though widespread in many contemporary and Eastern philosophies today, are based on what we would call natural or even sensual thinking. The spiritual in these cases becomes a special case of the natural and sensed worlds examined by physicists.

We need to separate our understanding from natural and sensual images. This separation may never be complete, but we can at least be aware of the way we presently think.

Let us try to form some more positive accounts. My immediate problem here is that you may be most happy if I produce a new *picture* which I claim shows discrete degrees most accurately. However, we have just seen that all pictures are based on spatial and temporal images and by that fact should be called into question. What can we do?

This is a problem that modern quantum physics has faced for much of the last century. Physicists have realized that pictures based on 'particles' or 'waves' are no longer satisfactory, but they have nothing satisfactory with which to replace them. Some among them have wisely said that 'we can no longer rely on naive pictorial thinking'. Thus, for spiritual degrees as well as physics, we have to rely on some different kind of thinking. Quantum physics can use its mathematical equations, but what can we use?

To understand discrete degrees in a specific way, we can either (a) build on and extrapolate whatever discrete degrees physics and philosophy have discovered, or (b) rely on our own intuitive understandings of causes and effects in ourselves, or (c) rely on revelation from God to guide us over a difficult impasse. This book has tried to present some combination of these. Let us examine the possible candidates for discrete degrees derived from physics and philosophy. Some of these have already been presented in Chapter 5. I list them as:

Degrees in Philosophy and Physics:

19. Form and substance are a pair of discrete degrees. For a given thing, such as a chair, the form is its position, orientation and shape. The form is not just the overall shape but also the shapes and arrangements of all its constituent parts. The substance of the chair is that of which the constituent parts are forms (are made of). Physics can give us some idea of substance such as a kind of energy or propensity to interact. Form and substance cannot be continuously transformed into each other.

20. End, cause and effect are a triplet of discrete degrees. The end (or purpose or 'final cause') is the original principle according to which a process starts. The cause is the formulation of means that is poised to act. The effect is the resulting action. End, cause and effect produce each other in sequence but cannot be reversibly transformed into each other.

21. Heat and light, strictly, are radiation in the same electromagnetic spectrum, making them a pair of continuous rather than discrete degrees. However, heat has a more general meaning: that of energy in general. Light has a more specific meaning, as a form of radiation that can be encoded with much information.

22. Energy and information do form a discrete pair of degrees. Note that 'light' is a particular form of energy, so we could approximately say that light is like form and heat is like substance.

23. Force and motion are discrete degrees. This was first realized by Boscovich and by Kant. Forces may be present even if no movement of matter occurs and vice versa.

24. Potential energy and force are discrete degrees. This was made clear with the discovery of electromagnetic fields by Faraday and Maxwell. Electric energy fields, for example, only produce forces if a charged particle is present within the field. Similarly, the gravitational fields of the earth and sun are not themselves forces but only produce forces on planets and satellites should these be present.

25. Waves and particles, or better waves and events are discrete degrees. This is the best way of understanding quantum physics: waves are a

description of causes, and specific particle positions (or events) are the actual effects of those causes.

26. Virtual and actual processes are discrete degrees. Electric fields, for example, are generated by a prior degree of virtual photons. I discuss this more in the next chapter.

Other discrete degrees are seen by our intuitive understanding of causes and effects, for example within ourselves, within our own minds, and they have been discussed in Chapter 5. These are related to those conceived of within theistic science:

27. Desire, cause and effect are a triplet of discrete degrees. The desire is the original impetus which motivates us. The cause is that motivation when it has formulated the means and is poised to act. The effect is the resulting action. Desire, cause and effect produce each other in sequence but cannot be reversibly transformed into each other.

28. Affection, understanding and action are discrete degrees. These are analogous to the previous set but generalized to all levels of the mind and soul.

29. Soul, mind, and nature, are the three discrete degrees describing the production of creation. This creation starts from what is spiritual. It then proceeds through minds which contain affections and thoughts. It finally has effects in nature.

The classifications 19–26 do describe discrete degrees, but only in nature. By themselves they do not indicate any spirituality. Nevertheless they reflect the true spiritual discrete degrees (27–29) more accurately than the continuous degrees (1–18) since they are themselves discrete and not continuous. I believe that trying to understand any kind of discrete degree is a useful education toward understanding what is spiritual.

Finally, we reject one specific proposal for the nature of spirituality that is increasingly common today:

30. Spiritual reality is not constituted by *consciousness*.

In Pfeiffer, Mack, and Devereux[4], for example, the spiritual and the material poles are distinguished according to whether the substance of something is consciousness, or whether it is matter. According to the current

---

[4] Pfeiffer, Mack, and Devereux, *Mind before matter*.

theism, however, Section 18.7 has that consciousness is a feature of the *operation* of love with wisdom, and it does *not* say that love or wisdom is made *out of* consciousness as if a substance. I argue that consciousness cannot itself be substance, on the basis of the Aristotelean 'metaphysical grammar' we are following. Only something dispositional like love or power can be a substance.

23.3 Sub-degrees of the spiritual

Let us return to the spiritual degree according to theistic science. As with the mental degree discussed in the previous chapter, the spiritual degree has its own sub-degrees. These are distinguished according to what the spiritual love is a love *about*. What is it that occupies the life and dreams of persons whose mentality is focused on each of these levels? The different sub-degrees correspond to the different answers. Is it a love of action, a love of wisdom, or a love of loving? These can be framed equivalently as a love of being useful, a love of truth, or a love of good.

According to the scheme of sub-degrees, the spiritual is divided into three sub-degrees. One, 1.3, is concerned with spiritual actions, another, 1.2, with spiritual thoughts in the understanding, and the last, 1.1, with spiritual loves in the will, all as shown in Table 23.1. This agrees with the reasons and presentations of Swedenborg (1976, ch. 5), who describes three heavenly states where the highest (1.1) is the 'celestial heaven', the middle (1.2) is the 'spiritual heaven', and the lowest (1.3) the 'spiritual-natural heaven'.

Note that these three correspond exactly to the three sub-sub-degrees

1: Spiritual degree love in the spirit	2: Mental degree thoughts in mind	3: Physical degree actions in the body
love of good: 1.1	thoughts of loves: 2.1	
love of truth: 1.2	thoughts of thoughts: 2.2	effects
love of action: 1.3	thoughts of actions: 2.3	

Table 23.1 *The 3 sub-parts of the spiritual degree are shown in the first column. This is a expanded version of Table 22.2.*

of the higher-rational described in Section 22.3. That, according to theistic science, is deliberate. There is a systematic correspondence of functions between the three spiritual sub-degrees and between the three sub-sub-degrees in the rational mind that is designed to have particular inputs from those spiritual levels.

23.4 Spirituality in life

Our spiritual life consists of the deepest and most fundamental loves that belong to us. These are the loves that make up the substances of our mind. These are the most fundamental substances that are part of ourselves rather than of God. Remember that God, as we postulated in Chapter 12, is life itself, so one essential part of our spiritual life is the first thing of ourselves: the first reception of life (love and wisdom) from God.

We need spiritual life and loves for everything we do since all our actions are motivated by some love or another (we are not machines that are motivated only by physical energies and forces). Some of our spiritual loves are good and unselfish, whereas some may be be evil and selfish. Some of us may erroneously think we can avoid considerations of spirituality by concentrating on everyday life and its demands and enjoyments. However we still have our own characteristic spiritual loves, even if we are not aware of what they are, let alone that we make any effort to improve them.

According to the theism being developed here, there must be *two* deep loves in operation. These will be termed the 'inmost love' and the 'permanent spiritual love'. The inmost love is constant at all times, and is the first recipient responsible for maintaining our identity as other aspects and loves of our life change. The second love, derived from the inmost love, is a life that is permanent only in the sense of being built up during the first adult parts of our lives and then remaining relatively constant.

Permanent spiritual love is formed in the same way that all mental life is formed. That formation uses the constraints built up by the physical actions in our historical past to make permanent mental and spiritual structures. These, respectively, make our mind and our soul. We can of course invent in our minds temporary mental and spiritual states (by thinking and desiring, respectively), but they will not last for long if there is no history or framework to preserve them. The historical actions that are the basis for our internal life are not every action or circumstance that we participated in. Rather, the important actions are just those particular actions that were the joint action of our own loves and our own deliberate thought. It is such actions that become part of our selves and contribute to making up what we are. Those actions are the products that come from inside us, not those that are involuntarily imposed on us from the outside.[5]

Spiritual development is based on what loves have deliberately entered into the actions of our lives. Such development does not depend only on knowledge or insight, not even on insight concerning spiritual things, unless those enter into actions. Neither is spiritual development based on meditation or development of an internal sight (either in daily life or in some dissociated state) unless that sight is used to discriminate and decide what actions are to be made in life. All these actions in life must be actual physical responses that make a difference to the world and are not confined to spiritual or mental decisions. Only physical events produce the 'outer layer' of our spiritual and mental lives that keep them permanently retained.

In a very definite sense, our spiritual loves define who we are, including what sort of person we are. In Section 11.3 we saw some of the ways by which we come to observe our loves, and the same procedure applies to our spiritual loves. Let me repeat what was written there: The loves are that which determine what we *would* do in various situations, just like the dispositions and potentialities of physics. Our loves may thus be discerned by one of the following procedures:

1. Seeing what we have done,
2. Seeing what we do now, especially when free,
3. Seeing what appears to us to be good,
4. Seeing our bodily and affective tone and responsiveness when various courses of action are considered,
5. Seeing where our desires take us when they are given free rein,
6. Seeing where our imagination leads us when it is free to wander.

All of these physical or mental 'experiments' must be conducted in some

---

[5] Matthew 15:11 and 18: "What goes into a man's mouth does not make him 'unclean', but what comes out of his mouth, that is what makes him 'unclean.' ... But the things that come out of the mouth come from the heart."

freedom, otherwise external restrictions will limit what can be seen in each case and hence limit the accuracy of our perception of ourselves.[6]

In all of spiritual development, we have the importance of actions in life. We can never achieve spiritual development by sitting quietly with our hands by our sides, waiting for God to act. Rather, we act, as if from ourselves, as then love and wisdom (from God) can enter into action and contribute both to the world and to our own inner life.

Religions should be addressing these issues. Many do, but do not always place sufficient importance on the difficulties. Since God is a God of love, and since God resides with us in our loves, the detailed perception and development of our spiritual loves is extremely important. It is crucial even in everyday life, since the whole tenor of our family, professional, social and political lives depends on our own spiritual loves permeating into all our decisions and actions. Religion should help us to deal with conflicting spiritual loves—as happens in states of temptation—and encourage us to rely on the truths and power of God in such situations.

There are clearly very many things to be discovered about the spiritual history of humans in various civilizations, cultures, religions and churches, much more than I could possibly know or even surmise.

23.5 Heavenly states

This chapter has discussed a spiritual degree, one made up of three subdegrees in which there are 'specialists' in the love of wisdom, the love of truth, and the love of good action in life. But do we experience these things in our everyday life? We may sometimes experience moments of grace and some brief insight into a spiritual state that seems far removed from our everyday life, but it certainly does not look like we are persistently aware of any of those three spiritual sub-degrees.

Maybe we come into these spiritual states in a more permanent way only after we die. Then, our physical body will have decayed, and there will no longer be the external constraints of selection on the actions of our inner spiritual and mental degrees. That is, provided of course, we built up

---

[6] For these reasons, spiritual development often requires the manifestation of unpleasant or selfish loves, as only then are they seen. In an extremely strict social or religious regime, some of our spiritual loves may never have had the opportunity to manifest themselves and may hence never become known even to ourselves.

suitable fixed structures in the spiritual degree by suitable physical actions in our life. Once that is done, we can imagine ourselves existing in *heavenly states* where we have many more possibilities to express our (fixed) spiritual loves in new ranges of mental experience. This is certainly what has been suggested by common belief about life after bodily death, even if it is not in the explicit doctrine of many of the leading churches.

Many thinkers deny the possibility of a spiritual existence for the soul because they think that persons in such states would have to be disembodied, and they can not conceive of anything like a normal life without any sense of body nor of relations of juxtaposition between distinct persons. They are mistaken, however, to think that the continued spiritual existence of a soul is without a body or any substance. Certainly such souls cannot continue to exist in physical space. We will never find them by searching under the earth or in the visible heavens. But in our multilevel theistic structure, spiritual beings will have their own kind of substance, namely love, and their own kind of relational space, namely the space defined by possibilities for interactions of distinct spiritual loves.

This is in contrast to Aquinas' view that souls are purely forms in conjunction with an 'act of existing' in the sense of being immaterial and having no matter. That view does indeed remove souls from physical space. It makes them completely absent from any space and also from any change, being, or consciousness. It is true that Aquinas' meaning of 'form' does include that of 'causal principle', and we both agree that souls are or contain the causal principles of our life. The question is whether the causal principles or forms (whatever make up the soul) are more akin to fixed mathematical forms or more akin to living forms. If they are like mathematical forms, they would not be of the kind to which any loving or lovable person would aspire, either before bodily death or afterwards.

The present view, by contrast, takes souls to be living forms of which spiritual love is their substance. This means that spiritual beings do have their bodies[7] and should well be visible by some appropriate kind of spiritual sight. Such beings will be composed of forms of love and will think by means of ideas, in manners presumably very similar to the way we do on earth. More details concerning this mode of living will have to depend on further insights, inferences, and investigations.

---

[7] Such a view is common in Christianity: "There is a natural body, and there is a spiritual body" (1 Cor. 15.44).

24

Discrete Degrees in Nature

WE COME to the third of the major degrees, in accordance with the initial image of God within creation. This third degree is the physical or natural degree. In it the full actualization of the previous degrees comes into existence. The full effects or actions of beings are manifest. This is the basis for those beings having a life of their own. We will investigate whether this overall function agrees with the specific details of physical reality that scientists have come to know. I begin by expanding what might be said about the nature of the physical world. I use theistic science as the basis. Then I see whether this agrees with modern physics. Sometimes it will not agree, so there will be opportunities for dialectical improvements either in our theistic science (according to the methods of Chapter 21) or in our physics. Theistic science would be making predictions that could be confirmed or falsified by future experiments, and a confirmation would encourage its acceptance within science as a whole.

According to the previous chapters, the physical degree has several functions. First, it receives the influx from the prior spiritual and mental degrees in order that those degrees have actual effects. Second, it maintains the more or less stable structures in physical space (such as our bodies) in order that there be similar stable structures within our minds.[1] Thirdly, it produces the final effects, in particular it makes the ultimate selections that govern which dispositions may operate. As for the degree containing the final selections, we described it as the bottom line of the whole set of discrete degrees. It is the level where the real choices are made and hence where the character of the whole is determined. Everything prior to these final selections is in some way composed of dispositions or

---

[1] As first argued in Section 20.6.

1: Spiritual degree	2: Mental degree	3: Physical degree
love in the spirit	thoughts in mind	actions in the body
love of good: 1.1	thoughts of loves: 2.1	effects of loves: 3.1
love of truth: 1.2	thoughts of thoughts: 2.2	effects of thoughts: 3.2
love of action: 1.3	thoughts of actions: 2.3	effects of actions: 3.3

Table 24.1 *The 3 sub-parts of the natural degree are shown in the third column. This is a further-expanded version of Table 23.1.*

potentiality for change. In that sense everything prior is 'less determinate' than the 'pure actualities' which I will argue are produced in the physical degree.

In contemporary physics there are two major unsolved problems. These happen to be related to our requirements above for the physical degree. The first unsolved problem is to know how space (or space-time) is produced. This is the question introduced in subsection 5.3.3, concerning how some pregeometry could be physically responsible for producing the geometry of space. The second unsolved problem is to know how quantum physical processes produce particular measurement outcomes, when many outcomes each have non-zero probabilities of occurring. This is the question introduced in subsection 5.3.1, concerning whether or not there is a reduction of the wave packet after quantum measurements, a phenomenon whose existence is much disputed.

I normally regard theistic science as producing a general framework for scientific theories and not detailed theories themselves. There may well be fundamental constraints on possible theories if they are to fit into a theistic superstructure. We will see in this chapter that theistic science does make suggestions and proposals for the nature of physics, and especially concerning pregeometry and quantum measurements.

24.1 Physical sub-degrees

In order to understand how these three functions of the physical degree might be accomplished, we have (as should be expected in theistic science) to consider the three sub-degrees of the physical. Let us continue our method used in the mental and spiritual chapters by seeing how the sub-degrees of each are related. Let us expand Table 23.1 by writing in the three sub-degrees of the physical, giving now Table 24.1. Because both the spiritual and the physical are images of God in their own ways, we should see some similarities in their respective sub-degrees.

In Table 24.1, we see first the sub-degree 3.1 called here 'effects of loves', or equivalently, 'effects from loves'. In physics we do not know so much about love, but we do know about organizing principles. In theistic science, because principles everywhere follow from love, we can think of this degree 3.1 as being where the spiritual and mental enter into nature and become an organizing principle for what is going to happen. Present-day physics does not know much about this mental influence. This is, however, the prediction based on science from our scientific theism.[2] We can think of the 3.1 sub-degree as 'effects of love on principles'. It must be 'soft' or 'receptive' to the prior degrees, as that is the way our desires and intentions enter into the world and have effects there (as they do in every moment of our waking life).

This sub-degree 3.1 has another important role, which is to fix the common space to be used in the universe. Remember that all the previous mental degrees had their own spaces and own metrics, which I speculated might be some kind of associative spaces of meanings. In the physical degree, however, the meanings are less apparent, and the space of the universe appears to be a large common manifold with no associative to its metric. In physical space, contrary things can exist close to each other and readily interact, so we conclude that there are no remaining psychological components in the space of the universe.[3] The question of how physical space comes to be and comes to have its metric is, in physics today, the field of quantum gravity. Theistic science will make some suggestions concerning the foundations of quantum gravity or (more generally) the investigations of pre-geometry (what exists before spatial geometries).

In Table 24.1, we see secondly the sub-degree 3.2 called here 'effects of thoughts', or equivalently, 'effects from thoughts'. Again, physics does not know much about thoughts but only about the rational laws that are often the content of thoughts. Because these laws describe the constant operation of causes, we can think of this 3.2 sub-degree as describing 'effects of thought on causes', in particular on regular and propagating causes. In

---

[2] We will learn more about that prediction when we get to its *its sub-sub-degrees* later in the chapter.
[3] There are only, we will see, something like 'shadows' or 'correspondences' or 'remnants' of those psychological meanings.

this physical sub-degree there must be quasi-deterministic physical laws of propagation, where 'quasi-deterministic' means still subject to the principles of the prior degree 3.1 (especially if those principles change from new mental intention or influx there).[4] In physics today, it is field theories of electromagnetism and quantum field theory which deal with 'quasi-deterministic physical laws of propagation'. Quantum field theory treats electromagnetism and other kinds of field interactions in terms of 'virtual particles' and 'virtual events'. We therefore expect theistic science to make suggestions concerning the foundations of quantum field theories.

Also in Table 24.1, we see the third sub-degree 3.3, called 'effects of actions', which deals with the production of final effects in the physical world by actualizing any remaining potentialities or propensities.

Here we are on the firmest ground about understanding this in terms of everyday experience and in terms of physical theory. We think that surely today's very successful physics is concerned with actual changes in our observations of those changes. If classical Newtonian mechanics were true, we would know exactly the final effects. They would be the motion of atomic corpuscles around in space, each atom having a specific location at any given time. However, the current theory is not Newtonian mechanics but quantum mechanics. In quantum theory, the individual bodies in the world do *not* have specific locations at each time but behave more like fields of propensity. These fields do give specific results but only intermittently: during what quantum physics calls 'measurements'. In Part II we began to discuss those features of the quantum world. Now we will see if they can fit into the sub-degree 3.3 at the end of our multi-level generative structure of the universe. To see what can fit into a sub-degree, we have to consider its sub-sub-degrees, and that means a whole new round of analysis. All the above sub-degrees (3.1 and 3.2) will have their sub-sub-degrees too.

24.2 Sub-sub-degrees of the physical

We now go through the exercise, similar to that of Chapter 22, of identifying as many as possible of the sub-sub-degrees of the physical degree. In

---

[4] There is of course also selection working in the other direction: the effects of changing principles in sub-degree 3.1 will be selected by what happens in the quasi-deterministic sub-degree 3.2.

3: Physical degree		
actions/effects/results in the body		
Effects of love on principles: 3.1		
Effects on principles of principles: 3.11	Effects on causes of principles: 3.12	Effects on actions of principles: 3.13
Effects of thought on causes 3.2		
Effects on principles of causes: 3.21	Effects on causes of causes: 3.22	Effects on effects of causes: 3.23
Effects of actions on effects: 3.3		
Effects on principles of effects: 3.31	Effects on causes of effects: 3.32	Effects on effects of effects: 3.33

Table 24.2 *The ennead of sub-sub-degrees within the physical degree. This is just the rightmost third column of Table 24.1, expanded to the next amount of detail.*
The phrase "effects on A of B" at all the 3.XY sub-sub-degrees means the "effects on (A of B)", which is the influence on B, in particular the A aspect of B.
The phrase "effects of A on B" at all the 3.X sub-degrees means the "effects on (A → B)", which is the influence on B because the place of B in the physical degree is the same as the place of A in the prior mental degrees.

Table 24.2 we write out the sub-degrees of the physical, from Chapter 19. This whole table is the third column of Table 24.1 above.

It takes a little effort to identify these sub-sub-degrees and parts thereof. We are dealing with the final remnants in the physical of spiritual and mental activity, and we do not have established sciences of psycho-physics to help us. However, it turns out that existing theories of physics do enable us to identify five of these nine sub-sub-degrees (3.21–3.32). Furthermore, current speculation in physics and quantum gravity is clearly oriented toward finding physical processes which would lead us to identify many of the remaining sub-sub-degrees, including the range (3.11-3.13) and the final step (3.33), as will be discussed in Section 24.4.

Fortunately we can exploit previous logical and physical investigations. We have at hand already the previous 9-fold of the exterior mind. All these correspond to each other in some manner, by which I mean that, since the mental and physical degrees are both structured in the image of God, we should expect that their interior structures have many similarities. The 3.1 (3.11, 3.12, 3.13) degrees will be discussed later when new physics is suggested. However, physics has already explored considerable detail of the 3.2 and 3.3 sub-degrees and sub-sub-degrees, in particular quantum physics. We must remember that intermediate results are not themselves the ultimate physical events but are more the preparation for such events. They provide, for example, the energy, the propensity or the circumstance for the final events. We are now making connections to the preliminary analyses of quantum field theory in Subsection 5.3.2, and of quantum mechanics in Subsection 5.3.1:

CAUSES (3.2):

1. **Effects on principles of causes: 3.21.** In the natural degree, the principles of causes are the general principles that guide the natural laws, such as general invariance requirements and more specifically the *variational principles* of least action for Lagrangians' that provide the starting point for many modern theories. This sub-sub-degree will be influential in the order of principles (3.21) → causes (3.2) → results (3.).

2. **Effects on causes of causes: 3.22.** The first result of the variational principles is the *dynamic laws* which govern the propagation of 'bare' particles and quanta, according to formal laws of time evolution. This sub-sub-degree will be influential in the order of causes (3.22) → causes (3.2) → results (3.).

3. **Effects on effects of causes: 3.23.** The next effect of the dynamic laws are *virtual events* of interactions of particles and quanta. These are reversible events whose role is the production of interaction potentials. This sub-sub-degree will be influential in the order of effects (3.23) → causes (3.2) → results (3.).

EFFECTS (3.3):

4. **Effects on principles of effects: 3.31.** The first effect of the interaction potentials is their interplay with kinetic *energy*, as expressed by the Hamiltonian operator in quantum physics. The operation of the Hamiltonian is the principle which generates the time evolution of the wave function in the quantum context as a direct consequence of energy balances. This sub-sub-degree will be influential in the order of principles (3.31) → effects (3.3) → results (3.).

5. **Effects on causes of effects: 3.32.** *The wave functions* generated by the 3.31 degree describe physical objects as wave packets. It hence leads to

sequences of their behavior by means of a residual propensity for selections that may be probabilistic. This sub-sub-degree will be influential in the order of causes (3.32) → effects (3.3) → results (3.).

6. **Effects on effects of effects: 3.33.** The final ultimate events are the selection of *actual outcomes* from the alternatives within the wave function. How this occurs is the 'quantum measurement problem', not fully solved yet; but note that the 2.33 degree (of sensorimotor observations and actions) corresponds with this selection process. This sub-sub-degree will be influential in the order of effects (3.33) → effects (3.3) → results (3.).

Combining these logical and physical identifications of the nine sub-sub-degrees of the external mind, we can redraw the previous figure as Table 24.3.

The divine source does not produce all these physical effects only directly but also indirectly via spiritual and natural stages that we see as natural dispositions or natural propensities in a 'trickle down' manner. That was discussed in Chapter 18. These dispositions or propensities are also known as causes, forces, powers, potentials, quantum propensities. They lead to the ultimate physical interactions and events. The physical dispositions are a *very* limited 'remnant' of Divine power. They operate in a way which is always related and always corresponds to the characteristic operation of the Divine Love: by all the patterns and sub-patterns we have seen above.

24.3 Existing physics

The above suggestions concerning quantum mechanics and quantum field theory give reasons for the interpretive ideas first presented in Section 5.3, reasons that come via theistic science from our scientific theism. We now have some basis for the simultaneous existence of both the ordinary and field-theoretic quantum theories. It is useful to explore in a little more detail some differences between these 3.2 (ordinary) and 3.3 (field theory) levels.

There are many similarities or correspondences between structures of the 3.2 and 3.3 sub-sub-degrees. Both levels have as their effect some kind of events. In both levels these events are produced after the propagation of

Discrete Degrees in Nature

Spiritual world: love 1.	Mental world: thought 2.	physical world: effects 3.		
Love of loves: 1.1	Higher Rational: 2.1	Reception: effects of love : 3.1 (reception of love): 3.11	(reception of thought): 3.12	(reception of decisions): 3.13
Love of thoughts: 1.2	Scientific Rational: 2.2	Scientific Laws: effects of thoughts: 3.2 Variational Principles: 3.21	Field Laws: 3.22	Virtual Events: 3.23
Love of actions: 1.3	External mind: 2.3	Material effects: effects of effects: 3.3 Energy: 3.31	Wave Functions: 3.32	Actual Selections: 3.33

Table 24.3 *The ennead within the physical degree.*

some field. Also, both have initiating principles that can be written as variational principles (the Schrödinger equation can be derived from a variational principle). However, the events and fields in the two levels are of rather different character. We will see that these character differences stem from their different places in the overall generative structure of the theistic universe.

The differences between levels 3.2 and 3.3 arise because they are in parts of the overall structure of discrete degrees. This is reflected in their being in different rows of Table 24.1. The bottom row is concerned with action and the middle row with forms and propagation of forms. The bottom row has *discrete* existences, and the middle row has *continuous* existences. This difference between discreteness and continuity pervades all their respective sub-sub-degrees.

The actual events in 3.33 (ordinary quantum mechanics) are therefore discrete, whereas the virtual events in 3.23 of field-theory exist in continuous collections. The actual events are the visible events in history (such as quantum measurements: see the next section), whereas virtual events are point events which are not measurements. The actual events of 3.3 have therefore finite time intervals between them, whereas virtual events occur continuously in time. Actual events definitely occur or do not occur, whereas virtual events contribute to preparing alternate futures for actuality and so cannot be definitely said to occur or not occur.

I will make two more predictions about these differences. One prediction concerns basic process philosophy. The other is from our theistic science and depends on the particular sub-sub-degrees suggested in Chapter 22 for the content of the mental sub-sub-degrees. The grounds for claiming these two predictions is weaker than much presented above, but it is arguably positive, as I will explain.

The philosophical prediction is: when events occur continuously in time, their evolution is deterministic, whereas when events occur intermittently or discretely, their evolution is indeterministic. By indeterministic, I mean that the time evolution for the future cannot be determined on the basis of what has already happened, and it perhaps may be that only probabilities can be given.[5] I do not know how to prove this correlation between continuity and determinism in process ontologies, but it

---

[5] We may think of this informally: when there are gaps in time between events, we may infer that there is necessarily wriggle-room between events.

seems to exist whenever I compare theories. The most obvious comparison is between classical and quantum physics. In classical physics, objects exist continuously in time and so the actual events describing them are also continuous in time. Classical physics is deterministic. By comparison, in quantum physics objects are only determinate at intermittent times, so the actual events describing them are discrete. Quantum physics is indeterministic. If this philosophical claim is true, then theistic science provides reasons why quantum mechanics has actual events which are indeterministic and require probabilities. It gives reasons for why quantum field theory has events which are deterministic, and, conversely, why quantum fields can be predicted indefinitely far into the future once their initial conditions are known. It is only the indeterministic actual events of 3.33 which may affect them by cross-level constraints or the prior reception processes of 3.11 by influx.

The theistic science prediction is that the virtual events of level 3.23 reflect the structure of the mental processes at the corresponding place (2.23) in the mental set of sub-sub-degrees. And what is the structure of the 2.23 mental level? Looking at the cognitive levels in Table 22.6, which reflect the discussion in Section 22.5, we see that this level deals with what Piaget calls 'operational thought'. This is the level of operations of one-to-one correspondences and reversibility. These operations are just those of mathematical *groups*, which are defined by laws of associativity, commutativity, identities, and inverses. The prediction, therefore, is that the virtual events of sub-sub-degree 3.23 have an internal group structure.[6] I am not saying what the group structure is in detail. I am only saying that virtual events are in *some* finite-group space. Such group structures are indeed already postulated in physics for virtual processes; the standard model for elementary particles of quarks, gluons and other bosons is built on group structures for electro-weak charge, color and charm variables, along with gauge invariances. This is in contrast to the actual events of 3.33, which are purely selective events.

---

[6] Strictly speaking, investigating the 'internal group structure' of a sub-sub-degree would require considering the sub-sub-sub-degrees within it.

24.4 Selections: new physics?

In Chapter 5 and in this chapter, I talked about the actualizing or selection events that make the bottom line of the whole multi-level world. I implied that such events are the same as the measurement events that are known in quantum physics, but this is not strictly true. There is still much debate in physics concerning whether there really are such events. Physicists do not yet have evidence for whether what is called the 'reduction of the wave packet' in measurements really occurs or not.

Many physicists, especially those in quantum cosmology who are used to thinking far from everyday life, claim that there is only ever the appearance of such actual selections, and that, *really*, they do not exist. Maybe, they say, the multiple options that are supposed to be selected from still continue to exist in 'worlds of their own' that can never interact with each other. Since, for all practical purposes, we are stuck in just one world, we therefore approximately exist (they claim) as if we made the selection that defines that world. The 'many worlds' interpretation of quantum mechanics by Everett[7], or the 'decoherent histories' interpretation by Gell-Mann and Hartle[8] and Halliwell[9], offer such views. These approaches have the feature of keeping only the Schrödinger dynamics and avoiding anything beyond that. In theistic science, this would be to advocate keeping only the propensity fields of degree 3.32 but without them ever being propensities *for* anything. The result of such interpretations is that each would-be-choice results in a set of multiple worlds, in which each possible outcome is manifested in each of the corresponding possible worlds. From any reasonable viewpoint (as Bell[10] eloquently argues), this must be considered an extraordinarily baroque speculation to avoid adding even the simplest formalism to allow precise outcomes, here the actualizations of propensities.

Theistic science must therefore go along with those who make some extension to quantum mechanics in order to allow and describe the *actual selection* between the multiple outcomes predicted by quantum mechanics. It is essential to the theory of this book that there are specific selection events made in physics. Only then can humans decide and can the resulting actions constitute the ultimate foundation of the theistic universe.

---

[7] Everett, "'Relative state' formulation of quantum mechanics."

[8] Gell-Mann and Hartle, "Classical equations for quantum systems."

[9] Halliwell, "A review of the decoherent histories approach to quantum mechanics."

[10] Bell, "Against 'measurement'."

There are a number of proposals for the selection mechanism in quantum mechanics. These are often called 'collapse' or 'reduction' mechanisms because the range of propensities existing before the selection is collapsed after the event to those compatible with which event actually occurred. I have investigated many of these proposals in Chapter 12 of Thompson[11], but I find no conclusive argument or evidence for a definitive conclusion on which is best. Within theoretical physics, the mathematics necessary to describe reduction events is plausibly given as some stochastic Schrödinger equation or an equivalent semi-group master equation with Lindblad operators: for details see the review by Bassi and Ghirardi[12] and references therein. The best known specific hypothesis is the proposal of Ghirardi, Rimini, and Weber[13], where fields are localized to narrow Gaussians. The GRW proposal has been criticized by Lewis[14] as not a true selection because of finite tails of the Gaussians, and indeed it does not give a strict selection between spatial regions. What is needed in the theistic account, however, is not necessarily a strict *spatial* selection but a strict selection between alternative outcomes, or *histories* as these are usually called.[15]

The prediction of theistic science is therefore that *some* actualizing or collapse events do occur, and so physicists should still be trying to find out where, when and how they happen. The present thesis states that there must be at finite time intervals some events in which these become *exactly* decoherent, but the thesis leaves open the precise conditions for such events. These actualization events are in addition to the results of environmental influence on quantum superpositions and will result in even fewer effects of superpositions, entanglement or interference effects than are predicted by Schrödinger dynamics. It is predicted that one day these will be observable effects in experimental physics.

A weighty objection to the possibility of actualizing events is based on how quantum mechanics fits into Einstein's special theory of relativity. That is because actualizing events may alter the causing field of propensity in one step, even if it is spread out over very large distances, possibly over light-years (say) for an intergalactic photon. This is one of many pos-

---

[11] Thompson, *Philosophy of nature and quantum reality.*
[12] Bassi and Ghirardi, "Dynamical reduction models."
[13] Ghirardi, Rimini, and Weber, "Unified dynamics for microscopic and macroscopic systems."
[14] Lewis, "Quantum mechanics, orthogonality, and counting."
[15] The quantum theory of 'decoherent histories' shows that *almost*-decoherent histories are easily generated according to quantum mechanics. Theism and common sense both only ask that histories become in fact decoherent, not just approximately.

sible effects of quantum non-locality. It is not yet certain that these are forbidden.[16] Relativity theory is commonly taken as forbidding all communications faster than the speed of light, since, in that case, the order of transmission and reception events would be different according to different observers in relative motion. That would appear to contradict one principle of causality, namely that a cause always comes before its effect. In our theistic science we do keep that property of causality: we never allow future events to influence what happens now. So does relativity forbid non-locality over spatial intervals within times less than the propagation time for light? (These are called 'space-like' intervals in relativity theory.) Should we follow relativity in its 'conventionality of distant simultaneity' by not allowing space-like separated events to have no intrinsic order?[17]

Theistic science, in reply, affirms that actual events must have an actual order. This response is based on the correspondence between non-local propensity fields and the non-locality of minds that follows because they are not themselves located in physical space-time (only their effects are). I surmise that any mind of a being has a complete ordering of its internal changes since since all events are 'seen' in the mind as they happen. Thus, if a non-local mind observes changes of propensity fields spread over space-like intervals, these observations will have some determinate order and so will the propensity-actualizing events that were observed.

What is not necessary is that the actual order of collapse events be determined by quantum mechanics, that is, by the Schrödinger equation. It is quite possible that actualizing events, since they occur probabilistically from their propensities, may also have a *probabilistic actual order*. This is to say, two space-like actualizing events will not have a predetermined order, but some order will be established *as they occur*. Only afterwards will it be clear that one event occurred before the other, when we see in which order changes were made to their common propensity field.[18] This theory is equivalent to making Lorentz invariance apply strictly to deterministic field propagations (the virtual fields of level 3.22 and the Schrödinger

---

[16] For more discussion, see Peacock (*The no-signalling theorems*) and Gisin ("The free will theorem, stochastic quantum dynamics and true becoming in relativistic quantum physics").

[17] As argued by Rietdijk ("A rigorous proof of determinism derived from the special theory of relativity") and Rietdijk (*On the explanation of matter wave interference*).

[18] As Gisin ("The free will theorem, stochastic quantum dynamics and true becoming in relativistic quantum physics") remarks, "quantum events must enjoy some sort of "freedom", and so "are not merely the realization of usual probability distributions, but must be thought of as true acts of creations (true becoming) ... The probability distributions of possible future [events] is time-order invariant, i.e. covariant. But the set of actual past [events] are not (and couldn't be)."

wave field of level 3.23) and to apply only statistically to indeterministic field actualizations (the actual events of level 3.33). That seems entirely fitting.

24.5 Pre-geometry: new physics?

The overall plan of generative levels being developed here leaves a whole sub-degree 3.1 for some kind of new physics between the mental degrees 2.X and those physical sub-degrees 3.2 and 3.3 that are already familiar from modern physics. This possibility was foreseen in the earlier discussion on Subsection 5.3.3, where the topic was how physical space and time came to exist. That discussion was driven by the continual modern research and speculation concerning quantum gravity. It is a research field that seeks to unify the dynamical processes described by quantum mechanics with the dynamical space-time processes described by general relativity. There have been many recent speculations about such things as superstrings, spin networks and causal sets. The aim has been to find a way to unify quantum mechanics and general relativity in order to develop a quantum theory about how space and time are produced. We want to know, for example, how the space-time metric comes to depend on mass and energy in space-time according to laws of general relativity. That is the way that gravity is described according to Einstein.

Starting in Section 24.1, we begin to see how such processes could arise in theistic science. The new sub-degree 3.1 has two major functions within the overall plan of generative levels. First it has to receive influences from the spiritual and mental degrees, since those are dispositions which cause the effects that are the physical world. The manner of this reception is not known in modern physics, but in theistic science it is quite definite that such influences must be effective, so there is a clear new prediction being made here. The second role of the sub-degree 3.1 is to be responsible for the creation and maintenance of a universe-wide manifold of space-time, where we start by envisaging a manifold conceived of as according approximately to general relativity.

In order to understand the details of operation of the new sub-degree 3.1, we begin by envisaging *its* three sub-sub-degrees 3.11, 3.12 and 3.13 and thinking about what they might do. If we are short of ideas here, we can (and should) consider them as simplified analogies or correspondences of the similarly-placed sub-sub-degrees 2.11, 2.12 and 2.13 with the top sub-degree of the mental degree outlined in Chapter 22. Those three sub-sub-degrees were concerned, respectively, with the reception into the mind of love, of wisdom, and of obedient action from the spiritual degree. According to our principles of correspondence, we should expect that the three uppermost physical sub-sub-degrees would be concerned respectively with the reception into the physical degree of intentions, of plans, and of determination to action from the prior mental degree. We can imagine how this might operate. There must be a first sub-sub-degree 3.11 that we imagine as 'soft', in that it is easily receptive of mental intentions for physical actions. There must be a second sub-sub-degree 3.12 that develops or propagates these intentions within some kind of projected space-time that is not itself physical space-time. There must be a third sub-sub-degree 3.13 of determination to actions that (I speculate) act to confirm or 'pin down' this projected space-time from all sources of influence, to make a fixed space-time manifold with the global metric that we know from physics. This would be the reason we have a shared space in everyday physical appearances. These last actions of 'confirmation' must be imagined as 'hard', or as having fixed effects, in that they produce a space-time that is no longer amenable to mental influences. The existence of space-time will itself constrain what future mental processes may occur, according with the principle in multi-level ontologies that actions at lower levels act to constrain or select what may happen in the future in prior levels.

Within this new multi-level structure of sub-degrees and sub-sub-degrees, we will ask how gravity may come about and how then general relativity may be an approximation to the behavior of our new physical structure. If we take gravity according to general relativity, it is the influence of spatial distributions of mass and energy on the metric of space-time. In our final Table 24.3, there are distributions of propensity for massive particles in sub-sub-degree 3.32, so it must be these distributions which constrain the metric-forming process in sub-sub-degree 3.12. This would make general relativity an example of how a 'lower' level (of propensity for particles 3.32) acts to constrain or select a similarly-placed 'higher' level (where space-time metrics are being formed in 3.12).

The role of the new sub-degree 3.1 is to generate physical space-time. It does not, however, generate it from a realm that has *no* space or time. It generates it from spiritual and mental realms that still have their own (non-physical) spatial structures and their own successions of state that give at least the appearance of time as we know it. Wheeler[19] started physicists on a more difficult problem than this. He asked how to produce physical space-time from a set of processes that had *no space or time* at all. Without anything like space or like time, we cannot have juxtaposition of distinct entities, and we cannot even have changes of state of those entities. Meschini[20], for example, calls into question the whole idea of pregeometry as trying to derive geometrical concepts from a realm which has absolutely none. That problem is too difficult. An easier problem is how multiple mental spaces (in which there are successions of states) may be received and combined by new processes in the sub-degree 3.1 in order to produce a unified global manifold of spaces and times that we know from physics.

The predictions of theistic science concerning physics are that we have very good reasons for the existence of a new sub-degree (3.1) and that the processes in this sub-degree will solve two long-standing problems: how mental intentions influence the physical world (in particular, our brains) and how space-time is generated as the global manifold known from general relativity. This will happen in a more general theory that also describes the processes of quantum field theory (3.2), and of ordinary quantum mechanics (3.3). Note that this is the very beginning of theistic science. We do not yet specify theories mathematically. Much work remains to be done. The present theistic science thus provides a general framework in which specific physical (or, better, generalized physical) theories may fit together with theories of mind. Theistic science does not at present determine the precise content of the theories of psychology and physics, but, as we have seen, it does constrain that content. Two previous chapters in this Part have described the extent to which I see psychology and physics being constrained by what theistic science we already can deduce.

[19] Wheeler, "Quantum gravity."
[20] Meschini, "A metageometric enquiry concerning time, space, and quantum physics."

25

Mind-body Connections

25.1 Relations between degrees

THE PREVIOUS three chapters have described the main degrees according to theistic science. This was done by identifying the structural degrees of scientific theism with actual processes in the universe, using the fact that some of these actual processes are known already and well described by modern science. Now we address more specifically the causal connections *between* those degrees. We need to consider the connections between the mental and physical degrees, between the spiritual and mental degrees, and between the divine and the spiritual. This is needed especially since, for many people it is controversial that such connections exist at all.

In fact, many current world views can be defined as the denial of the reality of one or more of these connections. There is a wide spectrum of such views. The three most common positions are as follows.

- Denial that there are any *mental-physical connections*: this is what it is to be a physicalist. This position used to be called materialism, but that name is less popular now because of the many not-material-like qualities within the physical.[1] To be completely consistent, physicalists should further assume that all rationality, thinking, feeling, deciding and consciousness must either be properties of physical (or material) objects in the universe or only be appearances that do not really exist. Some physicalists shy away from this conclusion. They attempt to formulate a 'non-reductive physicalism' that keeps the reality of rationality and consciousness while still allowing physics to be a complete descrip-

---

[1] Theistic science would claim that these qualities come from the multiple sub-degrees within physics.

tion of reality. Other physicalists contend that such compromise positions are actually inconsistent. Much current debate about physicalism
and consciousness centers around these issues.

- Denial that there are any *spiritual-mental connections*: this is to take the
  view of humanists that minds are 'natural phenomena' that are self-
  aware, self-motivating, and hence self-sufficient. Such people would
  therefore not allow for the existence of anything transcending normal
  thinking or feeling. They strongly dislike the idea of reducing mentality
  and rationality to physics. They seek non-reductive ideas of mind such
  as non-reductive holism or emergence in order to keep some real kind
  of mental-physical distinction.
- Denial that there are any *divine-spiritual connections*. This is to be a
  'spiritual-atheist', rather like the Buddhist view. Strictly speaking, the
  Buddhists refuse to confirm or deny the existence of a divinity, but they
  typically reject any talk of God or theism.[2] A similar view, one that allows for spirituality in an atheistic universe, has recently been advocated by Harris[3].[4]

Theistic science does assert the reality of *all* of the inter-degree connections which contrasts with these partial or limited views. Theistic science
goes on to describe the details of these connections in a scientific manner.
It draws on the general principles of the scientific theism described earlier in this book and is able to make predictions of how these connections
operate.

Between any pair of levels P and Q within the multilevel generative
structure that we have developed for theism, we can now begin to describe how P influences Q by generative causation and how the effects in
Q yet again affect what can happen in P by selections or constraints. This
standard pattern is not symmetric dualism because generation is distinct
from selection. We will see that the overall effects of such asymmetric connections result still in a rather close coupling between adjacent degrees. In
the end, the result is effectively an interactive dualism.[5]

---

[2] As described by Dalai Lama (*The universe in a single atom*).

[3] Harris, *The end of faith*.

[4] Harris (*The end of faith*), in fact, claims to draw on "new evidence from neuroscience and insights from
philosophy to explore spirituality as a biological, brain-based need, and invokes that need in taking a
secular humanistic approach to solving the problems of this world." Whether he is a physicalist,
humanist or spiritual-atheist will depend on the precise meaning of 'brain-based.'

[5] I am sure that Descartes would have been very happy to hear of such a theory of interactive dualism,
as he was often pressed to explain how souls and bodies could interact according to his theory. The
best he could say was that to interact was their intrinsic nature, without making a detailed hypothesis.

Let us look first at the details of mental-physical connections: those between our minds and our bodies (including our brain).

25.2 Mind-body connections

When we look at how minds are related to bodies, there are many questions we want answered.[6] We want to know (a) how intentions in the mind must be formed in order to have effects in the body, and (b) how the physical body can be affected by those intentions. We also need to know (c) how the mind can be influenced by the body, for example when it perceives the physical world or when diseases affect the operation of the mind, and (d) what it is about our body that makes it able to influence minds. Is it something in our brains which does this, or does all of our body influence the content of our minds? Are things outside our bodies also related to minds?

Finally, we need to solve what Kim[7] calls the 'pairing problem'. How can distinct non-physical minds be connected with distinct bodies if those relations are not mechanical or spatial? If we do not have detailed answers to these questions, we want at least to see the basis on which answers may be found after further investigations in theistic science. The ingredients of many of these answers can be found in the previous chapters of this Part, but here I bring them together.

Intentions affecting the physical

An answer to question (a), which concerns how intentions in the mind must be formed in order to have effects in the body, is straightforward within our generative level structure. The intentions, having been started from some love and developed by means of thoughts and considerations, must be carried forward to the external mind sub-degree 2.3, as described in Table 22.3. More specifically, they must be actualized all the way to the sensorimotor sub-sub-degree 2.33, as listed in Table 22.6. That there is such a level (or module) is a commonplace assumption in psychology.

---

[6] The historical lack of detailed answers has led many people to despair of dualism, as they wonder how minds and bodies—things so different—could possibly interact with each other. This bizarrely led them to deny even the possibility and evidence of interaction: the very thing that is so immediately obvious to us in almost every minute of our daily lives!

[7] Kim, "Soul, body, and survival."

It is called 'motor' because it is the last place in the mind where intentions must exist if they are to have neural and then muscular effects in the physical brain and then in the body.

How (b) the physical body can be affected by those intentions is a more complicated question. Neither theistic science nor ordinary science has a detailed answer. When discussing the components of the physical degree in Section 24.1 and again in Section 24.5, we saw that, according to theistic science, there is a sub-degree 3.1 which is concerned precisely with receiving mental intentions into the physical. This is exactly the process that would be forbidden if the physical degree were causally closed, but it is necessary within theism for the reasons given in Section 20.6 with reference to connections between divinity and nature. Theism implies that the conservations of energy and momentum are only approximations that hold when and where there is no reception of intentions. We may wonder whether such reception shows up as discrepancies in the conservation laws or by some other symptom. If we knew, then experiments would be possible to investigate this process, in our brains in particular.

To begin investigating how the physical world may function as not causally closed, I first note that the 'receptive sub-degree' 3.1 has its effects on the quantum-field-theory processes in sub-degree 3.2, in particular on the physical field Lagrangian in sub-sub-degree 3.21. I speculate that reception of intentions will show up as local spatio-temporal variations in the coupling constants that appear in the physical Lagrangian. The value of unit electric charge (or, equivalently, the fine-structure constant[8] normally labeled as α) could *vary* by rather small amounts according to received intentions, and such variations would certainly affect the operations of biochemistry and hence of organic physiology.[9] Local variations of the fine-structure constant should be easily measurable by magnetic resonance imaging if the time resolution of those measurements could be sig-

---

[8] The fine-structure constant is $\alpha = e^2/\hbar c$, where e is the unit electric charge, $\hbar$ is Planck's constant, and c is the speed of light. It has been measured to be $\alpha = 1/137.035999$, at least outside living organisms. Every atomic and molecular structure and reaction rate depends critically on the value of the fine-structure constant.

[9] Physicists, especially cosmologists such as Sandvik, Barrow, and Magueijo ("A simple cosmology with a varying fine structure constant") and Bekenstein and Schiffer ("Varying fine structure 'constant' and charged black holes"), are already considering the possibility of the fine-structure constant varying on a universe-wide scale, maybe depending, for example, on the age of the universe. Of course, it would not then be a constant, but a 'constant'. Murphy, Webb, and Flambaum ("Further evidence for a variable fine-structure constant from Keck/HIRES QSO absorption spectra") discuss astronomical evidences for such a variation. Theistic science considers *local* variations of the same kind. Re-imagining global symmetries or variations in a local form is a well-known technique in physics for suggesting new theories.

nificantly improved. This idea concerning the fine structure 'constant' is just one suggestion for what could vary within physics. Other possibilities should also be considered.

Perceptions affecting the mental

We next ask (c), how the mind can be influenced by the body when we (mentally) perceive the physical world. Let us consider perception first, since that is a familiar operation. When we perceive with our senses, with our eyes for example, we come to have ideas which depend on those physical things (light waves, sound vibrations, etc.) that have been perceived. How is this possible?

The process of perception seems difficult within the multilevel structure of generation and selection since the physical degree has no direct causal influence on the mental. Strictly speaking, the causation is always 'forward' from the mental to the physical and not the reverse. However, the process of selection, which is also part of the theistic scheme, can be organized so as to give perception, which is the influence of the physical on the mental. Theistic science makes a precise prediction for the manner of operation of the senses in giving input to the mind. The sensory part of the mind must be able to generate the whole (wide) range of possible perceptions, so the physical input may select which ones will actually occur and hence determine which perception will exist in the mind.

Perceptions are formed by senses causing the sensory cortical areas of the brain to have deterministically particular patterns of neural activity, so that these physiological effects can select the subsequent perceptual content of the mind as it generatively interacts with the brain. The process here is rather subtle. The mind must have a general disposition to see/imagine *any* of its possible percepts; the role of the sensory cortex is to *select* the particular content. This implies the general psychological principle that 'we see only what we are capable of and disposed to see'.[10] Since the mind can recognize things (such as a four-leaf clover) that it has never seen before, the ability of the mind to generate possible perceptions must accord

---

[10] This principle, that 'we only see what we want to see', might be considered already well known. One consequence is that we do not see what we are not expecting or attending to see. This is the well-studied phenomenon of 'inattentional blindness'.

with generative rules or procedures and not merely by associations with memories of what has been seen in the past.

There is a physical analogy between mental perception and physical sight here which may prove useful. It develops the idea discussed in Section 14.5. When we see things in the physical world, we use light to illuminate those objects, and our eyes receive the secondary light rays reflected, filtered and selected according to the nature of the seen objects. Our sight can only be accurate if the initial incident light is clear and composed of all colors equally since seeing things in colored light does not give an accurate picture. Similarly with mental perception: there must be received into our mental space a 'clear light' that contains all forms and sensations that can possibly be the means of seeing. Our perception depends then on filtering and selecting from this set of all forms, in such a way that what remains is according to the nature of what is seen. With mental perception, this 'clear light' must come from loves and wisdom higher in the mind and originally from God (according to Section 14.3). If our interior loves and/or wisdom are not clear but colored, not impartial but prejudiced, then our *mental* perceptions will similarly be not accurate. There is always the possibility of biasing perceptions whenever specific expectations or prejudices already exist in the mind.

25.3 Correspondences

We next ask (d) what is it about our body that makes it able to influence minds by selection? Is it something in our brains which does this, or does all of our body influence the content of our minds? Are things outside our bodies also related to minds? How do bodily diseases affect the operation of the mind?

We have to consider the spatial and time organizations of minds and bodies, which is not something considered yet in this book in much detail. There was some preliminary discussion in Section 20.6, where it was stated (in anticipation of a full theory) that our bodies are physical systems whose purpose within theism is to provide an overall container or enduring structure that can persistently select a rather complicated set of internal dispositions. We must now think about how this works and how details of 'enduring structure' of complex organic bodies could be important and be part of our answer to question (d).

Let us revisit the argument of Section 20.3 to consider the mental and physical degrees. Each has its own detailed set of constituent events. Because of all these microscopic events, there will be successive influx from the mental degree reciprocating with sequential constraints by previous events in the physical degree. I claim that this alternation will repeat itself longest if the *patterns* of the constituent events are most similar in the two degrees, and if they do not get out of step. By a 'survival of the fittest', the patterns remaining after a long time will be those that are common to both the mental and physical degrees. This commonality is not of shape or substance but of the 'network of events'. The two degrees in this case will be undergoing processes which execute similar overall functions because the pattern of internal events will be quite similar. In the long term this gives rise to *correspondences of function* between adjacent degrees.

In the arguments in the previous two chapters we often used the similarity of overall functions of sets of sub-sub-degrees that were in the same relative place within their own degrees. This was called a correspondence of function. Now we have something a little more general. There can be correspondences of function within two adjacent levels where the function is that of the complex organic and spatial structures in the two levels, in particular of the functional patterns of their events.

Thus we will have 'correspondences of function' between the mental and physical degrees. Our minds and brains will sustain each other by influx and constraint when psychological and neural processes are most nearly isomorphic to each other in their functional description, as Fingelkurts, Fingelkurts, and Neves[11] have for other reasons suggested. Thus the mind predisposes the brain to carry out those functions which 'mirror' or 'correspond to' the mind's own functions.

The answer to question (d) is that our bodies (as physical structures) are best able to influence minds (by selection) when they have a detailed internal pattern of events and functions which are most similar to the internal pattern of events and functions that go on within the mind. This is apparently much more likely within living bodies, and especially within brains, though the reasons for this are not yet fully clear.

There still remains the question of neurological diseases and their effects on the mind. There is the well-known example of Phineas Gage, whose

---

[11] Fingelkurts, Fingelkurts, and Neves, "Natural world physical, brain operational, and mind phenomenal space–time."

personality was altered when a large steel bar went through his brain in a railroad-building accident. For many people, the very existence of such effects is taken as evidence for materialism: that the mind depends on the brain. In theistic science, we agree that the mind does *in part* depend on the brain. How else could perception function at all? Though we do not have complete dependence or supervenience of all details of the mind on brain function, the brain does still have a significant role in the formation of the mind. Throughout this book, especially in Section 20.6, we have seen how the physical actions we perform are the basis for our having our own independent life. Our physical brains are intermediate steps in the operation of this basis. If this is true, then it is to be *expected* that neurological (and, in fact, all other physiological) diseases will have some effects in the development of our minds.

There is much to be learned by derivation and observation about the details here, not just in mind-brain functioning but throughout living organisms. Discrete degrees are never of a continuous substance with each other. Yet, we now see, they have functional relations that make them 'contiguously intertwined' at all stages and at all levels of detail at each stage.

The mind and brain thus fit together by approximate analogy with hand and glove, or, better, with subcutaneous tissue and its outer skin. The analogy is most precisely with the *functions* of tissue and skin and not so much with their material shape. The mind provides all the directed activity of the brain just as the tissue of the hand provides all the directed activity of the skin of the hand. When we look inside the physical head we see only the brain, just as we only see skin when we look at the hand. It *appears* that the skin of the hand does all the work, but we don't assume that that is all there is. It *appears* that the skin has life, but we know that all but the simplest life comes from the underlying tissue. The skin (like the brain) has simple capacities for action and reactions, but it is a mistake to imagine that all capacities for activity and information processing belong to the skin (or the brain).

This theory of mind and brain connection establishes an intimate relation between them. It is not a relation of identity or a relation of aspects or points of view. It is more a relation of inner and outer or of cause and effect. Propensities in the brain are the causal product of mental actions. We now understand better the claim of Bawden[12] that we wrote of in Sec-

---

[12] Bawden, "The psychical as a biological directive."

tion 4.8: "the role of the psychical in relation to the physical (in the living organism) is essentially the relation of the potential or incipient to kinetic or overt action." Admittedly, Bawden was thinking only of *physical* potentials, but we now see that his claim is true in theistic science once mental dispositions are allowed to exist.

25.4 Distinct minds and bodies

One question is what Kim[13] calls the 'pairing problem': how can distinct non-physical minds be connected with distinct bodies if those relations are not mechanical or spatial?

To begin to answer, we note a previous suggestion that the topology and metric of mental and spiritual spaces are associative with respect to meaning and function, since proximity is then determined by those features. This would imply that the connections of a mind with anything else should be based on the meaning and function of that other thing. This also implies that the connections of a particular mind to a particular body, according to theistic science, should be initiated and maintained by the particular *functions* that each particular mind and body accomplishes together, since the possibility of interaction always depends on proximity in the relevant space.

25.5 Spiritual-natural relations

All of the above descriptions of the connections between the mental and physical can be applied analogously to the connections between the spiritual and the mental. There will be widespread and thorough-going correspondences between functions of internal spiritual processes and the functions of internal mental processes. All of the processes (a)-(d) may be applied again to these connections in ways that are analogous to the above explanations.[14]

Using both these sets of correspondences, we can generate corresponding relations between spiritual and natural events. The correspondences

---

[13] Kim, "Soul, body, and survival."

[14] The elucidation of the details here and clarification of exactly how the analogies fail or prevail in the new applications is left as an exercise for the reader (or a later edition of this book).

of natural with spiritual things are very useful to give definite and permanent form to our ideas of Love (which otherwise tend to be vague and
nebulous). We have, for example, the idea that "the Divine Love operates
by means of Wisdom, to produce outgoing Spirit and actions". This *corresponds* to the pattern in the physical world, where "physical dispositions
(energies and propensities) operate by means of interactions in spatial relations to produce physical effects". Love is *like* a disposition or physical
energy or vibration, but it is *not identical* to anything physical. We have
many metaphors and analogies between the spiritual and the physical. To
forget this is to think physically and naturally of spiritual realities and thus
to make one or more of the ontological errors concerning spirituality that
are listed in Section 23.2.

Several of these correspondences have been used in this and previous
chapters as illustrations. They help visualize non-physical processes. They
are also often used in religious scriptures, as a means for representing spiritual processes in everyday language. This makes them memorable even if
spirituality itself is not yet recognized. I now present a list of candidates for
such correspondences. I have listed first the physical processes and then
the spiritual or mental processes to which they correspond:

1. The sun is the source of physical light in the world, and God (as Wisdom itself) is the source of understanding for us. We see physical things
   best by reflections of the clear light of the sun, and we understand (have
   'insight', or 'see') ideas best when we receive the clear light of rationality from God.
2. The first living reception of light from the sun is by green leaves, where
   (with other inputs) it is used for plant growth. This corresponds to our
   first reception of the clear light of rationality from God since this has a
   similar function.
3. Our everyday physical life is sustained (in part) by food that is swal-
   lowed and digested to give energy. This corresponds to our everyday
   spiritual life being sustained by reception of spiritual food which consists of new ideas and affections. Some food is from plants, which correspond to preliminary rational structures already built up.
4. Digested food is distributed throughout our body through blood vessels by means of the heart. This corresponds to the way new ideas and
   affections in our spiritual body are conveyed to where they are useful
   by the way we receive, store and re-enact loves.

5. Plants also produce oxygen, which via the atmosphere is received by us in our lungs and also conveyed through our blood vessels to where actions are produced in cells, especially in our internal and external muscles. This corresponds to the way rationality, after first reception, is conveyed to where it can inform the operation of loves.

6. The brain is the overall controller of what happens in the body. This corresponds to the way spiritual loves and principles are the general source of mental activities in our mind.

7. Our bodies are held together by an overlying skin. This corresponds to the way the physical degree acts as a 'container' and basis for our mental and spiritual life.

8. Our bodies are held together by internal membranes. This corresponds to the way there are internal sub-...-sub-degrees throughout our spiritual and mental bodies that have the role of the 'third sub-degree' that correspond, as images of God, to Action within God.

9. Animal bodies typically have bilateral (left-right) symmetry or near-symmetry. I speculate that this corresponds with the spiritual fact that every internal process requires the joint operation of love and wisdom, and that these must have been received in similar (but spatially distinct) manners before that joint operation.

I believe that all of these have some basis in reality, even if some at first seem far fetched. There are many more correspondences to be found and elucidated. I speculate that *all* of the physical world (from galaxies to solar systems to ecologies to physiology) will be found to correspond with internal spiritual functions and hence with images of God. This claim is based on the fact (within theism) that God is the original source of life of all these physical things, and hence that nothing can persistently exist that is not an image of God according to some correspondences of function. Since, in this case, all the parts of a mind will be similarly related to all the parts of the brain and/or body, there is much more to be investigated.

25.6 The human (functional) form

When we think about the correspondences proposed in the previous section, we see many details which are found in our human bodies. They are not found in the shape, size or mass of our body but in the *functional form* of humans. They are found in the patterns and networks of events within our human functional form since this network pattern is what sustains the connections with our mental and spiritual bodies. Other animals, even plants, have limited or simplified forms which are functional in their own individual ways.

Within theistic science, the hypothesis concerning the human functional form will have important consequences for the possibilities of, say, life on other planets and especially for the evolution of life on this planet. We do not predict that possible extraterrestrial beings will look exactly like humans, but that, though their bodies may be very different, their internal functions will have a 'topological' structure that is also an image of God and hence will have some similarities to our own.

Part V

Applications

26

Evolution

26.1 Causal explanations

WHEN WE look for an explanation of how life came to exist on earth, we want not just descriptions or a few reasons why life happened. We want to know about the *causes* for what has happened. Any theory of evolution must depend on a theory of what kinds of causes exist and of how these causes operate. If theistic science investigation proposes a new (and plausible) account of how causes operate in the world, we are obliged to reconsider the theory of evolution and revise it to take into account the proposed kinds of causes and their manners of operation.

Darwin, in fact, was motivated to develop his theory of evolution via natural selection because he precisely wanted to follow the then new naturalistic theory of causation. It was the theory in which God was *not* involved in the day-to-day running of the universe. From an early stage, Darwin looked for a theory in which a self-sustaining and self-developing natural world could produce all the living creatures seen today without God being responsible for its details and (in particular) not being responsible for the disease, predation, and parasitism that he saw. We may debate whether or not Darwin's theory is plausible or successful with its causal explanations. However, within the absent-God causal scenario, it is clear that it is more or less the only possible explanation. As a result, it has today a very large number of followers. Many of them are still seeking the detailed causal explanations but uniformly agree on the 'sanctity' of the laws of nature within a naturalist philosophy.

There are many scientists who do profess religion and think that theism and Darwin's theory can co-exist. This compatibility is possible since theism means to them that God sustains the world, and Darwin has described how creatures *in* the world have functioned and developed together.[1] This view, however, is equivalent to deism, not theism. It holds that God is not involved with the world once its operation has started (except, perhaps, in special events such as the founding and/or culmination of new religions). Once 'laws of nature' are assumed to be inviolate, Darwinism can accommodate such deistic views.

Within our new scientific theism we are unable to follow Darwin, in either the naturalistic or deistic world views. When God sustains the universe, this is *not* accomplished 'at a distance' by 'merely sustaining' the universe according to laws of physics but (we now conclude) by the *presence* of God in some degree. There can be no power without substance and no substance without present existence, as was argued in Chapter 4. This means that any sustaining action of God in the world will necessarily require the reception of life from God, not abstractly but as a substance really existing. This life is not always according to fixed physical laws. It necessarily has spiritual and mental components that will be effective if a suitable receptive form (e.g. a human form) is present. The fitness of a living organism is not purely a function of its interactions with the physical world and other organisms. It depends *also* and *at least* on the fullness of its reception of life from God. This implies that, within a proper theism, it is impossible to have a purely naturalistic account of evolution. Fitness, and hence selection, are not entirely natural. They are subject also to spiritual and mental considerations.

One common alternative to the theory of natural selection is the theory of intelligent design. The intelligent design theory, however, is deliberately limited, as it does not attempt a causal explanation. It tries to develop techniques to examine physical organisms and then to determine whether or not that examination provides evidence for the existence of an intelligence in the coming to be (or design) of those organisms. Strictly, it is neutral on whether the intelligence is God or whether it might be previously-existing extra-terrestrial beings who have (say) genetically-engineered the organism. Because intelligent design theory does not produce causal accounts, it is often criticized as lacking in predictive power. It does make general 'structural' predictions about the forms expected to occur within living organisms, but it will never, it seems, yield the detailed prior and condi-

---

[1] They remind us of Galileo's phrase, "Scripture teaches us how to go to heaven, not how the heavens go."

tional probabilities necessary to form Bayesian arguments of the kind that many scientists use to assess the likelihoods of the hypotheses they are considering. See, for example, the discussion by Sober[2].

Intelligent design theory has generated an extraordinary amount of animosity from mainstream (naturalistic) scientists. They often accuse it of being false. Then they simultaneously accuse it of being non-scientific because non-falsifiable! By comparison, theistic science is advocating a much *stronger* theory than intelligent design since it cannot be neutral about 'the nature of the designer'. We start from the assumption that God exists, as being itself and life itself.

Another common alternative to natural selection is creationism, where different species are created individually and specifically by God according to the first chapter of Genesis that culminates in the creation of man (and woman). These acts of creation, with whole new populations of plants or animals coming into existence, would have been rather spectacular to watch! Are such special creations possible according to theistic science? The answer, we next see, is *no*.

26.2 God needs evolution

On the basis of the arguments developed in theistic science, I conclude that God can *not* create immediately.

First of all, God cannot create self-sustaining organisms immediately for the reasons given in Section 12.2. Any new self-sustaining organism will (by definition) have life in itself. Snce God is life itself, such an organism cannot be essentially distinct from God but really must *be* God. That is indeed logically possible, but then God could not love that being unselfishly because it would not be sufficiently distinct from God. In fact, God is not us (we can tell by examining humanity's behavior) , and God loves us unselfishly, so this direct route is not used by God.

Secondly, God cannot create robust theistically-sustained organisms immediately. By 'theistically sustained', I mean like us (humans, animals, and plants), sustained by reception of all the discrete degrees of life according to theistic science. By robust, I mean organisms that can fend for themselves in the physical world. For this, the organisms must be sufficiently

---

[2] Sober, "Intelligent design and probability reasoning."

'thick skinned', rather than 'thin skinned' and overly susceptible to contrary influences from outside. That God cannot create robust individuals immediately can be discerned from this idea of 'thickness of skin' and the correspondences of skin as outlined in Section 25.5. Let me explain the argument in more detail:

Suppose someone creates a new spiritual affection or a new mental idea. This can be done rather easily, and then we may have that affection or idea in our mind. But be careful, lest we forget it! Forgetting can done even more easily than formation. Forgetfulness is common if we do not constantly pay attention and if we do not make some memory to remind us in the future. Memories make a permanent physical trace that is caused by the idea. New content in the mind is evanescent and disappears quickly if there is no physical effect either from producing an outward action or from an internal memory trace. This would not construct robust individuals with an apparent life of their own. To be created immediately like this is to have no 'skin' at all. A lack of skin is the condition which *corresponds* to having no physical basis for the permanence of one's spiritual life.

Some religious people ask, but did not God create Adam rather quickly, and was he not a whole person? In reply, I first note that I believe that the first 11 chapters of Genesis have only a meaning based on correspondences and *not* a literal or historical sense. Let us examine the story of the creation of Adam and Eve for its spiritual meaning. In that story, God did create Adam almost immediately. Adam (and Eve) were 'very good' and lived full of innocent, unashamed and wonderful love in the Garden of Eden. But look what happened next: there was a 'fall' within the first generation! This was hardly a robust life. Adam and Eve were thin-skinned rather than thick-skinned individuals. And look what prompted their fall in this story: it was the desire of Eve to 'be as gods, knowing good and evil'.[3] To want to 'be as a god' is to fail to realize that one can *not* be a god. It is to argue from appearance and to forget that one has life *only* 'as if' from God. These newly created individuals lacked a robust intellectual discrimination concerning even a fundamental truth of theism. They were therefore easily led astray by superficial and erroneous conclusions.[4]

To create permanent and robust individuals, they must be developed so

[3] Genesis 3:5.
[4] Such superficial conclusions are those reached on the basis of only appearance and external knowledge and not on understanding or wisdom. To conclude on the basis of only appearance is to have eyes not looking up but only at ground level, like a snake.

that, at every stage of their life, they are *thick*-skinned, which is to have a substantial history of physical actions in the past and mental and spiritual lives built on that. Since not even God can create history, this means that a longer and slower process of creation is needed if a race of people is to be developed who have fully-developed and long-lasting characters to be loved and to love in return.

The creation of such people must be gradual, by means of a series of beings that themselves have their own personal histories. The process may only start by some simpler physical action by God if one could be found that did not require a history of its own. Once such an *ab initio* physical event has occurred, all subsequent actions must be gradual and by means of successive modifications of what already exists. This is what we (should) call *evolution*. It is *needed* by God. There can be no immediate creation of new beings, neither plants, nor animals, nor humans. There are no instant adults. There can only be gradual internal modifications of already-existing beings. God has to be patient.

These arguments concerning biological evolution may hardly be known by religious people or theologians today, but surely they can see the same logic at work in the development of individual spiritual lives and in the creation of new religions or churches. When developing our spiritual life, God works with what we are and tries to improve that. Such changes cannot be sudden, or we would lose our sense of individual existence. That certainly could not be permitted. Some will argue that the influx of grace may have a sudden effect and that the creation of a new religion by revelation or incarnation is surely a sudden process. My answer is that gratuitous grace has indeed dramatic influence, but the real task of religion is *afterwards*, when we return to our original lives and diligently seek to modify our previous habits into the new pattern that was briefly glimpsed.[5] With Paul, the well-known recipient of grace, the assimilation took more than ten years, probably fourteen years![6] It is similar with new religions. Miracles do convert quickly. Jesus always asked beforehand whether the person was prepared: whether he or she 'had faith'. That meant there would be some continuity even in these miraculous cases. It is well known

---

[5] Most people in similar situations are only too well aware of the conflicts between the old and the new loves. This conflict (and the resulting temptations) is often painful and never very quickly resolved. That is because, since our being is our deepest love, it is ultimately a question of identity: of who we are. Are we our old or our new loves? We never change instantaneously from one to another, but only by means of bridges.

[6] 2 Corinthians 12:2 and Galatians 1:2.

that the receivers of a new religion are often recalcitrant in keeping their old rituals that are supposed to be given up. The greatest number of religious conversions are by assimilation rather than by replacement precisely because of the need for continuity in our most permanent biological and spiritual lives.

26.3 Descent by modification

Since God needs to develop living creatures by means of a continuity of physical forms, evolution must proceed by means of descent by modification. This phrase is often taken to *define* Darwin's theory of natural selection, to distinguish his theory from that of immediate, special and separate creations. Now, however, different terminology is needed. Since Darwin thought of his theory as natural selection, let us describe ours as containing *theistic selection*. Where he talked about survival of the fittest, we agree, as long as we do not forget that fitness also depends on reception of life from God, a reception that also depends on our organic structures. Thus, in theistic selection, we have also a survival according to reception. We are talking here only about what factors influence the survival of plants or animals in the world. We especially mean those that are in addition to physical and ecological factors already known. Theistic selection must include all the considerations of natural selection as well since the natural or physical degree is an essential part of our theistic structure.

The details of the *causes and means* of modifications remain an open question within theistic science. Two limiting cases for these causes can be called the 'hands on' and 'hands off' treatments by God. The hands-off case is when the only sources of modifications are random mutations, genetic drift and genetic recombinations during reproduction, just as in present-day neo-Darwinism. That is, God would wait for suitable new forms of organisms to naturally arise, and then the degree to which these new organisms are physically, mentally and perhaps spiritually fit will mean that they live longer and be more likely to reproduce. There is therefore both natural and theistic selection, but the actual *origin* of the species is explained in the same way as by contemporary evolutionary theory.

According to the 'hands off' explanatory theory, we would see why the *forms* of organisms are not arbitrary. The theistic component of the selection process means that creatures who are able to successfully receive and retain life from God are more likely to survive and hence to reproduce. Over the long term, organisms that have the human form will tend to be produced because they will be favored numerically in any competition for limited resources or (say) in resistance to diseases. Their mental perceptions and thoughts will more accurately portray reality. This hands-off view is one kind of theistic evolution. Let us call it *theistically-filtered evolution* to distinguish it from the common view of 'theistic evolution' wherein God does not have any kind of causal or filtering role in evolution at all.[7]

The other limiting case is that of 'hands on' management by God. In this limit, God is continually involved in the day-to-day influx of divine life and hence also in the long-term management of genetic and physiological structures. That is, God would be not infrequently be producing modifications to the molecular structures of organisms, but in such a way that this is not directly noticed by the creature. The creature is never deprived of its sense of living *as if* from itself. In Chapter 12 we saw that this was a fundamental requirement for all life on earth, with the result that any new modifications must in some way be hidden from having immediate effects, at least until the being develops new loves that want and correspond to the new molecular structures. We could call this limit *theistically-driven evolution*. We should expect some 'driven nature' of evolution if we think that God has a particular interest in or desire concerning its result. In the 'fully driven' limit, which we might expect if God is completely benevolent, unselfish, and diligent in wanting us to develop, God will be doing everything possible to manage the detailed generation of genetics, species, and ecologies to accomplish first what is good and later what is very good.

All of these kinds of theistic evolution imply that the actual causes of evolution are internal. If we watch evolution in progress, we always see *continuous* changes in living organisms. And even if we could examine the physical and molecular structures of the organisms during that evolution, we would still only see continuous paths of the molecules. There is never any 'popping into physical existence' of a new creature or species where there had been empty space. Neither is there any sudden creation of new creatures 'out of dust'. Even the very simplest bacterium has a complex internal structure that must already correspond to some simple mental sub-degree and therefore cannot be created immediately by God. Other-

---

[7] That common use of the term 'theistic evolution' should more precisely be called 'deistic evolution', since deism is the view that, once God created the world, the universe developed in time according to purely natural laws and without any so-called 'interference' from God.

wise the non-physical sub-degree would be missing its 'skin' of previous historical actions as the basis for that bacterium's independent life. This necessary physical continuity what is meant by 'descent by modification', by gradual modification. Descent by modification, we conclude, cannot be used to characterize Darwinism or neo-Darwinism, since now we see that it is a necessary component of any theory of evolution within theism.

We may think of theistically-driven evolution as intelligent design since God is intelligent and God is continually working on and modifying species. However, it is certainly not part of the 'design and build' procedure as we know it in, say, engineering. God is always working with existing biological creatures and doing the best that is possible to pull creatures into life, always according to knowledge of the physical structures that will successfully receive and retain their mental and spiritual life. Patience is clearly needed. Sometimes beings, once developed, are invaded or eaten by others (infection and predation) if that helps the function of the overall ecology though perhaps not some of the individual beings. The requirement of physical continuity means that the beings possible within a given time scale have genetic or epigenetic[8] relics from previous creatures whose genes were modified to make the present creature. This must happen often since no creature is a creation *ab initio*. There is always a development from what already exists towards what is desired in the future.

26.4 Why evolution is true

There are many similarities of theistically-driven evolution with raising a family or raising democracy in a nation. We never begin from scratch. Sudden changes are rarely successful. Everyone must gradually develop his own character, as if from himself. Molecular designs will have been selected, not only for physical efficiency, but *also* for their ability to receive theistic influx and so represent some small part of the human functional form in the mental and spiritual degrees. It may be that putative examples of 'bad design' have their good uses when the needs for reception are taken into account. We certainly cannot decide 'good design' on purely physical grounds since the overall purpose is always the coming into existence of human-like beings who are able to spiritually receive, retain, and delight in (and hence return) the love of God. When evolution comes

---

[8] In the cell, but not part of the genome.

to the spiritual stage where actions during the life have very long-lasting consequences, then phenomena of disease, predation, etc take on new importance and have to be managed to minimize their occurrence.

Many scientific investigations are still needed, even given the concept of theistically-driven evolution. We still have to understand the history of life on earth and the frequencies of genes in the various populations. We still have the problem of finding transitional species. Even in the hands-on limit, there must still be transitional forms between the main taxa of life in the various eras. There are the same needs here for evidence as in Darwinian evolution. The development of a new species may now seem easy to explain, perhaps too easy, but speciation is still a difficult process to understand and to accomplish. There must have been preparatory collection and harboring of new genetic information in the non-functional parts of existing genomes until these new sections could be activated together to give birth to a new species. How, given what we know of molecular genetics, could that have been managed? And managed simultaneously in several creatures of a species (especially if there is sexual reproduction)? Apart from that word 'managed', the questions of the continuous variations of genetic structures are very similar to those asked by Darwinian evolutionists. Therefore such research work is still needed.

The origin of life is still difficult to understand, even if now it is not so astronomically improbable as it would be according to a purely naturalistic account. We need to understand how the materials for life were assembled together into a form that keeps some perpetuating structure of its own. If you watch these materials in detail they will not follow exactly the laws of physics of inanimate bodies. Only the very simplest structures can be directly assembled (for reasons explained above). After the first assemblies, all else must follow by driving 'behind the scenes' to make these evolve gradually into new forms of life. The difficulties, even for God, of assembling organisms (as if from themselves) are sufficiently numerous that the idea that all the world's creatures came from just one ancestor ('universal common descent') seems (to me) to be rather plausible. Whether it is also true must be the subject of scientific investigations, but, certainly, universal common descent cannot be used as distinguishing feature of only Darwin's theory.

We will look again at the meanings of religious scriptures such as the first chapters of Genesis to properly understand the manner in which living beings come into existence.

26.5 Evidence

Three theories that should be compared with observational and experimental evidence are

A. **neo-Darwinian theory:** random mutations, genetic drift and recombination, natural selection,

B. **theistically filtered evolution:** random mutations, genetic drift and recombination, natural *and theistic* selection,

C. **theistically driven evolution:** *preselected and* random mutations, genetic drift and recombination, natural *and theistic* selection.

Most evidence for neo-Darwinian evolutionary theory is based on continuous but gradual changes of physical form, especially of genetic information. All that evidence can no longer discriminate between the Darwinian theory, A, and the B and C theistic theories above. Still, it ought to be possible to devise statistical tests to distinguish between the three theories.

Detailed predictions for the theistic selection theory B will depend on advances in theistic science, especially concerning the manner in which variable theistic influx influences the behavior of organisms and concerning the manner in which partial 'images' of the human form may function mentally and physiologically. The mental aspect of this functioning will be discussed further in Chapter 27.

The detailed predictions for the theistic mutations theory C are more difficult to make. They depend God's 'management policy' for biological evolution. Probably, we will have to examine and make predictions for specific limiting cases for this policy, such as mutations confined to the DNA sequence or mutations concerning the gene expression mechanisms or mutations affecting other epi-genetic control mechanisms of cells.

Since the theistic theories are fully-fledged causal theories of evolution and therefore are not arbitrarily disqualified before evaluation, the questions to be answered are the relative probabilities of the three theories in light of the empirical evidence available. According to Sober[9] and Sober[10], this assessment should use Bayesian arguments in probability theory, using what is called the Law of Likelihood:

Observation O favors hypothesis H_1 over hypothesis H_2 precisely when $Pr(O|H_1) > Pr(O|H_2)$. And the strength of the favoring relation is to be measured by the likelihood ratio $Pr(O|H_1)/Pr(O|H_2)$.

Here, the expression $Pr(O|H)$ means "the conditional probability of O, given H."

In order to compare the three hypotheses A, B and C above, we need to determine the three conditional probabilities $p_A = Pr(O, H_A)$, $p_B = Pr(O, H_B)$, and $p_C = Pr(O, H_C)$, where O denotes the sum of the empirical evidence concerning the history of life. We determine whether either of the theistic hypotheses B or C is favored over the neo-Darwinian theory A by seeing whether either of the ratios p_B/p_A or p_C/p_A is larger than unity.

Most neo-Darwinists say that if evolution were repeated, it is very unlikely that humans as we know them would be produced again. They agree that the probability p_A of producing rational humans is extremely low because of the occurrence of the many fortuitous mutations, drifts and selections that occur without any oversight. Given Darwin's theory A, therefore, we insist that the occurrence of human life, though not impossible, is still clearly an extraordinary event and hence one that must *require* an extraordinary explanation.

Our first estimates of these ratios p_B/p_A and p_C/p_A place them much larger than unity since the theistic additions in B and C compared with Darwin's theory A do indeed make the likelihood of life on earth much greater than that predicted by theory A. In this case, both the theistic theories are judged to be favored over Darwinian theory. I will then be reminded, and admit, that this requires an independent and robust prediction of 'theistic selection' on independent grounds and not one based merely on observations of existing forms. Otherwise the prediction of the success of human forms would be entirely circular. Making such independent predictions is the task of theistic science.

A more detailed likelihood analysis should also consider the relative 'prior probabilities' that enter into Bayesian arguments of likelihood. I con-

---

[9] Sober, "Intelligent design and probability reasoning."
[10] Sober, "Did Darwin write the origin backwards?"

cede that the prior probability for theism is less than for any naturalistic account of the universe and may well be as low as 10%, 1%, or even lower, at least in the eyes of modern-day scientists. Such prior probabilities should be taken into account, therefore, in any full calculation of the likelihood of theistically-filtered or theistically-driven evolution in relation to observations and also in comparison with neo-Darwinian theories.

27

Consciousness

QUESTIONS of what consciousness is, who or what is conscious, and what they are conscious of, have been touched on in previous chapters. Now we focus on these issues specifically and compare our answers to what has has been suggested by philosophers and scientists over the years.

27.1 The hard problem

Chalmers[1] has divided the problems of understanding consciousness into two kinds. There are 'easy problems' about sensations, discrimination of patterns, information processing, and deliberate control of behavior. These are associated with the notion of consciousness. Chalmers thinks there is no real issue about whether these phenomena can be explained scientifically, for example by computational or neural mechanisms. These easy problems are to be contrasted with the 'hard problem' concerning the nature of *experience*, of *qualia* (the appearance that sensations present to our mind). The actual *awareness* that is part of consciousness appears to be a kind of 'inner glow' that accompanies and illuminates sensations and experiences but in a way that is mysterious to computational scientists and neurologists. What is missing, when we just discuss the mechanisms, is 'what it is like' to actually *be* the organism in question and to experience these qualia as our own.

The work of Chalmers initiated a minor industry that speculates about such questions as whether organisms can function without any accompa-

---

[1] Chalmers, "Facing up to the problem of consciousness."

nying consciousness. Can be 'zombies' that live as we do except without consciousness? If you say no to zombies, what reasons can you give? Are they impossible logically, or psychologically, or neurologically, or linguistically? Some philosophers (including Chalmers) have tried to formulate a 'property dualism', whereby consciousness is a property of natural objects alongside other physical properties of mass, charge, etc., but yet does not affect the causal closure of physics, which most of them want to preserve.

Consciousness or awareness does not seem to have a causal role in psychology that is independent of the causal mechanisms that underpin whatever may be the basis for thinking and feeling. Whether these causal mechanisms are in the brain or in some other substance to be determined, consciousness itself does not appear to have causal roles in our mental life. We are sure it is *there*, but what does it *do*?

One philosophy that gives a definite answer is that of Aquinas. He asserts that consciousness is a property of the immaterial intellect and is moreover an *essential* property of the intellectual mind. He does not allow for a mechanistic explanation of the operation of consciousness because the mind is to him a *simple substance*, not composed of any parts, and so has consciousness (and intellection, will, etc.) by its very essence. A simple substance mind with such essential properties would indeed solve the hard problem. However, it would solve it at the cost of not allowing science to investigate the detailed processes of thinking and feeling or of perception of truth or loving what is good. These are the processes that we actually investigated in Part IV, on the basis that the mind was *not simple* but was composed of parts in some mental spaces, in several discrete degrees. Therefore, we do not accept the Thomist view of mind as a simple substance. We instead seek a more scientific understanding of all the detailed processes that go on in our minds. It is not impossible to have simple minds, but they do not fit within the theistic science that is now being developed.

27.2 Awareness

We adopt Postulate 17, from Section 18.7, as the basis for further discussion within theistic science concerning the existence and content of consciousness. This is the postulate that "Whenever love acts by means of wisdom, that action is a conscious action. There is consciousness of the production of the result and also of the delight that arises from the achievement of that production." Since love and wisdom are both received from God, as derivative dispositions, this postulate claims that whenever those two received things act again *together*, the result is a conscious action.

According to this postulate, consciousness accompanies all processes and actions within the mental and spiritual degrees. Of course, not all of these will be *our* processes and will not be within *our* consciousness. To understand the limits of our own consciousness, we need to know the limits of whatever love it is that defines our own identity (as discussed in Section 20.4). We must conclude that we are conscious only of those actions that follow (as from derived dispositions) from our own identifying love. We might yet be influenced by many other processes, with other loves of their own, but until they are assimilated within us and act 'as if' from our own love, we are not aware of them but only of their effects. Such things just 'pop into our minds', we say to ourselves. We may keep some of these new things for ourselves, adopted to be under the care of our own loves, and we become conscious of them. Other things not adopted are ignored in 'un-awareness' and fall away.

Sometimes, the love and wisdom within a level[2] seem to be *already* united. This happens, for example, after a procedure or habit has already been formed. To start with, all procedures require conscious attention, but, after practice, the constituting ingredients seem to stay united most often. The procedure becomes like a 'module' that functions without conscious attention to its internal sequence. We no longer have the distinct awareness of the kind described above. Rather, the module becomes simply part of the action. When consciousness focuses on the result of a conscious action, it sees not just the immediate effect in its own level but also the further effects that result from all the unconscious operations of derivative dispositions in modules that are invoked. This is the perfectly normal pattern when we learn a skill. To start with we have conscious awareness of the initial ingredients and their effects. After the skill is learned, it is like invoking a unitary module in the mind. The result is that the conscious awareness of the action is now very much focused on the *final* effect. A good workman does not focus on his tools. He is instead aware of the effects of his tools on the target of their operation. The conscious presence

---

[2] That is, love and wisdom, or whatever corresponds to them at the level being considered.

has then moved from inside the mind to the final effect, which may be outside the body.[3]

One consequence of the kind of consciousness of Postulate 17 is, that we are *not* immediately aware of the love that leads to our action, *nor* are we automatically aware of our understanding which was instrumental in selecting that particular action. We can usually make an effort to be re-flectively aware of our relevant ideas, in a kind of 'higher order' manner. That effort is needed, however, because we have to deliberately raise our level of awareness to a prior or higher level in order to 'look down' on the thought processes that we originally used. Attaining such a reflective awareness is very useful, but obviously it is not automatically a part of nor-mal consciousness at a given level. It is more difficult to become aware of our constituting loves, since, even if our reflective awareness can be based on a higher level, we still only see forms and effects, not causes. We have to *infer* our loves, even our own loves, by collecting evidence for how we feel and how we behave in a wide variety of circumstances. We are never directly conscious at a given level of the loves operating at that level. Nev-ertheless, those things are still accessible to our awareness if we can also operate at the next higher level in the generative structure.

Phenomenal consciousness consists of the appearances things have for us in our minds. We certainly have that kind of awareness of things, as well as the action consciousness and the reflective consciousness defined above. There is a current trend, started by Damasio[4], of reducing phenom-enal awareness to reflective awareness and claiming that all awareness of things, even of our own emotions, is to be reflectively aware of ourselves as having these conscious contents. This is one way we can come to know our own loves, but only one way of many. Both reflective and phenome-nal consciousnesses are special cases of the action consciousness defined by Postulate 17. The previous paragraph outlined how this reduction is possible for reflective awareness, but this is not immediately so clear for phenomenal consciousness.

To see the nature of phenomenal consciousness, we recall how theistic science conceives perception in general. All kinds of perception must in-volve a part of the mind generating a wide range of possible or potential sensations. Then the sensory organs (existing as structures in a derivative

---

[3] See Riva et al. ("From intention to action") for further discussion of consciousness and presence within series of several derivative intentions and also when external technologies are used.

[4] Damasio, *The feeling of what happens*.

degree) cause structures to exist which select which sensations are to be actually manifested on that occasion. When we look at perception according to this theory, we see that it is a theory of constraints on action. If those actions are the operation of love by means of wisdom, then they will be conscious actions. The content of that consciousness will be the nature of each action, in this case the production of a sensation. This is what we claim as the nature of phenomenal consciousness. Our visual field seems to be like a sheet of phenomenal consciousness. This is possible if we have an equivalent sheet of potential sensations and the corresponding layout of constraints to select particular sensations everywhere on that sheet.[5]

27.3 What awareness is not

According to Postulate 17, consciousness is not a property of physical objects alongside other physical properties. We do not have property dualism. Neither does consciousness emerge from complicated structures of physical objects such as brains. It *appears* that this emergence might be what is happening, because, in theistic science, the existence of suitably complicated brain and processes is a prerequisite for the operation of the corresponding mental functions. The brain structures form a physical degree that is a good correspondence with the mental degree and therefore act (as a skin) to contain and manifest those mental processes. This appearance of emergence is not actually emergence, since (in reality) the mental and spiritual degrees are appearing from God, not appearing from physical processes or natural objects.

Neither is consciousness something internal to us, a monad, as Leibniz thought, that runs in a parallelism to physical processes. "Monads have no windows," he said, and thus he required God to set up parallel sequences of events in separate mental and physical entities. According to theistic science, there is *some* kind of parallelism. We do have reasons for the mental-physical correspondences described in Section 25.3. But the reasons for the parallelism are completely different. We do not have God setting it up in advance, but rather have the parallelism arising dynamically for specific causal reasons, namely because of the generation of derivative dispositions and the reciprocal actions of constraint back on the causal degree.

---

[5] Of course, talking of a 'sheet' is talk of a two-dimensional surface, but, at some level we are mental functionalists, and hence we know that all we need is that kind of functional structure, not an actual two-dimensional arrangement of neurons, of ideas, or of minds.

In theistic sciences, decisions in minds do really cause their effects. There is no parallelism which implies merely the appearance of such causality. Leibniz's view led to Malebranche developing his view of occasionalism (as discussed in Section 18.2) whereby all power belonged to God alone and none to created creatures or objects. Because of intermediate derived dispositions, we do not hold this view within theistic science.[6]

In theistic science we therefore have a kind of dualism. It is certainly not Cartesian dualism, since Descartes' conception of a rational soul as single non-physical substance is excessively crude and simple compared with our theory of spiritual and natural discrete degrees. Even his idea of a rational soul is not correct. It ignores the essential role of love in defining the substance of the mind.

We do have awareness coming about by reception from God, but it is not awareness itself which is received. Some forms of Hinduism have in Sanskrit the phrase Sat-cit-ānanda, or truth-consciousness-bliss, to describe the nature of Brahman (the divine source) as experienced by a fully-enlightened saint. In our scientific theism, God (the divine source) certainly has truth and consciousness and delights in divine actions, but our consciousness and our delights are *with us*, whenever we act by bringing love and wisdom together again into action.

27.4 Awareness in animals and plants

Because our theory of consciousness depends on the unified action of love and wisdom within the spiritual and mental degrees, the *quality* of the consciousness will depend on the details of which specific love and which specific wisdom are acting together and in which sub-degree or sub-sub-degree (etc.) the action is taking place. The quality of our wills and understandings (to receive love and wisdom, respectively) will influence the quality of our consciousness. This dependence of consciousness on the nature of our mental structures that receive life from God means that all living beings—those that receive divine life—have consciousness in all their varying mental and spiritual degrees.

This implies that animals and plants are all conscious, but with many varying degrees of consciousness. They will have varying degrees of

---

[6] See Section 18.2 for the argument here.

awareness and many varieties of clarity in perception. Since it is difficult for us to directly examine the consciousness of animals and plants, let me begin by describing some general considerations to help us predict what those levels of consciousness are. These considerations will be based on examining the various roles of different parts of the human functional form (see Section 25.6 and related discussion), and ascribing different levels of awareness as necessary for the operations of these different parts.

Animals are primarily those creatures which ingest and digest food aerobically and have powers of locomotion. As a first approximation, we may say that all animals are aware of *affections* that derive from love. Hence they also have the necessary sensory awareness and cognitive discriminations that accompany these affections as many of these are necessary for the operation and delight of those affections. Animal powers of motion enable them to to move around to satisfy their desires. We predict that each individual species of animal corresponds to a particular kind of desire or affection. The enormous range of animals on earth demonstrates the great range of possible desires and affections. We may sometimes find many of those affections within ourselves.

Plants do not have locomotion, but they receive and retain the energy of light from the sun and grow into stable structures. Typically, they convert water from the earth and carbon dioxide from the air into plant body and oxygen with the help of sunlight. Correspondences to these processes were begun to be described in Section 25.3, and were found to be related to perceptions of truth of some kind. This implies that, on earth, plants have rather simple consciousnesses that are essentially kinds of perceptions but with hardly any consequential discrimination. Those awarenesses may be at most at sub-sub-degree 2.32 and 2.33, but at no higher degree. We can imagine plants being first aware of the sunlight, then of water, and then of some underlying impetus to bring these together to make a 'body of awareness' which is the growth of the plant itself. In the overall ecology (both spiritually and physically, in correspondence), this body of awareness becomes in turn the food for animals: for rational thought in humans and actual food on earth. The plant kind of consciousness presumably does not use perceptual constancies. Because plants do not move, they do not need to discern invariances under changes of perspective.

Biologists today may insist that they can perfectly well explain the reactions of plants to light by purely biochemical means, and that therefore no 'plant awareness' is needed to explain the phenomena. Theistic science will admit this may be true in large part, but it is not the whole story nor even the whole causal explanation. Naturalistic explanations may be largely true, because organized natural process are precisely *needed* in order to make a firm foundation or skin for interior mental processes, even in plants. Then, in order for those specific mental processes to be attached to *this* plant and not another, say, there must be causal influence from that mentality into the operation of the plant. This causal influence must occur to some extent, no matter how 'low down' is the sub-...-sub-degree of that mentality and no matter how limited is the range of effects that can be generated in the physical by generative dispositions from plant mentality. Again, we presume that the wide variety of plants portrays in part the even wider variety of possible structures of mental perception. We should not think that God is restricted to a small number of suitable organic forms.

Since the number of plants and of animals is finite in comparison to the infinite varieties of loves and truths within God, they are still practically nothing. We need not be upset that forms of organisms may be temporarily created, to live for an era but die out again. The number of new creatures fossilized in the Burgess Shale or the number of dinosaurs is still small compared with the much larger number of possible creatures that may yet represent distinct divine loves and truths. The overflowing nature of God's love is more than sufficient to generate all the animals, plants, insects and bacteria that have ever existed.

27.5 Timing issues

Experiments in measuring electrical signals from the brain have recently cast doubt on the role of consciousness in making decisions in humans. Experiments by Libet et al.[7] found that onset of an electrically observable cerebral process (the readiness potential, or RP) *preceded* the appearance of the subject's awareness of the conscious wish to act, by at least 350 msec. That appears to indicate, Libet claims, that the volitional process is initiated unconsciously.

The scenario and subject consciousness used in these experiments has been examined in more detail by Batthyany[8], who shows that the subjects

---

[7] Libet et al., "Time of conscious intention to act."
[8] Batthyany, "Mental causation and free will after Libet and Soon."

were asked to be a state of intention to make a random finger movement at some later time. That first intentional state, even if it did not yet include a specific decision, was therefore existing for some period of time before the final result. With theistic science, we know that states of intention are states of love or desire to act, and that the persistence of such states must be maintained by patterns of neural activity. We can surmise that these neural patterns can be detected, as very plausibly of the form for which Fingelkurts, Fingelkurts, and Neves[9] cite experimental evidence, and are hence very likely to be what Libet has measured.

27.6 Parapsychology

Within our theistic framework, all physical processes are the successive products of prior spiritual and psychical processes. Just from the direction of this causation, we might expect very many parapsychological phenomena to occur and even many events that appear to be miraculous. However, unambiguously parapsychological results appear to be rare, and successful parapsychological experiments seem to be getting rarer. Why is this?

The main reason is that, despite causation proceeding from the mental to the physical, it is certainly not the case that thereby we 'create our own reality' (as many have speculated and believed). Rather, there is a physical level of fixed and actual events that act to select, constrain, and retain our mental and spiritual processes, as I have argued. Therefore, in normal life, there are few parapsychological phenomena and even fewer events which could be considered miraculous. Instead of our minds creating our reality, it is clear that it is our external reality which is essential in constraining our minds to operate only within the boundaries of our own bodies. According to theistic science, our spiritual life is only possible if we have a spiritual container (soul) for the spiritual life we receive from God. Our spirituality is not automatically spread out across the whole universe, or across all times, or at 'all frequencies'. It is closely connected to the functions we perform with our bodies in the world.

The main times that parapsychological events seem to occur is in periods of strong feelings and emotions such as stress from grief, exuberance,

---

[9] Fingelkurts, Fingelkurts, and Neves, "Natural world physical, brain operational, and mind phenomenal space–time."

accident, injury, or sickness. Brain death also produces such occurrences, called near-death experiences. In these and in other cases, there seems to be a spontaneous spilling over from the normal containers of mental and spiritual life. Then the reasons listed in Section 25.4 no longer apply so strictly, and our consciousness can extend to people, events, and or actions outside the limits of our skin.[10] Such cases of strong feelings and emotions tend to be spontaneous and difficult to reproduce in laboratory settings. In fact, the sheer numbers of spontaneous cases showing external connections of consciousness are overwhelming whenever these are diligently investigated. They used to be collected more reliably in the early days of psychical research. Now, with more public skepticism, many people keep their experiences to themselves. Near-death experiences appear to be more acceptable currently, though perhaps not in all scientific circles.

We should also consider the possibility advocated by Swedenborg[11], that miracles and other effectuating events are deliberately kept from our view so as not to force rational thought to conclusions it cannot assimilate. This would be quite possible even in our 'scientific era', since such things are under the management of God. Miracles may still occur in interior degrees, out of view, but 'external miracles' might perhaps only now occur when they can be interpreted in many ways. It seems to be the story of parapsychology: quests for definitive and forceful demonstrations make the phenomena retreat. Instead we may be supposed to freely and rationally understand the operations of God, spirituality and mentality in the world. I therefore leave open the question of whether reliable parapsychological experiments will ever become commonplace.

---

[10] That is, outside our spiritual and mental 'skin' as well. We can think of this as speaking (or shouting) in spiritual space to others existing outside our spiritual body.

[11] Swedenborg, *Miracles*.

28

Spiritual Growth

28.1 The need for spiritual growth

B Y SPIRITUAL growth, I refer to all development towards the maturity of our own spiritual loves and their associated wisdom. Sometimes that growth is described in religious language, for example in terms of a path or pilgrimage guided by the love and grace of God, as we are being reborn or regenerated into a new life with God. Others consider spiritual growth in humanistic terms, as the development of integrity concerning what is loving and true in our lives. Some think it comes from God. Others think of it as the unfolding of human potentialities.

In all cases, it is clear that we need spiritual growth since we start life when newly born, without explicit knowledge of these things and without any sense of our own spiritual loves. It is commonly accepted that spiritual growth comes about during our adult life, starting in early adulthood when we first take responsibility for our own actions. It then depends on both the internal decisions and external actions we make during our life.

Theistic science will in particular examine the development, progression and operation of our spiritual loves, which are the processes that exist and operate in the spiritual degree 1. These processes are primarily loves, according to our generative structure, but they must have associated thoughts and understandings in order to be effective. In Section 23.5, it was surmised that most of us do not come into the fullness of our spiritual life until after bodily death. That would mean that there will be two kinds of understanding that should be associated with and guide our spiritual life. The first is the understanding in those spiritual degrees 1.1, 1.2 and 1.3 themselves, and the second is understanding in our mentality, in particular in the corresponding degrees 2.11, and 2.12 and 2.13. The first understanding can be called truly spiritual wisdom. The second understanding is the internal or higher rational in our minds. It is this second kind of understanding which is (or should be) readily accessible and usable to us in our ordinary lives. It is the primary instrument for guiding us in our spiritual growth while we live on earth.

28.2 Permanent development

We want spiritual growth that has permanent effects in our lives. According to theism, permanent changes in our life depend on the actions *we* perform: actions for which our loves and our understanding are directly responsible, and have made their own. Let us continue the discussions from Sections 23.5 and 26.2 about how spiritual growth is not instantaneous but has to be gradually worked into our lives. The new loves and new understandings that come with spiritual changes have to be attached to us in some way. They should be strongly rooted into our lives by being appropriated to ourselves. They are appropriated *as if* to ourselves, since, in reflective consciousness, we should be aware that all life, love and wisdom are derived from God.

It is true that love, influx and grace from God are essential to everything we do. They are essential to our spiritual growth, but there are some actions needed from us in response. Even if we follow Calvin and regard ourselves as the stump of a tree with no life of our own, we must still at first allow, and then encourage and later nurture the new life that grows in us as the result of grace from God. God gives us whatever we are able to retain. In fact, we are given sometimes a little *more* for a short while, in order that we remember vividly and be encouraged to persevere.

Permanent growth, according to our theory, comes from the joint action of (good) love with (true) wisdom. This conjunction of love and wisdom must moreover have had effects through all the discrete degrees, right down to actual effects in the physical degree. Only those complete actions have all the connected ingredients to have permanent effects for our spiritual life. [1]

---

[1] Note that I am *not* addressing here the question of whether or how it is possible to *change* our spiritual life once it is already permanently formed according to the above scheme. That question involves issues of repentance, temptations and salvation which are beyond the scope of this book.

28.3 What spiritual growth is not

Permanent spiritual growth comes from the joint action of (good) love with (true) wisdom, according to theistic science. Unfortunately, that view has not been widely understood, and a variety of simplified theories has been promulgated in the past. Those theories claim that spiritual growth depends on much simpler requirements that we now see are insufficient.

Permanent spiritual growth, for example, does *not* come from any one of the following things *by itself*:

Belief: since this is just in the understanding and does not change loves in the will.

Knowledge, even of truths (wisdom): knowledge of what is true, even of what is good, is no use unless it is used to reform the will. It is 'faith alone' to think that only knowledge is efficacious.

Blind obedience: obedience to truth is fruitful, but blind obedience has no input from wisdom in the understanding.

Good intentions or love: love needs wisdom in order to act for good purposes. Good intentions 'mean well' but often stray through lack of insight, even lack of common sense.

Suffering: suffering by itself is something that happens to us not something we do. There are many causes of suffering (natural and human); what is spiritually significant is how we respond to these.[2]

Personal imputation of the suffering of others: The suffering of others, even of Jesus, cannot help us unless we examine our life and bring it into agreement with the good that he is bringing to us.

Elevated, expanded, rotated, vibrated (etc.) consciousness: Expanding our consciousness even to the whole universe and over all time, or making it run fast or slow, does not show us what is spiritual, let alone help us regenerate our spiritual nature.

The point is that within theistic science none of these things can even *exist* by itself. I am not saying that the presence of the above things has no effect on spiritual growth. I want to contradict some existing theories which say that one of these things is *all* we need for permanent spiritual development.

---

[2] See, for example, Matt. 15:17-20.

28.4 Stages of spiritual growth

In Chapter 23, we made a sketch of the sub-degrees 1.1, 1.2 and 1.3 that should be expected in the spiritual degree. They are the degrees related to love of good loving, love of good understanding, and love of good actions, respectively. Since all physical and mental growth begins from the third degree 3, and works up towards the first degree 1, the same pattern must hold for spiritual growth. The pattern can be used to infer the stages of proper spiritual growth, no matter how it is described by the person himself. That growth starts in our mental understandin-, in sub-sub-degrees 2.13, 2.12 and 2.11, and then carries on in our spiritual will specifically, in sub-degrees 1.3, 1.2 and 1.1, in those orders. These various sub-(sub-)degrees are illustrated in Table 28.1. The progression of spiritual growth proceeds by means of steps through these degrees.

The first step (S1) is to acknowledge that there *does exist* a spiritual degree(!). Many people who adhere to naturalist or humanist world views deny even the possibility of spiritual processes (as we discussed in Section 25.1). The first step, therefore, is to break out of the ideological constraints of those world views (in sub-sub-degree 2.31, in the scientific rational) and allow that there is 'light'. Let a new day dawn by accepting that there exists somewhere something absolutely good and true.

Once that step has been made, there is a progression of three further steps as our understanding is reformed and raised up. We come to understand next (S2) that these new ideas of good and truth are of two kinds. There are those within us that are mixed up with all our habits of thinking and, separate from these, also further understandings (not belonging to

1: Spiritual degree love in the spirit	2: Mental degree thoughts in mind	3: Physical degree actions in the body
love of good: 1.1	thoughts of love of good: 2.11 thoughts of love of truth: 2.11 thoughts of love of action: 2.13	physical effects
love of truth: 1.2	scientific rational: 2.2	
love of action: 1.3	external mind: 2.3	

Table 28.1 *Stages of spiritual growth: the relevant 3 sub-degrees of the spiritual on the left, and the 3 sub-sub-degrees of the higher rational in the center.*

us) that are unconditionally good and true. After this, actions may begin (S3) that are guided by knowledge from that unconditional source, even if we do not always act this way because we are not yet acting from love. Then (S4) our understanding finally begins to see the source of these things as love (like a sun), and a good faith is founded that begins (like a moon) to reflect that love and truth into our lives.

The above stages of growth are with sub-degree 2.1 and are hence primarily concerned with our understanding. They result in a life that is managed from our understanding of truth. That is, we always have to be thinking about what to do and consequently make mistakes when our attention wanders. It would clearly be better if our life could be guided by a good love, rather than (rather consciously) forever by our intellectual understanding of what we should be doing.

The next three stages (S5, S6 & S7) involve the growth of love in our will and the conjunction of our understanding with those new kinds of love. The first stage (S5) involves the first formation in the will of good loves (in 1.3) leading to obedient action and to the new life of our understanding that comes from conjunction with this love that is good for the first time. Our understanding is now able to understand the deep principles of spirituality and religion and also think 'high flying' thoughts about these things.

The following stage (S6) is where our loves achieve a life in degree 1.2, and hence a good love of understanding is now readily achieved. Now all those deep and high thoughts are integrated into the human form as an image of God. Insights concerning everyday life are now easily visible, and these guide our spiritual life. Finally, stage (S7) is where our loves have been regenerated to the first spiritual degree (1.1), and hence our life is then governed (as it should be) by actions from love (not merely from insights). In that way we are more completely in the likeness of God.

Those acquainted with the story of Genesis Chapter 1 may see a pattern of correspondences in this progress of spiritual creation. Examining the details of possible correspondences of these stages with natural progressions is left as an exercise for the reader. Never forget that the spiritual degree is equally as real as the physical and mental degrees.

29

Errors and Evils

29.1 The problem of evil

EVERY BOOK about a good God should explain how it is that we have evil in the world. This book is no exception. We will address these issues, even though we have not properly defined good or evil, since for many people these questions are obstacles to belief in theism. Like Charles Darwin, they say they do not want to believe in the existence of a God who could be responsible for the evil in the world. Along with evil actions by people and their effects on innocent victims, they see many 'natural evils' such as earthquakes, floods, and asteroid impacts. They ask questions about genetic defects and sickness in living beings as well as allegedly bad design in animal physiology. We should also add to this list the mistakes that come during the growth of humans, since we all are born in states of such great ignorance.

I will not claim to provide a complete answer to these questions. Any answer must depend on God's management policy concerning all these defects and on our trust (or otherwise) in the goodness of that policy. This is the policy normally called providence. It governs *how quickly* God will deal with all those difficulties and also governs the balance between our short-term objectives and God's long-term objectives. Impatience will commonly give rise to negative views of apparent strategies.

This chapter will confine itself to the philosophical foundational questions and scientific details that need to be understood before any conclusions (positive or negative) can be confirmed as real and not just speculation or wish-fulfillment. I will not attempt to provide a solution to the problem of evil, partly because any proposed solution would be read in some quarters as a justification for evil in the presence of God.

29.2 Mackie's logical problem of evil

Perhaps the clearest exposition of the problem of evil in recent years is that of Mackie[1]. He presents the 'logical problem of evil' as understanding how all the three propositions:

1. God is wholly good (benevolent),
2. God is omnipotent,
3. Evil exists,

could be true simultaneously. If God is omnipotent, he should be *able* to remove all evil, and if he is benevolent, he should not hesitate to do so. Mackie argues that if any two of the propositions were true, the third would be false. Hume[2] states the problem about God as follows: "Is he willing to prevent evil, but not able? Then is he impotent. Is he able, but not willing? Then is he malevolent. Is he both able and willing? Whence then is evil?"

We may agree with Mackie that certain proposed solutions are fallacious. Some argue that evil is necessary for creation, others that evil is necessary for good works to be done, and others that good cannot exist without evil. It is not orthodox theology that evil is needed for good to exist or that is is necessary to creation. Evil might be the occasion for good works to be done but we can still insist that it would be better if such good works countering evil were not necessary to start with. In all cases, therefore, we should be able to agree that it would be a better universe if evil did not exist in the first place or if particular evils could be removed.

We can consider the view that evil is due to human *free will*. Many philosophers and theologians follow this view and hold that human freedom is a 'great good' that God insists must be present in creation, even if the side effects are so many and so damaging in terms of the injuries that we inflict on each other every day. Mackie asks, therefore, why God "could not have made men such that they always freely choose what is good?" He confesses, though, that in the end he finds incoherence in the notion of freedom of the will.

[1] Mackie, "Evil and omnipotence."
[2] Hume, *Dialogues concerning natural religion.*

I agree that it is difficult to understand how we have free will, especially in a world where God has complete foreknowledge of our future actions. Nevertheless, I claim that our actions are freely chosen. It would clearly help the theistic case if there were an understanding about the existence of evil that did not depend on the freedom of the will. I argue below that the reasons relating to evils can in fact be expressed in much simpler terms, and that free will can also be derived from these simpler reasons. We will see that a theodicy can be formulated that does not directly depend on the concept of free will.

29.3 Divine versus Absolute omnipotence

There is a simple argument related to divine omnipotence which has a direct bearing on the problem of evil. In its light the argument will be seen in a different way. Mackie agrees that this will be a possible line of reasoning for a theodicy as long as, he reminds us, we are not still "thinking, in other contexts, that [God's] power is really unlimited".

There are already well-known 'paradoxes of omnipotence' that date back to medieval times, and Mackie[3] reminds us of them. One such paradox is 'can God create a stone he cannot lift?' If he can then he is not omnipotent, since there is something (a lifting task) he cannot do. If he cannot, then he is not omnipotent since there is something (a creation task) he cannot do. A common response is that since God is supposedly omnipotent, the phrase 'could not lift' does not make sense, and hence, in relation to God, the paradox is meaningless. However, since science cannot permanently tolerate paradoxes or denials of sensible questions, we do have to come to some resolution of this problem in theistic science.

The only solution to the paradox that I can see is to deny that God is absolutely omnipotent. Since any assumption of absolute omnipotence leads to a contradiction with that presupposition, it is clearly self-contradictory, as argued by Cowan[4]. Nothing self-contradictory can be attributed to God. We are thus logically obliged to distinguish *divine omnipotence* from *absolute omnipotence*. Then we can coherently claim that 'divine omnipotence is not absolute' and that there are (indeed) some things that God cannot or will not do. This logical argument does not tell us *what* precisely these

[3] Mackie, "Evil and omnipotence."
[4] Cowan, "The paradox of omnipotence."

limits are. It is more a kind of existence proof, driven by the inconsistency of a non-existence.

The limits of divine omnipotence have been touched on in previous chapters, so we do already have some idea of what God's limits might be. Most of these limits stem from love, in particular from divine Love. The limits come from the fact that God's Love always overrides his omnipotence. That is, perhaps he in fact does have many of these powers to be listed, but (from Love) he never does these things. Then God's omnipotence is effectively reduced. The resulting 'effective omnipotence' is what we should henceforth call 'divine omnipotence'.

There are many things *A* that an absolute omnipotence can logically perform, but God does not do those things, for reason *B*. Let me list some of these:

A1. Create beings that live from themselves.
  B1: No, because these beings would then be divine and not lovable unselfishly, because not distinct from God. See Section 12.2.

A2. Create theistically-sustained beings suddenly *de novo*.
  B2: No, because they would be missing their own history of actions and hence would not be robust with their own 'skin'. See Section 26.2.

A3. Remove all evil from the world existing today.
  B3: No, because much of that evil consists of the loves that make persons, and *all persons* are loved by God, so none can be removed. See Section 20.4.

A4. Remove all the evil loves from inside all existing persons.
  B4: No, because some people are (very sadly) substantially constituted by their evil loves.

A5. Stop all persons from choosing evil, even though they still *can* do it.
  B5: Maybe some but not all, since influencing persons is done by the *presence* of some substance, not remotely, so such persons will be hemmed in and will clearly *feel* constrained. Some small fraction of these will certainly rebel against those internal constraints and end up in more evil than before.

A6. Stop all persons *intending* all evil, even though they love it and still *can* do it.
  B6: No, because if a person's love could not intend what is loved, then their loves would have no form in their understanding and so could

not permanently exist. God loves all persons, and he wants them all to exist permanently.

We see that, in all these cases[5], God's omnipotence is ruled by Love. This is as it should be. So the answer to whether God can create a stone which he cannot lift is 'yes'. And that stone is us.

It is because of the basic need for all conscious creatures in creation to be able to act as if from themselves and to enjoy the delights from those actions, that most of these limits arise. Also, from these principles, we have the need for freedom of the will for us (supposedly rational) humans. It is always necessary that our actions be our own and not imposed on us. As discussed previously, we cannot ever be allowed to think of ourselves as predestined or unfree, as then our actions would not even *seem* to be our own.

29.4 Real questions

In light of the above understanding of divine omnipotence, which follows logically from the understanding of God as Love, we can discuss some real questions that concern the creation of the universe. The arguments above concerning omnipotence focused on the continued existence of our world which already has evil in it, but how, we ask, does evil even exist in a theistic universe? How can God thereby be still good? How could evil have arisen in the first place?

The first question is therefore whether we involve God in some way in *all* physical processes, including those that might be random, destructive, or even evil. This is a problem if we believe that God is wholly benevolent.

Here, we do begin to reply by means of the free will defense, despite Mackie's objections. With our generative level structure, God is not 'acting through' the world but gives all natural beings freedom and life to act as *they* wish. As Christian belief has in Matthew 5.45, "he makes his sun rise on the evil and the good, and sends his rain on the just and the unjust". This does not mean that 'the just and the unjust' are treated identically and have the same sets of dispositions and intentions. Rather, as they will perform different acts and have different actual forms, by Postulate 10 they

---

[5] I admit that the reasons B5 and B6 are not yet fully argued within this book.

will have different dispositions and then lead the different lives of their choice. Just because God sustains the consequences of many actions, does *not* mean that God *wants* them to happen that way, only that God seems to prefer the continued existence of the people concerned, rather than their non-existence.

We may also ask how certain beings have dispositions which act contrary to divine intentions, given that all dispositions derive from the divine and given that there are no evil or contrary intentions in the divine life. We agree that a benevolent God could *permit* certain contrary intentions, but we wonder how these could ever *persist* in a universe governed by Postulate 10. One may wonder for example how selfish dispositions could be sustained, when there is no selfishness in God. I believe the answer lies in seeing that certain dispositions, to look after oneself for example, have a good use in certain contexts and may well be derivable from the divine life in certain discrete degrees. They only perform *good* uses, however, when they are coordinated and governed by *prior* derivative dispositions, such as intentions to be useful to others. This is the way they may be linked in the divine life, but it is possible that some persons may be such that they can only receive the dispositions to look after oneself and not receive the prior dispositions that are supposed to govern them. If these persons are still to live, they can only be alive with a restricted fragment of the divine life, a fragment that in this case will act with regard to one person only. This fragment (by itself and with derivatives from it in its 'uncoordinated' state) may well be disposed contrary to the original divine intentions. These subsequent contrary derivatives are only indirectly generated from the divine life, *via* the continued existence of the persons concerned. Divine benevolence is maintained, provided we do not forget that these contrary dispositions are *derived* via the (good) disposition to give (some kind of) life to all persons, and that they are *not* a permanent component of the original divine.

The third question is how evil came to exist in the world for the first time. The question, therefore, is:

Could God not create a world in which all persons (no matter that they evolved gradually biologically, developed gradually psychologically, and regenerated gradually spiritually) still never made decisions against God, still never entertained false thoughts or evil intentions, and still never desired delights that cannot come from God, and (moreover) never aspired to *be* gods but always knew that they were separate from God?

Remember that all 'gradual progressions' were through incomplete stages of ignorance and partly egotistical desires, and that those ignorances and egotisms are only balanced and restrained by a suitably-managed influx of love and wisdom. Were those balancing and restraining processes *always* successful?

Or did some people, in some galaxy far, far away, diverge from what is good and true? Is that us? Are *we* the people who have the most need to shun evils?

As anticipated at the start of this chapter, these discussion sections do not really provide answers to the problem of evil. There is no reason given for natural disasters, etc.,[6] except that God must work with the materials that respond best in their reception and longest-term retention of divine life, even if those materials are not perfect.[7] We have merely established various divine and natural principles which, given theistic science, any future answer should take into account.

---

[6] We have already considered the question of possible biological 'bad design' on page 238.
[7] Only God is perfect.

Part VI

Discussion

30

Metaphysics

Let us now, in the light of the proposed theistic science, look back at that the philosophical issues that are often debated, especially those discussed in Chapter 2. We need to compare present with previous theories, concerning in particular the *metaphysical* issues–about what exists and how it functions.

30.1 Rational theology

One traditional approach to metaphysics in rational theology is to define God as "that than which no greater being can be conceived". Although this definition may or may not yield Anselm's proof for the existence of God, it can certainly be used to determine the attributes that should be ascribed to God. In careful hands, Ward[1], for example, shows how to, from this starting point, derive a theology in good agreement with our scientific theism. The need for careful hands arises because of the difficulty in this method. How do you decide which attributes are 'greater' than certain other attributes? Is it greater to be unable to suffer or to be able to suffer? Aquinas thought that God could not suffer (that God is impassible), whereas Whitehead (with many since him) holds to the contrary that it is better that God suffers with the suffering of his creatures.[2] Swedenborg holds the intermediate position that God does not suffer but may at most grieve. These three views follow directly from their respective ontologies: the God of Aquinas is Pure Act; the God of Whitehead is within a process ontology; and the God of Swedenborg is Love Itself. In our scientific

---

[1] Ward, *Religion and creation.*
[2] Whitehead (*Process and reality*) has that God "is the great fellow-sufferer who understands".

theism, since God is characterized by being life itself, he is certainly not unable to change, and hence he is not Pure Act because he can respond to our love.

The theism and science presented in the previous sections attempt to explain the relation between God and the world in a way that is rationally comprehensible. The scheme must be devoid of self-contradiction or inconsistency, as otherwise anything whatsoever could be proved. A *reductio ad absurdam*, for example, could then be used to disprove any additional hypothesis. We acknowledge, of course, that it is God we are here talking about, so we freely admit that there are infinite depths and heights to God that we may take an eternity to try to understand. But we insist that the further existence of these depths and heights does *not* contradict our best rational understanding. We insist on this, in part, because our best rationality comes from God (who is Wisdom itself) precisely for that purpose.

In requiring *some* rational comprehension to be faithfully true,[3] scientific theism cannot include any kind of non-rational assertion that verges on the self-contradictory. We cannot follow Plotinus, for example, in declaring God to be beyond both being and non-being. Nor can we include the assertion of Aquinas that in God essence and existence are identical, nor similarly that his substance and form are identical. Nor do I see a non-contradictory manner for asserting that God consists of three persons and yet is Absolutely Simple. Nor do I follow Aquinas in saying that love and wisdom are not truly predicated of God except by analogy. Perhaps some theologians feel free to add in such non-rational assertions as *addenda*, but, unless it can be shown how such declarations may be consistent, they cannot be part of any rational theism.

Part of the impetus for these assertions by Plotinus, Aquinas, and others is their belief that God is greater when his unity is beyond not only all *division* but also beyond all *rational* distinctions. To have to distinguish between being and nonbeing or between essence and existence was 'beneath' God, they thought.

I reply that, while we may agree that God is "that than which no greater being can be conceived", we are definitely *not* claiming that God

---

[3] We remember here the discussion at the end of Section 14.2, concerning how a proper wisdom, as distinct from 'mere' understanding of causes, requires our thinking to be fully linked with love. From Section 23.5, we note that it may be some time before we obtain in ourselves this linking in its fullest form.

is "greater than can be conceived". It would clearly diminish God if these inflated unities necessarily involved contradictions![4]

30.2 Firsts and lasts

A big tension, between the reality of God (as firsts) and the reality of everyday nature (as lasts), was shown in Chapter 2 to have influenced many philosophers to go to one side or the other. Using theistic science as a basis for what kinds of connections between God and nature can be known, we see that most of the philosophers discussed in Chapter 2 do not describe those connections. Only Aquinas and Swedenborg appear to make consistent and more-than-abstract arguments that go from God to material nature, and from the material back again to God. Both of these systems place mind within that connection, as in our theory.

I do not include Plotinus in this short list because of his tendency towards non-dualism, wherein the natural world does not exist in the normal sense of containing material objects. Descartes did not even attempt to elucidate the connections between God and the world, in part because he wanted to keep science separate from religion. Kant claimed that we never know about those connections since they involve, he said, knowledge of things in themselves beyond human reach.

Any theory that gives a unified account of first things with God and of last things in nature will thereby be able to explain why creation is needed by God and what it is that can be done by means of a created world that God cannot do immediately. That particular explanation is missing from nearly all the metaphysical theories that have been examined, but is clearly needed. It would be good to know why God is so slow in creating planets, biological life, humans, and spirituality. Most accounts of divine omnipotence imply that God can and will create all these things immediately and moreover, if he is benevolent, heal them immediately if they are flawed. Yet, this does not happen! Can you explain why not? In the light of this book's explanations of evolution and human development, only something like Swedenborg's account remains capable of giving sufficient explanation.

---

[4] Indeed, I would insist that everyone needs some kind of rational and consistent understanding as the basis for religion. A person's faith, for example, should be based on what is true and consistent, even if the understanding of those truths is slow in coming. Faith based on what can *never* be comprehended is hardly useful.

30.3 Rationality and love

Other sources of debate are the relation between 'rationality in the under-standing' and 'love in the will' and also the assessment of which is 'higher' or 'better' in some sense. Which should describe the essence of human nature? Philosophers (naturally) have very often taken rational thought to be highest expression of humanity, so much so that the 'God of the philosophers', for a long time since the Greeks, is taken as Pure Intellect and is therefore in contemplation of whatever is eternal (which is only the divine itself!). Others, perhaps influenced more by religion, have taken Love to be at the heart of God. This debate may be exactly like a squabble between the two brothers Esau and Jacob, each seeking their father's birthright blessing, but it has important consequences concerning human nature as well. Aristotle, Plato, Aquinas, Descartes and Spinoza all took rational thought as the highest, most-godlike human activity, and hence they assumed human life should be understood as the product of rational agents. Others, such as Hume, Swedenborg, Schopenhauer and James, saw that love and desires were the deeper motivating factors for human life and often also for the life of God. Of course, we now remind ourselves, *both* love and rationality should work together, with love motivating rational thought and rational thought guiding love towards its desired actions.

This debate even has consequences for physics. If philosophers see rationality as the only principle in God and humans, they tend to see what can be comprehended by rationality as the only principle that should govern physical processes. Rationalists tend to characterize physical nature in terms of forms. Pythagoras thought the essence of nature was number. Descartes thought the essence of nature was extension. Many *theoretical* physicists today think that nature can be characterized as information, group structures, or binary digits (bits). If pressed, they may explain that they are talking about 'active information'. They then think that if they could produce a mathematical theory for the universe, the universe itself would be explained! If, however, a philosopher sees love as an essential principle in God and humans, then he realizes that forms and mathematics are *not* enough to explain existence: some further *being* is needed to constitute any existence (whether physical, mental, or divine).

Understanding that 'further being' that embodies forms has not proved easy. Most traditional concepts of 'being' are either static (like Parmenides) or else almost devoid of content (like the 'pure potency' of Aquinas). There has been a widespread rejection of *static* being in the last century, in favor of *becoming* as primary, as witnessed by the development of pragmatic and process philosophies. Theistic science claims, however, that this is still not enough. We need not just a philosophy of becoming as Whitehead gave. We need a philosophy of the love or propensity that *generates* that becoming at the appropriate moment. Aristotle always emphasized potentialities for becoming, and while Aquinas knew of these, they were not fully integrated into his theology. These considerations bring us back to love, as a universal principle, that exists (in various likenesses) in nature, minds, and (where we started) also in God. Not only does our theology become different (and better, we claim), but so also do physics and psychology.

In contrast to Descartes, we see now the need for active powers in nature and *also* in minds. If he talks of the physical as extension only, he forgets half the story and so does not allow for real causes. Then, as most people realize, although Descartes was talking of passions and emotions, he was completely missing the nature of mental substances such as love and will that would be capable of being the subject of passion and emotion. In contrast to Whitehead, we now need continuing substances and not just events. For the continuation of objects, we need efficacious causes, not retrospective perception.

30.4 Divine immanence

Theism has always maintained that the universe does not exist in its own right, but is sustained (every moment of every day) by the continuing power of God. The question is: does God do this 'at a distance', or is the divine more closely involved in the universe and even present (immanent) within it? We would like to compare this 'general Divine action' with the less frequent 'special divine action' that occurs when God acts specifically in the world in a manner not consistent with its regular behavior. Religions have always insisted on the possibility of special divine action, Saunders[5] reminds us, as only in this way do divine revelation, incarnation or intercession become possible. If special divine action is at any time possible, what does that mean for the 'sanctity' of natural laws?

One common argument follows Leibniz[6], who claimed to Clarke that "if

---

[5] Saunders, *Divine action and modern science*.
[6] Quoted in Brooke (*Science and religion*), p. 149.

God had to remedy the defects of His creation, this was surely to demean his craftsmanship", and that "when God works miracles, he does it not to meet the needs of nature but the needs of grace."[7] This argument has often been used to support Darwinian evolution when talking to the religious: it must have been possible to arrange the details of evolution in advance.

The response to Leibniz is to remember that *all* human life, whether moral, rational or spiritual, must in fact come from the grace of God. We have to insist, with Aristotle, that action (grace, in this case) comes about only from power and presence. This means that all human life depends on the (closer or further) presence of God. Since God must be constantly making changes to the spiritual and mental worlds, the physical world must also be frequently affected by God' actions. Leibniz's mistake is to think that *material* creation is the only objective of God's actions in the world. It is not. The natural laws of the physical world are only approximate and valid subject to *ceterus paribus* (other things being equal). When God is present, other things are not equal.

God is therefore immanent everywhere in creation and especially active where there are mental beings. This implies that there is no strict distinction between general divine action and special divine action. The laws of nature were never strictly and uniformly adhered to in the first place. The only laws that *are* strictly followed are the multilevel generative laws, which is why theistic science concerns itself with knowledge of them.

30.5 Mental dualism

We have the incompleteness of physical laws not only from divine action, but also from actions of the mind. Since we have derived a fully-fledged account of mental substances that is completely non-reductive, those substances (that is, our own minds) must be able to influence the course of physical things. Within the multilevel generative structure that is deduced within theistic science, we certainly do not have physicalism, whether reductive or non-reductive. Neither do we have an emergence theory, since this is usually taken to be emergence from material brains. If, instead, we could consider emergence by creation or generation from God, then perhaps the name could be appropriate. We now have reasons for something

---

[7] From Letter 1 to Samuel Clarke, November 1715.

like a transmission theory of consciousness, as James[8] suggested. We begin to know where that consciousness comes from and its nature when it arrives, so a realistic and more accurate psychology may begin. Neither do we have a dual-aspect monism as James[9] proposed, as followed by many from Russell[10] to Polkinghorne[11], since we do not have a monism in the first place but rather a multi-level reality that includes both God, minds and nature as well as the principles of their interconnections.

---

[8] James, *Human immortality.*
[9] James, "Does 'consciousness' exist?"
[10] Russell, *The analysis of mind.*
[11] Polkinghorne, *Exploring reality.*

31

Formal Modeling

31.1 Is modeling possible here?

Traditionally, science has depended on mathematics in its attempts to describe phenomena in detail, and, more recently, on the ability to make formal models of the systems it is examining. This process began in astronomy, where numerical predictions are important, and progressed with Galileo and Newton to describe the motion of bodies on earth. It has taken a while, but now there are extensive computational models for all kinds of physical processes, from atomic nuclei to chemical combustion to stellar and galactic evolution. In recent decades, detailed statistical and formal models have been constructed for genetics, cell and neural activities, and now cognitive and connectionist models have been simulated on computers to describe psychological processes. The question is whether such models are still useful in theistic science. Or does the range of 'qualities' in all the various degrees and sub-degrees render mathematical models impotent?

I will certainly claim that no mathematical or formal model could *completely* represent the whole theistic universe, even if we do not include the Divine itself. But let me suggest some ways in which mathematical models may still be useful, even if they only partially portray some aspects of each degree and sub-degree. After all, modelers claim that they are 'only modeling' and not producing complete descriptions, and that hence we should never confuse their models for reality.

The reason that models may still be descriptive in many places in our theistic multi-level generative structure is because it is *forms and structures* which are intellectually knowable, and hence are formally knowable.

Loves and dispositions can be known in terms of forms only in so far as they are characterized by their *effects*. Formal models will hence be accurate in some part, just as long as they describe forms and structures faithfully. To be accurate they must make comprehensive attempts to describe all the possible effects of the dispositions, desires or loves.

Formal models must ultimately fail, however, because the possible effects at any level are ultimately from the life which derives from God. They hence may have an 'aspect of infinity' which cannot be captured by listing finite sets of effects or even by functional rules for generating formal mappings from causes to effects. In reality, because all loves come from an infinite God, there will always be the possibility of new and creative responses. Mathematical modelers should not forget that their models are only partial and finite. Subject to this proviso, this chapter considers what kinds of partial and finite models may be usefully constructed.

31.2 Physical models

Physicists have already demonstrated that the physical degree (3.), without consciousness, can be modeled mathematically. Because of the rather uniform metric of physical space, theories of virtual processes can be mathematically formulated and solved for the 3.2 sub-degree, either using perturbation theory or some all-order lattice models on a discretization of space and time that approximates continuous spacetime. In the 3.3 sub-degree of quantum mechanics, instances of the Schrödinger equation have been spectacularly successful in describing low-energy phenomena in nuclear, atomic and chemical physics. In this sub-degree, spacetime is directly taken as continuous, and differential equations are solved to represent the evolution of wave-functions describing propensity fields.

The pre-geometric sub-degree 3.1 has proved more difficult to describe, not least because physicists do not know exactly what processes should be modeled here. As mentioned in Chapter 5, proposals have suggested 'spinors' by Penrose and Rindler[1]; 'loop quantum gravity' as described

---

[1] Penrose and Rindler, *Spinors and space-time. volume 1.*

for example in Rovelli[2], Rovelli[3] in terms of spin networks, and 'causal sets' according to Bombelli et al.[4] and Brightwell et al.[5]

Rovelli[6] interestingly characterizes loop quantum gravity in terms of superpositions of different-sized lattices, which implies that the 'true' quantum dynamics of the 3.1 pre-geometric sub-degree will involve (in sub-sub-degree 3.11) some kind of propensities for producing geometric spin lattices of various sizes. These are largely speculations still being developed.

31.3 Causal sets

Causal sets are models which describe sets of events (regarded as fundamental), some of which are related to others by an 'influenced by' or 'informed by' relation. This relation can be regarded as that of some primitive causation. Following Bombelli et al.[7] and subsequent work, we assume that those relations are non-circular and transitive. That allows us to partially order all the events, making up a 'causal set' of all events in a network structure defined by causal relations.

Physicists then want to recover a uniform space-time with the invariance properties of Galileo and/or Lorentz, so they proceed to assume a 'uniform sprinkling' of events over all space and time such that the events have 'unit density' in some natural units usually taken to be that of the very small Planck length ($\ell_p = \sqrt{\hbar G/c^3} = 1.6 \times 10^{-35}$ metres). Further, Knuth and Bahrenyi[8] show how to use counts of links to define pair intervals, from which a scalar measure can be found that could be an invariant metric under Lorentz transformations. This can be thought of as leading to (or even deriving) Einstein's special relativity.

[2] Rovelli, "Loop quantum gravity."
[3] Rovelli, "Loop quantum gravity."
[4] Bombelli et al., "Space-time as a causal set."
[5] Brightwell et al., "'Observables' in causal set cosmology."
[6] Rovelli, "Loop quantum gravity."
[7] Bombelli et al., "Space-time as a causal set."
[8] Knuth and Bahrenyi, "A derivation of special relativity from causal sets."

31.4 Associative spaces

What I find interesting concerning causal sets is that they may be used to model the general operation of dispositions even in the non-physical spaces. It is not now necessary that sprinklings be generated over a uniform space-time, so causal sets could be used to model the networks of causal processes within the spaces for higher-level operations, spaces which do not have uniform metrics. It could be feasible to define the partially-ordered sets of events for the operations of mental dispositions where the space, we have presumed, has some kind of associative metric associated with types of mental meanings or relations.

To extend causal set theory for this purpose, we will have to generalize the theory in order that *new* events can be indeterministically generated since the existing theory assumes we are already given a full network of events extending through all space and time. It is in the process of generating new events that the details of the metric become important. The likelihood of interaction depends on proximity. Proximity depends on the metric.

More specific investigation of the possible nature of mental spaces is needed. There has been some work on this by Smythies[9] and Smythies[10], but we should not assume (as he did) that the mental spaces are in a higher-dimensional manifold that also includes physical space. To begin with, we have to develop the formulation of causal sets to allow for non-deterministic causation to produce links, so that we are able to distinguish the links connecting actual events from those which have only some propensity of occurring.

31.5 Cognitive and connectionist nets

For some decades now, cognitive psychologists have modeled mental processes in terms of cognitive or connectionist networks. These have often been formally defined in terms of semantic associations. My question now is whether these semantic networks can be re-worked to explicitly derive the manner of existence of ideas or thoughts in some kind of associa-

---

[9] Smythies, *Analysis of perception.*
[10] Smythies, "Space, time and consciousness."

tive space. What kind of metric would be implied for such an associative space?

Part of the answer here depends on which kinds of *operations* are needed describe cognitive processing. Operations are the modification of those ideas and those semantic connections. Very often these are defined in terms of algorithmic procedures attached within the semantic net itself. From the viewpoint of theistic science, however, these procedures should be taken as approximate treatments of the dispositional character of the several dispositions then present and active. Section 22.2 has discussed how the theistic science ontology may give rise to functions and procedures. Now we are asking whether existing procedural modeling in cognitive psychology could be mapped back onto ontologies of dispositions.

Most existing work on cognitive nets involves what theistic science would regard as a single level and perhaps also the neighboring levels in order to implement procedures and memories. To understand the general operation of multilevel structures, we could look for guidance at the work of Pacherie[11], who draws up the flow diagrams of intention, action control and feedback involving at least three levels of psychological processing. Suggestions have been made to generalize the structure of cognitive or connectionist networks. Thompson[12] has talked about 'layered networks', and Commons[13] has talked about 'stacked neural networks', but neither has yet been implemented or tested.

31.6 Self-aware artifacts?

According to theism, organisms or minds do not, strictly speaking, have either self-awareness or self-control. This is because a given discrete degree cannot be aware of itself, and any apparent self-awareness must have come by reflective awareness in a higher degree. We are not in control both of ourselves and of the manner of this controlling, since all life and love comes from God. This means that all (apparent) self-awareness comes from reflection in some prior degree and that all (apparent) self-control comes from love and wisdom operating together in some prior degree.

These considerations will have impacts on the kinds of artificial intel-

---

[11] Pacherie, "The phenomenology of action."
[12] Thompson, *Layered cognitive networks.*
[13] Commons, "Stacked neural networks must emulate evolution's hierarchical complexity."

ligence machines that some may wish to construct. We note, of course, that, strictly speaking, all minds and all machines are equally unable to be self-aware and self-controlled, since they are all systems within the theistic universe. What has to change, therefore, is the rhetoric which broadcasts the likelihood of self-managing devices. This fact is already obvious to some researchers, such Abel[14] for example. He makes the correct stronger argument that physical dynamics "alone cannot organize itself into formally functional systems requiring algorithmic optimization, computational halting, and circuit integration."[15]

31.7 The recursively nested hierarchy

It is also worthwhile to investigate formally the whole hierarchical structure of degrees, sub-degrees, etc that has been deduced from scientific theism, according to the recursive principles described in Chapter 19.

Some questions might be, for example, is it reasonable to use this structure at only a finite depth, by which I mean $n \geq 0$, when we talk about (sub-)^{n}degrees? What is the limiting form of this structure as $n \to \infty$? Does it form a continuous set on a line or in a square? Should we form 'coarse-graining' approximations for finite creatures if we cannot make restrictions to finite n? Formal arguments may help us see how this structure induces qualitatively new dispositions everywhere, at every depth of analysis. Do we, in the 'fine-grain' regime, end up with a continuous spectrum of qualities, or do they forever remain discrete degrees?

Perhaps there is generated some kind of *fractal* structure, even if it is as simple as the Cantor fractal obtained when lines are divided and extended in their central thirds. I certainly use many self-similarities between (sub-)^{n}degree triples and (sub-)^{m}degrees triples for $m \neq n$: these represent possible correspondences of function assumed to occur (in individual ways) at all all levels and between all levels. But what is the full range of self-similarities within the complete structure? What is the range of correspondences, mathematically speaking?

Finally, we would like to know how the full generative structure of

---

[14] Abel, "The capabilities of chaos and complexity."
[15] Abel then notes that "a single exception of non trivial, unaided spontaneous optimization of formal function by truly natural process would falsify this null hypothesis", and that no putative demonstrations are yet close to demonstrating formal controls.

(sub-)^{n}degrees may be represented (in whole, or in parts) by means of physical structures such as a biological body. Are there any formal guidelines for how this may be efficiently accomplished? How is this related to the mapping assumed when I talked in Section 25.6 of how the human functional form is represented and retained in the physical body according to correspondences of function?

32

Possible Objections

32.1 Logical formulation

What is the evidence for your theory? What can be measured, or at least observed, to confirm or refute it? Is it falsifiable, and hence (according to Popper) possibly scientific? My theory is being published for the first time and needs time to grow and to make predictions. I have already stated two predictions about new physical processes that should be measurable (see Chapter 24). There is also one prediction about psychology that could refute my theory, as it predicts that no artificial intelligence machines could be built with equal rational and motivational capacities as humans. That is because only God is the source of understanding and will, and having those capacities requires the full biological details for the human functional form. If mechanical AI machines could be successfully operated, that would refute my theory.

Are the ideas in this book analytic or synthetic? A priori or a posteriori? The ideas here are analytic deductions from the several Postulates of theism. All I have shown strictly *a priori* are the logical connections between those ideas. Later I examined how plausible consequences of these ideas begin to provide possible explanations for mental and physical phenomena. My selection of those phenomena is clearly *a posteriori*, as are those attempted scientific explanations.

You claim to know the nature of things in themselves, as love or whatever. Did Kant not show that this is impossible for us mere mortals? In his pre-critical phase, Kant tried to find the nature of things in themselves along the lines suggested Part II: see Kant[1] for one of his attempts. In Kant, Johnson, and

---

[1] Kant, "Kant's inaugural dissertation."

Magee[2], however, he became conflicted concerning whether knowledge of spiritual things could be possible and (especially) could be possible with mainstream empirical rationality. In the end, he reacted against the presentation of spiritual ideas as presented by Emanuel Swedenborg, apparently in order to appear conventional. I do not react against Swedenborg's presentations of spiritual ideas in the way Kant did.

You have a general scheme with 'generation and selections', but the details are scarce. In fact, anything from wish-fulfillment to strict epiphenomenalism could be made to fit into your framework, depending on the relative powers of generation and selections. It's the details that matter! Yes, I admit that is true. The formal structure of the 'scientific theism' does *not* make specific predictions about the relative influences of previous events (instrumental causes) compared with generative powers (principal causes), so many different detailed scientific theories are possible within its framework. I think of the situation in this manner: quantum mechanics in physics is not a detailed theory but rather a theory-framework in which such theories may be formulated (e.g. by defining the Hilbert space, the observables, and the Hamiltonian). Similarly, the theistic science here is not a specific theory-framework. It is rather a general ontological and philosophical structure in which such theory-frameworks may find a home. It leaves it to empirical investigation and related theorizing to determine what exactly is true within its framework.

32.2 Philosophy

Your view, that everything comes by means of minds that are not God, must be a kind of idealism: that only mental things are real, and that we make our own realities! Do we not refute that, as Samuel Johnson did, by the simple fact of kicking a stone? I agree that everything does come into existence via minds. What is made explicit, however, is that this is not idealism. Actual physical things can be derived from what is spiritual and mental. We are talking here of real (kickable) material things and not just the appearance of them!

I agree that it *appears* that we are creating our own reality in a 'new age' sense, but I must insist that that would be only an inadequate and partial description of the whole story. It would be to forget that actual physical events are the ultimate products of all actions and are necessary for the

---

[2] Kant, Johnson, and Magee, *Kant on Swedenborg.*

continued existence of permanent mental and spiritual forms. That is, we are severely constrained in *how* we create our reality.

In any case, the process of creation is not purely personal or individual, but communal, in fact common throughout the physical universe, and in fact managed by the One God.

Your view, that everything is causal and exists in some space, must be a kind of physicalism. Especially since I believe that everything which has a physical effect must be physical. I agree that, if you wanted to follow this rule to define causality, then everything would be physical.[3] But the physicalities thereby introduced would be unrecognizable to today's naturalistic scientists and philosophers, since these physicalities include love, wisdom, will and understanding, in fact all of spiritual and mental life in an entirely *non-reductive* manner. Those scientists would be very unwilling and unhappy to hear their beloved 'natural laws' extended to include such things. I, therefore, choose a different meaning of physical: as that which is not living and not conscious.

You claim that God knows the future, even if that future does not yet exist. If so, what is the truth-maker for that knowledge? There must be one, if the knowledge is true! And if there is one, does that not imply that there are already facts which imply the character of future events, so (in particular character if not in actualities) they already exist, in contradiction to your claim? It indeed appears that if God did know truly what was going to happen in the future, then, as Johnson[4] argues, there must be true facts existing now which are the truth-maker for that true belief. Hence, even if the future does not yet exist, it must already be definite what that future will be. My preferred response to this objection is to insist that it is not true that God knows what will necessarily happen in the future, but *only* that he knows what *would* happen if there were *no* divine intervention to change it. And then I insist that God is ontologically free, in the sense that not *all* future divine events are the subject of divine foreknowledge. Admittedly, that is difficult for outsiders to determine (without asking).

---

[3] This issue relates to the discussions about the definition of 'physical' in Chapter 7. I once entertained the definition of physical as everything that exists and changes, in which case minds and souls would be physical. Or, following Aristotle, we could define the physical as that which has its source of change inside itself, and then even God is physical (and, depending on what you mean by 'inside', perhaps *only* God is physical!).

[4] Johnson, "God, fatalism, and temporal ontology."

How can you be so sure that there are no *spatial relations between distinct sub-degrees? Admittedly there is discreteness between God and the world, but why within the world?* Perhaps we could consider the theoretical proposals of Smythies[5] and Carr[6]. John Smythies insists (as do I) that there are mental spaces in order to contain the distinct and concurrent existences of our mental content. But he goes on to insist that such mental spaces are subspaces of a higher-dimensional reality that also includes our familiar three-dimensional space and one-dimensional time.

This is not my view. Mental spaces should have a completely different topological and metric structure, based for example on similarities of meaning, and so should be associative spaces rather than physical spaces. I also do not follow Smythies' theory, because I hold that mentality and physicality are two distinct and discrete degrees without any possibility of continuous transformations between them.

32.3 Theology

Is this theory Bible based? Or, does it contradict the Bible in places? The theism here is admittedly not based directly on the interpretation of specific verses in the Bible, Torah, or the Qu'ran, but, I claim, is based on the principles by means of which those sacred scriptures may be understood as the product of a Loving God. I admit that those texts sometimes appear to contradict such a nature of God, but I claim that those contradictions arise because it is *us* who are angry, not God, and, in that case, we *think* that God is angry.

Furthermore, we now know that we have to take into account the existence of internal or spiritual meanings of those texts. It may be (even if we do not all agree with this) that God's intended meaning of various parts of the texts reside in the internal sense rather than in the literal sense. On the basis of understanding the various texts as 'multilayered' or 'thick' documents, I confess that I take those books that have multiple levels of meaning as indeed the Word of God.

Is this view an ex nihilo *creation?* Traditionally, creation *ex nihilo*, creation out of nothing, is taken to mean that, prior to the first creation, nothing existed. God did not make the universe from pre-existing building blocks but started from scratch. Creation *ex nihilo* refers thus to a supernatural

---

[5] Smythies, *Analysis of perception.*
[6] Carr, "Mind and the cosmos."

event which was the beginning of the universe. The theism of this book is strictly in accordance with all these requirements, so the term should be appropriate.

However, the philosopher in me queries the correctness of the term 'creation *ex nihilo*'. Since, as we know, nothing comes from nothing, how can there be creation out of nothing? It does not make sense, and Parmenides would strongly object to non-being changing to being. How is this query usually responded to in theology? I should think that theologians insist that before the universe, it was not the case that 'nothing existed', since in fact *God existed*. That is, there was the *being* of God even before the being of the universe. The correct significance of the phrase 'creation *ex nihilo*', therefore, must be to deny 'creation not out of previous ingredients' but still to affirm 'creation from God'. It should insist on creation that proceeds *from* an immaterial source without being constructed or assembled *out of* pieces of that source. The 'being' of creation is new, and it derives from the being of God, not from previous materials. This should be the standard meaning within theism.

Do you deduce scientific conclusions from religious doctrine? Is this not a kind of fundamentalism? If religious doctrine is to fully agree with scientific theory, then one or both of them has to be changed. They certainly do not fully harmonize with each other at present! So the answer to the first question is yes, but we must specify *which* religious doctrines are being used as the basis.

However much scientists declaim against 'fundamentalists', we should note that scientists are themselves very much in favor of a fundamentalism of their own: the one that bases scientific knowledge on a unified theory of everything. They say, of course, that this is the good kind and admit it is their wonderful dream to produce such a *fundamental* theory. So fundamentalism, as such, is not the problem.

Are you not bringing God in to solve even the simplest interpretation problems in quantum mechanics? Even maybe in classical physics? It may indeed seem like this, but most often I am not bringing in God to solve problems in physics, but using principles derived from God to make theories in terms of which those problems are solved.

And I admit indeed that, sometimes, there may be direct or indirect influences from God, souls and/or minds that influence outcomes in quantum mechanics, so even those derived theories are only valid within a larger picture. Maybe physicists are unhappy with this, but they should remember that, according to theism, even the smallest particles of nature are sustained in their being and their interactions by God, and that happens not abstractly but by the real presence of God.

Theist and dualist traditions say that minds and God are without parts, simple and indivisible. Here also? I do note that many traditional philosophical views of minds and God take those beings as *purely simple*. This was the view of Aquinas and his followers and was used by Descartes with respect to his rational soul. It continues to be used today by those who argue, for example, from the incorrigibility of introspective knowledge. God, they insist, must not be made out of parts, but must be simple, since there is no other being to assemble any parts. According to Descartes, thought is the essence of minds or souls and is the entirety of that essence. A soul simply *is* thinking, and that is all it is, they say.

My response to this query concerning God is given in Chapter 13, and concerning minds in Section 27.1.

Are we humans not now living ourselves? Is my life not my own? Can I not have some privacy? The whole theism here is built on the basis that we at least appear to ourselves to be living from ourselves, that my life is my own, and that the mental contents of humans are private to themselves. It is on that basis that we enjoy life, love to live, and hence can grow to love what good and true. Nevertheless, we must admit that truth tells us that God is life itself, and that (in reflection) we must acknowledge that fact if we want to avoid serious mistakes in our spiritual development. Even if we follow theistic science and believe that minds are objectively real, our everyday thoughts are not automatically broadcast to our neighbors. Telepathy may be theoretically possible, but in practice it will be no more frequent than before.

Is the world now a part of God (panentheism)? You can certainly argue that the substance of the world flows from the substance of God, and that hence we are really part of God, which is panentheism or even pantheism. However, the 'flowing' is *not continuous*, but a serious of *discrete* steps, and the discreteness of those steps means that, in the end, we have a life that is distinct from God (see Section 18.2). In fact, we can even use our life to turn away from God and to act against God. Since God is one and is unselfish love, that implies we are certainly not part of God.

Only humans are said to be an 'image and likeness of God', not even animals. But you apply it to everything: atoms and all! The verses of Genesis 1:26-27 certainly only use the 'image' and 'likeness' in connection to humans, and not in connection to the plants and animals that were previously created. I argue at some length in Chapter 10, however, that even a very preliminary inspection shows some similarities between plants, animals and humans. Recent results in molecular biology and genetics show very many even deeper similarities. I conclude that as long as we pay attention to the *limits* of the similarities, we can find new levels of meaning for 'image and likeness'. In Islam, for example in Unal[7], it is equivalently claimed that the universe is "the realm where God's Names are manifested".

Could you say more about the trinity? It appears everywhere in this book! I agree that the concepts here of Love, Wisdom and Action within the being of God are very similar to the concept of the Christian Trinity (see Section 14.7). It may be possible for Christians to extend the ideas here, using them as a model for how their Trinity may be understood. They may take the Father as referring to the Divine Love that is the original source, the Son as the Wisdom that is the human face of God, and the Holy Spirit as the Action or Proceeding which goes out into the world. However, in order to focus on core or generic theism, I can neither confirm nor deny this interpretation of the triad nature within God.

This issue is complicated by some theologians who insist that the Trinity is only to be accepted, not to be understood. If someone claims to understand what it means, those theologians are immediately suspicious that some serious error has been (thereby) made. That complication seems to make a mockery of serious intellectual effort towards comprehension of what really is the case.

I am not religious (or, not a monotheist, or Buddhist), so how can I believe what you say? It must be clear that the entire derivation presented has been based on theism. If, however, it points to anything true about spiritual reality, then we must expect that previously enlightened teachers will have come across similar views, in part if not as a whole.

It is relevant to examine the Buddhist concept of Śūnyatā, taken to mean 'emptiness' or 'voidness' with respect to the inner being of humans. It asserts that nothing possesses an essential or enduring identity and that the

---

[7] Unal, *The Qur'an.*

realization of this fact leads to wisdom and inner peace. This is clearly related to the theistic claim that we humans have no life or being that belongs to ourselves since all Life and Being strictly belong only to God. Our reflection that this is true is, within theism, part of the path towards wisdom.

What about the problem of evil (natural and/or man-made)? Now God does not just create the universe at the beginning, but is involved with every step, so is He not more responsible for evil of all kinds? The problem of evil is discussed in Chapter 29, but not in the sense of explaining how all evils are created in a world controlled by God. Rather, I explain from general principles that God is *not* willing to be omnipotent and to remove from existence all those people who have made selfish, dominating, possessive or evil loves as an non-negotiable part of their own life, as part of the their own principal love. This means that many evils in the world have to be managed, rather than eliminated, by God.

32.4 Psychology

How do you solve the 'binding problem': how the mind can be unified when the brain has many parts? In theistic science, this difference of numerical quantities is solved because a mind is a small collection of mental substances (in one of the mental sub-degrees) that is responsible for *generating* a large number of neurological activities in the brain. There is no requirement in the theory of generation and selection that one cause cannot have many effects, either simultaneously or successively. The binding problem is only serious when identity or reductive theories of minds are attempted, and neither of those theories is part of theistic science.

Have you really explained what are mind, consciousness, feelings, soul? Have you solved this 'hard problem.' Not really: it is more like a homunculus explanation, always deferring to something else not explained! I agree that I have not really explained what consciousness is and why it is necessary. So, in some sense, the hard problem still remains. What theistic science does, however, is to very plausibly assert that consciousness is, in essence, the awareness of the *doing* when love and wisdom act together in the spiritual or mental degrees. Any such doing is essentially conscious, and the essence of any consciousness is the occurrence of such doing. This is, indeed, a kind of identity theory but not a reductive account and certainly not a mind-brain identity theory!

Mind-body dualism is still incomprehensible me! How can there be such connections as you are claiming, between things so incompatible? This question is really about how minds can *ever* be related to bodies, since they seem so different. This query has been at the heart of much resistance to mind-body interaction theories over the years, despite that interaction being observed by everybody in every waking minute of every day. Any answer to this query must allow that mind-body connections, as well as being observable and frequent, are also law-like, are based on some comprehensive and rational theory of the world, and are similar to other processes which are (ideally) already well known. This book contains, I believe, the ingredients for formulating such an answer.

How can minds be disembodied? I cannot make sense of a whole person living without a physical body. One frequent belief is that our minds and souls are necessarily involved with our bodies. That is certainly our common experience during life on earth. Nevertheless, theistic religions have commonly asserted that we will still have some kind of life after the death of our body and that this non-physical life may be available in other circumstances as well.[8] According to theistic science, however, we have physical, mental and spiritual *bodies* whenever we have physical life, mental content in our mind, and our own spiritual awareness, respectively. This implies that the descriptions 'embodied' and 'disembodied' are not sufficient to distinguish physical from non-physical existence.

The Christian resurrection is believed to be 'resurrection of the body' and is commonly taken to be resurrection of the physical body, but now, however, the nature of the resurrection body is not entirely obvious. Paul, for example, had the idea of resurrection as a spiritual body[9], and this has been the source of considerable debate over the centuries.

How can minds be embodied? I cannot make sense of mental life living with even a non-physical body. Another frequent belief is that our minds and souls are necessarily distinct from our bodies. We can then possibly exist in states

---

[8] The religions claim that heavenly states are particularly accessible during separation from the physical body, but (with more work) are also available without such a separation.
[9] 1 Cor 15:44.

out of our body which may reasonably be called 'non-physical', 'supernatural' or 'spiritual'. Descartes took our souls to be essentially distinct from physical things, which he defined as the extended. This view has persisted with the belief today that our minds are entirely non-spatial. We never see ideas in physical space. We never meet the number three on the street, for example.

Nevertheless, the actual experience of those who have had some active life apart from their physical body does point to this life being based on a particular person's point of view in some space, with the person himself or herself possessing some apparent body. In a mental world, appearing to have a body means you *do* have a body.

I therefore see life at all levels (physical, mental and spiritual) as essentially involving a personal body, though of different kinds of substances, in different spaces, at each level. I claim that this involves no reductive treatment or possible denigration of those respective manners of living.

32.5 Biology

You seem to be bringing back 'life' as a something non-physical. Surely science has long ago shown that living organisms are entirely explainable by their physical constituents! It is true that theistic science does not ascribe all biological activities to the operation of physical laws in a causally-closed physical universe because it treats living creatures as under the influence of mental or spiritual influx from distinct discrete degrees. This treatment, however, does not introduce 'life' as some new factor about which we know nothing. It introduces only the possible affects of mental activity, about which we already know quite a lot. We are certainly capable of investigating this in more detail in the future.

32.6 Physics

Physicists have shown the conservation of energy. This shows the closure of the physical world! It is a basic principle! How do you escape that? It is true that the principle of conservation of energy for isolated systems is one of the most faithfully believed principles in the physics of the last 150 years. It is taken as a rigorous principle, for example, for the rejection of possible perpetual-motion machines. Certainly, no violations of this principle have been discovered. In special relativity, this generalizes to the conservation of 4-momentum, which includes conservations of energy and 3-

dimensional vector momentum. The validity of the principle can be derived from invariance under spatial translations and time shifts.

However, as discussed in Section 20.6, within theism we must take into account that no physical system is strictly closed. Every substance of every discrete degree is necessarily and always open to the reception of divine life. Secondly, space and time will not be isotropic if there are spatiotemporal variations of the spacetime metric or of coupling parameters (see Section 25.2). We already know how to treat some metric variations, namely those that occur according to general relativity and generate gravity, but others may be possible.

The generalization of the conservation laws according to general relativity may well happen again if more general and new laws of nature are predicted and/or discovered. Theistic science essentially predicts that this will occur, and, moreover, that the new laws will not be purely physical but will describe possible influences from mental activities. We await with eagerness to see what experimental evidence may support this prediction.[10]

---

[10] If you have more penetrating objections or think my responses are not adequate, please email me at ijt@ianthompson.org, and I can revise this chapter.

33

Conclusions

This book introduces connections between theism and the sciences, and so it enables us to begin what can be called 'theistic science'. On the way, it had to clarify exactly what the essential parts of theism were, making what was called a 'scientific theism' built on deductions from basic postulates about God. Connections have been made between theistic science and the sciences of physics and psychology. There will be further consequences for biology, neurophysiology, and the theory of evolution. I admit that we only have a skeleton for a scientific theory, not the detailed structures and mechanisms that come from further observations and analyses, but a body without a skeleton cannot stand.

This progress has been enabled by recent advances in the theory of dispositions. One primary new step is taking 'loves' and 'propensities' seriously as kinds of dispositions, with the ontological framework that allows such dispositions to be the substances underlying objects (physical as well as mental). A second step is to take seriously some ideas of practical religion, such as that 'God is Love'. The third new step is to systematically apply a theory of 'derivative dispositions', in order to enable a general theory of 'multiple generative levels', some of which are already known in physics and psychology. Such a theory of multiple levels has been deduced as a consequence of theism. We interpreted this as the spiritual, mental and physical that we already know (or at least, should know). The existence of a multilevel theory including the mental and physical degrees, as distinct but related, goes a long way to formulating an alternative metaphysical view to naturalism. It should enable scientists to consider a wider range of theories than hitherto, when trying to understand the phenomena they observe in and outside themselves.

Overall, the presentation of this book has a bearing on the validity and possible acceptance of theism as a coherent theory. We see specific elements of psychology and specific relationships in physics that are better explained with the theistic postulates than before. The theistic claims can provide novel predictions or at the very least explain what we already know with more rather than less understanding. Theism may also make some things that are left still contingent (but factually certain), like evolution, growth and development, be necessary with the addition of theism. I am offering a way to be theists and still be scientifically respectable, and maybe I am also showing that there is a better explanation of science, and that we might have to accept theism to have that explanation. Which it is will depend your underlying prior dispositions (your loves), and on how successful these explanations will be in the light of further research.

Appendix A
Theistic Postulates

Here is a list of the theistic postulates as presented in the earlier chapters:

Postulate 1 *God exists.*

Postulate 2 *God is One.*

Postulate 3 *God is Being Itself.*

Postulate 4 *God loves us unselfishly.*

Postulate 5 *All the world, and each of its parts, is a kind of image of God.*

Postulate 6 *God is Love.*

Postulate 7 *God is Life Itself.*

Postulate 8 *We all live from God's life, as if from ourselves.*

Postulate 9 *Our actions (what we actually do) are our own.*

Postulate 10 *The life we have from God is in accordance with what we have actually done.*

Postulate 11 *God is a unity, in which there is an infinity of what may be intellectually distinguished, but what is not in fact separated.*

Postulate 12 *God is Wisdom Itself.*

Postulate 13 *God contains proceeding Actions.*

Postulate 14 *God exists eternally.*

Postulate 15 *What is unified and continuous in God is imaged as discrete distributions.*

Postulate 16 *The relations between created realms is an image of the relation between God and creation.*

Postulate 17 *Whenever love acts by means of wisdom, that action is a conscious action. There is consciousness of the production of the result, and also of the delight that arises from the achievement of that production.*

The above postulates are not all logically independent, since often later postulates are refinements and applications of earlier postulates. In particular,

- Postulate 3 implies Postulates 1, 2, and 14.
- Postulate 7 implies Postulates 6 and 4, once that life is understood as unselfish love.
- Postulate 10 implies Postulates 8 and 9.
- Postulate 11 implies Postulate 2.
- Postulates 15 and 16 are particular applications of Postulate 5.

Simplified Theistic List

A simplified list of postulates may therefore be given, after reordering to lead from God down to us, as follows:

Postulate' 1 *God is Being Itself.*

Postulate' 2 *God is Life (unselfish Love) Itself.*

Postulate' 3 *God is Wisdom Itself.*

Postulate' 4 *God contains proceeding Actions.*

Postulate' 5 *In God, there is an infinity of what may be intellectually distinguished, but what is not in fact separated.*

Postulate' 6 *All the world, and each of its parts, is a kind of image of God.*

Postulate' 7 *The life we have from God is in accordance with what we have actually done.*

Postulate' 8 *Whenever love acts by means of wisdom, that action is a conscious action. There is consciousness of the production of the result and also of the delight that arises from the achievement of that production.*

Here, again, Postulate 2 may be taken as implying Postulate 1, once the nature of Love itself is understood as substance and Being.

Appendix B
Further Resources

Related works by the author

Websites:

- This book: http://beginningtheisticscience.com
- Blog: http://blog.beginningtheisticscience.com
- Ontology: http://www.GenerativeScience.org
- Dualism: http://www.newDualism.org
- Theism: http://www.newTheism.com
- Theistic sciences: http://www.TheisticScience.org
- Spiritual growth: http://www.7DaysofCreation.info
- Personal: http://www.IanThompson.org

Books:

1. I.J. Thompson, *Philosophy of Nature and Quantum Reality*, Pleasanton CA: Eagle Pearl Press, 2010.
   This book, written in 1993, develops a first-principles ontology for processes with only one generative level, and hence very simple compared with the multilevel structures here. It does, however, include a detailed description of the relations between potentiality and actuality, extensiveness and space, and how 'being' remains constant during changes.

Articles:

1. I.J. Thompson, *Two Ways of Looking at Time*, Cogito **1** (Jan 1987) 4-6
2. I.J. Thompson, *The Nature of Substance*, Cogito, **2** (1988) 17-19.

3. I.J. Thompson, *Real Dispositions in the Physical World*, British Journal for the Philosophy of Science, **39** (1988) 67-79.

4. I.J. Thompson, *The Consistency Of Physical Law With Divine Immanence*, Science & Christian Belief **5** (1993) 19-36.

5. I.J. Thompson, *Are Quantum Physics and Spirituality related?*, New Philosophy, **107** (2002) 333-355.

6. I.J. Thompson, *Discrete Degrees Within and Between Nature and Mind*, pp. 99-123 (2009) in Antonietti et al. (eds.) *Psycho-Physical Dualism Today: An Interdisciplinary Approach*, Lanham MD: Lexington Books, 2009.

7. I.J. Thompson, *Derivative Dispositions and Multiple Generative Levels*, in M. Suárez (ed.), *Probabilities, Causes, and Propensities in Physics*, Synthese Library, Springer, 2011.

Works Cited

Abel, David L. "The capabilities of chaos and complexity." *Int. J. Mol. Sci.* 10, no. 1 (2009): 247–291.

Armstrong, D. M. *A world of states of affairs.* Cambridge; New York: Cambridge University Press, 1997.

———. "Dispositions are causes." *Analysis* 30, no. 1 (1969): 23–26.

Baars, Bernard J. *A cognitive theory of consciousness.* Cambridge [England]; New York: Cambridge University Press, 1988.

Bassi, Angelo and Giancarlo Ghirardi. "Dynamical reduction models." *Physics Rep.* 379 (2003): 257–426.

Batthyany, Alexander. "Mental causation and free will after Libet and Soon: reclaiming conscious agency." In *Irreducibly conscious: selected papers on consciousness*, edited by Alexander Batthyany and Avshalom C. Elitzur. Heidelberg: Universitats-Verlag Winter, 2009.

Batthyany, Alexander and Avshalom C. Elitzur, editors. *Irreducibly conscious: selected papers on consciousness.* Heidelberg: Universitats-Verlag Winter, 2009.

Bawden, H. Heath. "The psychical as a biological directive." *Philosophy of Science* 14, no. 1 (1947): 56–67.

Bekenstein, Jacob and Marcelo Schiffer. "Varying fine structure 'constant' and charged black holes." *Phys. Rev. D* 80, no. 12 (2009): 123508.

Bell, J.S. "Against 'measurement'." *Physics World* 8 (1990): 33–40.

Bielfeldt, Dennis. "Can western monotheism avoid substance dualism?" *Zygon* 36 (2001): 153–177.

Bird, Alexander. *Nature's metaphysics: laws and properties.* Oxford; New York: Clarendon Press; Oxford University Press, 2007.

————. "Structural properties revisited." In *Dispositions and causes*, edited by Toby Handfield. Oxford; New York: Oxford University Press: Clarendon Press; 2009.

————. "The dispositionalist conception of laws." *Foundations of Science* 10, no. 4 (2005): 353–370.

————. "The ultimate argument against Armstrong's contingent necessitation view of laws." *Analysis* 65, no. 286 (2005): 147–155.

Bolton, Robert. "Dualism and the philosophy of the soul." *Sacred Web* 4 (1999).

Bombelli, L. et al. "Space-time as a causal set." *Physical Review Letters* 59, no. 5 (1987): 521–524.

Boudry, Maarten, S Blancke, and Johan Braeckman. "How not to attack intelligent design creationism: philosophical misconceptions about methodological naturalism." *Foundations of Science* 15 (2010): 1–18.

Brainerd, C.J. "The stage question in cognitive-developmental theory." *Behavioral and Brain Sciences* 2 (1978): 173–182.

Bratman, Michael. *Intention, plans, and practical reason*. Cambridge, Mass.: Harvard University Press, 1987.

Brentano, Franz Clemens. *Psychology from an empirical standpoint*. London; New York: Routledge and Kegan Paul; Humanities Press, 1874.

Brightwell, Graham et al. "'Observables' in causal set cosmology." *Phys. Rev. D* 67, no. 8 (2003): 084031.

Broad, C. D. *Examination of McTaggart's philosophy*. Cambridge, U.K.: The University Press, 1933.

————. *The mind and its place in nature*. London: Paul, Trench, Trubner, 1925.

Brooke, John Hedley. *Science and religion: some historical perspectives*. Cambridge; New York: Cambridge University Press, 1991.

Brown, Richard. "Deprioritizing the a priori arguments against physicalism." *Journal of Consciousness Studies* 17 (2010): 47–69(23).

Carr, Bernard. "Mind and the cosmos." In *Science, consciousness and ultimate reality*, edited by David Lorimer, 33–64. Exeter, UK; Charlottesville, VA: Imprint Academic, 2004.

Cartwright, Nancy. *How the laws of physics lie*. Oxford; New York: Clarendon Press; Oxford University Press, 1983.

Chakravartty, Anjan. "The dispositional essentialist view of properties and laws." *International Journal of Philosophical Studies* 11, no. 4 (2003): 393 – 413.

Chalmers, David J. "Facing up to the problem of consciousness." *Journal of Consciousness Studies* 2, no. 3 (1995): 200–19.

Cobb, John Boswell. *A Christian natural theology. Based on the thought of Alfred North Whitehead.* Philadelphia: Westminster Press, 1965.

Commons, Michael Lamport. "Introduction to the model of hierarchical complexity and its relationship to postformal action." *World Futures* 64, no. 5 (2008): 305–320.

———. "Stacked neural networks must emulate evolution's hierarchical complexity." *World Futures* 64, no. 5 (2008): 444–451.

Corcoran, Kevin, editor. *Soul, body, and survival: essays on the metaphysics of human persons.* Ithaca: Cornell University Press, 2001.

Cowan, J L. "The paradox of omnipotence." *Analysis* 25 (1965): 102–108.

Coyne, Jerry A. *Seeing and believing the never-ending attempt to reconcile science and religion, and why it is doomed to fail.* The New Republic, 2009.

Dalai Lama, The. *The universe in a single atom: the convergence of science and spirituality.* New York: Morgan Road Books, 2005.

Damasio, Antonio R. *The feeling of what happens: body and emotion in the making of consciousness.* New York: Harcourt Brace, 1999.

Davidson, D. "Causal relations." *Journal Of Philosophy* 64, no. 21 (1967): 691–703.

Dawkins, Richard. *The God delusion.* Boston: Houghton Mifflin Co., 2006.

Day, Vox. *The irrational atheist: dissecting the unholy trinity of Dawkins, Harris, and Hitchens.* Dallas, Tex.: BenBella Books, 2008.

Elder, Crawford L. "Laws, natures, and contingent necessities." *Philosophy and Phenomenological Research* 54, no. 3 (1994): 649–667.

Ellis, Brian D. "Causal laws and singular causation." *Philosophy and Phenomenological Research* 61, no. 2 (2000): 329–351.

———. "Causal powers and categorical properties." In *The metaphysics of powers: their grounding and their manifestations,* edited by Anna Marmodoro, 133–142. New York: Routledge, 2010.

———. *Scientific essentialism.* Cambridge; New York: Cambridge University Press, 2001.

Ellis, Brian D. and Caroline Lierse. "Dispositional essentialism." *Australasian Journal of Philosophy* 72, no. 1 (1994): 27 –45.

Emmet, Dorothy. *The effectiveness of causes.* London: Macmillan, 1984.

Erikson, Erik H. *Problem of ego identity.* New York: International Universities Press, 1956.

Erikson, Erik H. and Joan M. Erikson. *The life cycle completed.* New York: W.W. Norton, 1997.

Everett, Hugh. "'Relative state' formulation of quantum mechanics." *Phys. Rev. D* 29, no. 3 (1957): 454.

Feldman, D.H. "Piaget's stages: the unfinished symphony of cognitive development." *New Ideas in Psychology* 22, no. 3 (2004): 175–231.

Feser, Edward. *Aquinas*. Richmond: Oneworld, 2009.

Fetzer, James H. "World of dispositions." *Synthese* 34, 4 (1977): 397–421.

Feyerabend, Paul. *Against method: outline of an anarchistic theory of knowledge*. London: NLB, 1975.

Fingelkurts, Andrew A., Alexander A. Fingelkurts, and Carlos F. H. Neves. "Natural world physical, brain operational, and mind phenomenal space–time." *Physics of Life Reviews* 7, no. 2 (2010): 195–249.

Fischer, Kurt W. "A theory of cognitive development: the control and construction of hierarchies of skills." *Psychological Review* 87, no. 6 (1980): 477–531.

Gell-Mann, M. and J.B. Hartle. "Classical equations for quantum systems." *Phys. Rev. D* 47, no. 8 (1993): 3345–3382.

Ghirardi, Giancarlo, A. Rimini, and T. Weber. "Unified dynamics for microscopic and macroscopic systems." *Phys. Rev. D* 34, no. 2 (1986): 470.

Gisin, Nicolas. "The free will theorem, stochastic quantum dynamics and true becoming in relativistic quantum physics." *arXiv* quant-ph (2010). eprint: 1002.1392v1.

Godel, K. "An example of a new type of cosmological solutions of Einstein's field equations of gravitation." *Rev. Mod. Phys.* 21, no. 3 (1949): 447.

Goswami, Amit. *God is not dead: what quantum physics tells us about our origins and how we should live*. Ahmedabad: Jaico Pub. House, 2009.

Goswami, U. "Cognitive development: No stages please—we're British." *British Journal of Psychology* 92, no. 1 (2001): 257–277.

Gould, Stephen Jay. "Nonoverlapping magisteria." *Natural History* 106 (1997): 22–27.

Gowan, John Curtis. *Development of the creative individual*. San Diego: R.R. Knapp, 1972.

Halliwell, J J. "A review of the decoherent histories approach to quantum mechanics." *Annals of the New York Academy of Sciences* 755, no. 1 (1995): 726–740.

Handfield, Toby, editor. *Dispositions and causes*. Oxford; New York: Oxford University Press: Clarendon Press; 2009.

Harré, Rom and Edward H. Madden. *Causal powers: a theory of natural necessity*. Totowa, N.J.: Rowman and Littlefield, 1975.

Harris, Sam. *The end of faith: religion, terror, and the future of reason.* New York: W.W. Norton & Co., 2004.

Hartshorne, Charles. *A natural theology for our time.* La Salle, Ill.: Open Court, 1967.

Heisenberg, Werner. *On modern physics.* London: Orion Press, 1961.

Herbert, Nick. *Quantum reality: beyond the new physics.* Garden City, N.Y.: Anchor Press/Doubleday, 1985.

Hume, David. *Dialogues concerning natural religion.* London, 1779.

Inhelder, Bärbel and Jean Piaget. *The growth of logical thinking from childhood to adolescence; an essay on the construction of formal operational structures.* New York: Basic Books, 1958.

Isham, C.J., R. Penrose, and D.W. Sciama, editors. *Quantum gravity; Proceedings of the Oxford Symposium, Harwell, Berks., England, February 15, 16, 1974.* 1975.

Jacobs, J.D. "Powerful qualities, not pure powers." *Monist* 94, no. 1 (2011): 81–102.

James, William. "Does 'consciousness' exist?" *Journal of Philosophy, Psychology, and Scientific Methods* 1 (1904): 477–491.

———. *Human immortality: two supposed objections to the doctrine.* Boston; New York: Houghton, Mifflin and Co., 1898.

Johnson, David Kyle. "God, fatalism, and temporal ontology." *Rel. Stud.* 45, no. 04 (2009): 435.

Kaempffer, F. A. *Concepts in quantum mechanics.* New York: Academic Press, 1965.

Kant, Immanuel. *Kant's inaugural dissertation and early writings on space.* Chicago; London: The Open Court Pub. Co., 1929.

———. "Thoughts on the true estimation of living forces." In *Kant's inaugural dissertation and early writings on space.* Chicago; London: The Open Court Pub. Co., 1929.

Kant, Immanuel, Gregory R Johnson, and Glenn Alexander Magee. *Kant on Swedenborg: dreams of a spirit-seer and other writings.* Vol. no. 15. West Chester, Pa.: Swedenborg Foundation, 2002.

Katzav, Joel. "Dispositions and the principle of least action." *Analysis* 64, no. 3 (2004): 206–214.

Kim, Jaegwon. "Lonely souls: causality and substance dualism." In *Soul, body, and survival: essays on the metaphysics of human persons,* edited by Kevin Corcoran. Ithaca: Cornell University Press, 2001.

Knuth, Kevin H and Newshaw Bahrenyi. "A derivation of special relativity from causal sets." *arXiv* math-ph (2010). eprint: 1005.4172v1.

Leibniz, G. W. *Monadology*. La Salle: Open Court, 1902, 1714.

Lewis, Peter J. "Quantum mechanics, orthogonality, and counting." *The British Journal for the Philosophy of Science* 48, no. 3 (1997): 313–328.

Libet, Benjamin et al. "Time of conscious intention to act in relation to onset of cerebral activity (readiness-potential). the unconscious initiation of a freely voluntary act." *Brain* 106, no. 3 (1983): 623–642.

Lightman, Alan. *Does God exist?* Http://salon.com/a/sfiWaAA, 2011.

Lorimer, David, editor. *Science, consciousness and ultimate reality*. Exeter, UK; Charlottesville, VA: Imprint Academic, 2004.

Lund, David H. *Persons, souls, and death: a philosophical investigation of an afterlife*. Jefferson, N.C.: McFarland & Co., Inc., Publishers, 2009.

Mackie, J.L. "Evil and omnipotence." *Mind* 64, no. 254 (1955): 200–212.

Marmodoro, Anna, editor. *The metaphysics of powers: their grounding and their manifestations*. New York: Routledge, 2010.

Martin, C. "The need for ontology - some choices." *Philosophy* 68, 266 (1993): 505–522.

Maxwell, Nicholas. "Is the quantum world composed of propensitons?" physics.hist-ph (2010). eprint: `1101.4479`.

———. "Quantum propensiton theory: A testable resolution of the wave/particle dilemma." *Br J Philos Sci* 39, no. 1 (1988): 1–50.

Menzies, Peter. "Nature's metaphysics." *Analysis* 69, no. 4 (2009): 769–778.

Meschini, Diego. "A metageometric enquiry concerning time, space, and quantum physics." *arXiv* gr-qc (2008). eprint: `0804.3742v1`.

Molnar, George. *Powers: a study in metaphysics*. Oxford; New York: Oxford University Press, 2003.

Mumford, Stephen. *Dispositions*. Oxford; New York: Oxford University Press, 1998.

———. "Ellis and Lierse on dispositional essentialism." *Australasian Journal of Philosophy* 73, no. 4 (1995): 606–612.

———. "Intentionality and the physical: a new theory of disposition ascription." *Philosophical Quarterly* 49, no. 195 (1999): 215–225.

Murphy, M, J Webb, and V Flambaum. "Further evidence for a variable fine-structure constant from Keck/HIRES QSO absorption spectra." *Monthly Notices of the Royal Astronomical Society* 345, no. 2 (2003): 609–638.

Pacherie, E. "The phenomenology of action: a conceptual framework." *Cognition* 107, no. 1 (2008): 179–217.

Paley, John. "The Cartesian melodrama in nursing." *Nursing Philosophy* 3, no. 3 (2002): 189–192.

Palmquist, Stephen. *Parapsychology, philosophy and the mind: a festschrift in honour of John Beloff's 80th birthday.* Jefferson, N.C.: McFarland Press, 2002.

Peacock, Kent. *The no-signalling theorems: a nitpicking distinction.* Http://people.uleth.ca/~kent.peacock/FQXi_v2.pdf, 2009.

Pennock, Robert T. "Supernaturalist explanations and the prospects for a theistic science or 'how do you know it was the lettuce?'" "*Naturalism, Theism and the Scientific Enterprise*" Conference (1997): 1–25.

Penrose, Roger and Wolfgang Rindler. *Spinors and space-time. volume 1, two-spinor calculus and relativistic fields.* Cambridge [England]; New York: Cambridge University Press, 1987.

Pfeiffer, Trish., John E. Mack, and Paul Devereux. *Mind before matter: visions of a new science of consciousness.* Winchester, UK: O Books, 2007.

Place, Ullin. "Intentionality as the mark of the dispositional." *Dialectica* 50, no. 2 (1996): 91–120.

Plantinga, Alvin. "Evolution, neutrality, and antecedent probability: a reply to Van Till and McMullen." *Christian Scholar's Review* XXI, no. 1 (1991): 80–109.

Polkinghorne, J. C. *Exploring reality: the intertwining of science and religion.* New Haven: Yale University Press, 2005.

Prior, E.W., R. Pargetter, and F. Jackson. "3 theses about dispositions." *American Philosophical Quarterly* 19, 3 (1982): 251–257.

Psillos, Stathis. "What do powers do when they are not manifested?" *Philosophy and Phenomenological Research* 72, no. 1 (2006): 137–156.

Rescher, N. "The revolt against process." *Journal Of Philosophy* 59, 15 (1962): 410–417.

Rietdijk, C. W. "A rigorous proof of determinism derived from the special theory of relativity." *Philosophy of Science* 33 (1966): 341–344.

———. *On the explanation of matter wave interference. towards the end of indeterministic physics.* Assen: Van Gorcum, 1973.

Riva, Giuseppe et al. "From intention to action: the role of presence." *New Ideas in Psychology* 29, no. 1 (2011): 24–37.

Rives, B. "Why dispositions are (still) distinct from their bases and causally impotent." *American Philosophical Quarterly* 42, 1 (2005): 19–31.

Rovelli, Carlo. "Loop quantum gravity." *Living Reviews in Relativity* 1, no. 1 (1998).

———. "Loop quantum gravity: the first twenty five years." *Arxiv preprint arXiv:1012.4707* (2010).

Russell, Bertrand. *The analysis of matter*. London; New York: Paul, Trench, Trubner, 1927.

———. *The analysis of mind*. London; New York: Allen & Unwin, 1921.

Ryle, Gilbert. *The concept of mind*. London; New York: Hutchinson's University Library, 1949.

Sandvik, Håvard, John Barrow, and João Magueijo. "A simple cosmology with a varying fine structure constant." *Phys. Rev. Lett.* 88, no. 3 (2002): 031302.

Sartre, Jean-Paul. *Existentialism is a humanism*. New Haven: Yale University Press, 2007.

Saunders, Nicholas T. *Divine action and modern science*. Cambridge, UK; New York: Cambridge University Press, 2002.

———. "Does God cheat at dice? Divine action and quantum possibilities." *Zygon* 35, no. 3 (2000): 517–544.

Shoemaker, Sydney. *Identity, cause, and mind: philosophical essays*. Cambridge [England]; New York: Cambridge University Press, 1984.

Smythies, John R. *Analysis of perception*. London: Routledge and Paul, 1956.

———. "Space, time and consciousness." *Journal of Consciousness Studies* 10 (2003): 47–56(10).

Snobelen, S.D. "Isaac Newton, heretic: the strategies of a Nicodemite." *Beyond Cartesian Dualism* 32, no. 04 (1999): 381–419.

Sober, Elliott. "Did Darwin write the origin backwards?" *Proceedings of the National Academy of Sciences* 106, Supplement 1 (2009): 10048.

———. "Intelligent design and probability reasoning." *Int J Philos Relig* 52, no. 2 (2002): 65–80.

———. "Why must homunculi be so stupid?" *Mind* 91, no. 363 (1982): 420–422.

Stapp, Henry P. *Mindful universe: quantum mechanics and the participating observer*. Berlin; New York: Springer, 2007.

Steiner, M. "Events and causality." *Journal Of Philosophy* 83, no. 5 (1986): 249–264.

Steinkamp, Fiona. *Parapsychology, philosophy, and the mind: essays honoring John Beloff*. Jefferson, N.C.: McFarland & Co., 2002.

Stenger, Victor J. *God, the failed hypothesis: how science shows that God does not exist*. Amherst, N. Y.: Prometheus Books, 2008.

Swedenborg, Emanuel. *De miraculis: miracles*. Swedenborg Society, 1947.

———. *Heaven and hell*. New York: Pillar Books, 1976.

Swedenborg, Emanuel. *The divine love and wisdom.* Everyman's library the-
    ology and philosophy. London: Dent, 1912.

Swoyer, Chris. "The nature of natural laws." *Australasian Journal of Philos-
    ophy* 60, no. 3 (1982): 203 –223.

Thompson, Ian J. *Layered cognitive networks.* Http://www.
    generativescience.org/ps-papers/layer7.html, 1990.

———. *Philosophy of nature and quantum reality.* Pleasanton, CA: Eagle
    Pearl Press, 2010.

———. "Real dispositions in the physical world." *Br J Philos Sci* 39, no. 1
    (1988): 67–79.

———. "The consistency of physical law with divine immanence." *Science
    and Christian Belief* 5 (1993): 19–36.

Thorpe, Lucas. "The realm of ends as a community of spirits: Kant and
    Swedenborg on the kingdom of heaven and the cleansing of the doors
    of perception." *Heythrop Journal* (2011): 52–75.

Tillich, Paul. *Systematic theology.* Chicago: University of Chicago Press,
    1951.

Unal, Ali. *The Qur'an: with annotated interpretation in modern English.* Som-
    erset, N.J.: The Light, 2007.

Ward, Keith. *Religion and creation.* Oxford: Clarendon Press, 1996.

Wheeler, J.A. "Is physics legislated by cosmogony?" In *Quantum gravity;
    Proceedings of the Oxford Symposium, Harwell, Berks., England, February
    15, 16, 1974,* edited by C.J. Isham, R. Penrose, and D.W. Sciama, 538–605.
    1975.

Whitehead, Alfred North. *Process and reality, an essay in cosmology.* New
    York: Harper & Brothers, 1929.

Index

Lightning Source UK Ltd.
Milton Keynes UK
UKOW031842170613

212392UK00017B/1151/P